How to Start A Small Business
in
Canada

All paid jobs absorb and degrade the mind.

(Aristotle)

How to Start
A Small Business
in
Canada

Your Road Map To Financial Freedom

Editor

Tariq Nadeem

ISBN 0-9733140-6-0   (paperback)
ISBN 0-9733140- 7-9   (e-book)

Cataloguing in Publication (CIP) data is with
National Library of Canada

This book is printed on acid free paper.

This publication is designed to provide accurate and authoritative information that is up-to-date and current at the time of this publication. It is sold with the understanding that the publisher is not engaged in rendering professional services.

Self-Help Publishers does not endorse any product or service in this publication. Any service or services provider listed in this publication assume full liability for their products and services and any claims arising from them. Clients will indemnify and hold harmless Self-Help Publishers for any liability arising therefrom.

Send your wholesale inquiries in U.S.A to Ingram Book Group, Baker & Taylor, and Nacscorp.
In United Kingdom and Europe send your wholesale inquiries to Bertram and Blackwell's.

For retail purchase visit your local Amazon and Barns and Nobles online bookstores or
checkout with your local bookstore.

For reprint/co-publishing rights contact Self-Help Publishers at 3-445 Pioneer Dr. Kitchner ,ON, N2P 1L8 Canada or
visit www.selfhelppublishers.com

Manufactured in United States of America and United Kingdom simultaneously
by arrangements with Self-Help publishers Canada.

Cover designed by Smart Prints,

Acknowledgement & Credits

© Her Majesty the Queen in Right of Canada, represented by the Minister of Public works and Government Services, 2005.

CIA-The World Fact Book
Department of Finance Canada (http://www.fin.gc.ca/budget04/brief/briefe.htm)
Invest in Canada(http://www.investincanada.gc.ca/)
Canada Business Service Centres (http://www.cbsc.org)
Workplace Safety and Insurance Board Ontario (http://www.wsib.on.ca)

"Minding Your Own Business: Becoming an Entrepreneur"- HRDC
"Guide for Canadian Small Businesses" Canada Revenue Agency Reference No. RC4070
(http://www.ccra-adrc.gc.ca/E/pub/tg/rc4070/rc4070eq.html)

Reproduced with the permission of the Minister of Public Works and the Government Services Canada 2004

Secret of Success Adopted from "21 Secrets of Success" by Brian Tracy

I also thank to **Mr. Fawad Chughtai**, Ms. Ambreen Tariq, Mr. M. Ashraf Khan and Mr. M.A Ghouri for their assistance, cooperation and help in dealing with technicalities of this publication.

Disclaimer

DEDICATION

This book is dedicated to Ms. Nicole Hudon (Licensing Officer) of Public Works and Government Services Canada and to Mr. Patrick Chartrand, a Labour Market Manager with Scarborough Community and Social Services and his staff. They have provided me guidance and advise whenever I knocked on their door. A big thanks to all of them!

CONTENTS

PART ONE

Chapter 1

AN OVERVIEW OF CANADA

Chapter 2

REASONS FOR INVESTING IN CANADA

Chapter 3

MINDING YOUR OWN BUSINESS

Chapter 4

BUSINESS ESSENTIALS

PART TWO

TAXES, DUTIES AND REGULATIONS

Chapter 1

Chapter 2

Chapter 3

Chapter 4

Chapter 5

Chapter 6

Chapter 7

Chapter 8

Chapter 9

HOW TO DOUBLE YOUR PRODUCTIVITY

IN CLOSING

LIST OF USEFUL WEB SITES

PART ONE

Chapter 1

AN OVERVIEW OF CANADA

*Only through focus can you do world-class things,
no matter how capable you are.*

(Bill Gates(Fortune, July 8, 2002))

CANADA
AN INTRODUCTION

Background: A land of vast distances and rich natural resources, Canada became a self-governing dominion in 1867 while retaining ties to the British crown. Economically and technologically the nation has developed in parallel with the US, its neighbor to the south across an unfortified border. Its paramount political problem continues to be the relationship of the province of Quebec, with its French-speaking residents and unique culture, to the remainder of the country.

GEOGRAPHY

Location: Northern North America, bordering the North Atlantic Ocean on the east, North Pacific Ocean on the west, and the Arctic Ocean on the north, north of the conterminous US

Geographic coordinates: 60 00 N, 95 00 W

Map references: North America

Area:

total: 9,984,670 sq km
land: 9,093,507 sq km
water: 891,163 sq km

Area - comparative: somewhat larger than the US

Land boundaries:

total: 8,893 km
border countries: US 8,893 km (includes 2,477 km with Alaska)

Coastline: 202,080 km

Maritime claims - as described in UNCLOS 1982 :

territorial sea: 12 NM
continental shelf: 200 NM or to the edge of the continental margin
contiguous zone: 24 NM

exclusive economic zone: 200 NM

Climate: varies from temperate in south to subarctic and arctic in north

Terrain: mostly plains with mountains in west and lowlands in southeast

Elevation extremes:
lowest point: Atlantic Ocean 0 m
highest point: Mount Logan 5,959 m

Natural resources: iron ore, nickel, zinc, copper, gold, lead, molybdenum, potash, diamonds, silver, fish, timber, wildlife, coal, petroleum, natural gas, hydropower

Land use:
arable land: 4.94%
permanent crops: 0.02% *other:* 95.04% (1998 est.)
Irrigated land: 7,200 sq km (1998 est.)

Natural hazards: continuous permafrost in north is a serious obstacle to development; cyclonic storms form east of the Rocky Mountains, a result of the mixing of air masses from the Arctic, Pacific, and North American interior, and produce most of the country's rain and snow east of the mountains

Environment - current issues: air pollution and resulting acid rain severely affecting lakes and damaging forests; metal smelting, coal-burning utilities, and vehicle emissions impacting on agricultural and forest productivity; ocean waters becoming contaminated due to agricultural, industrial, mining, and forestry activities

Environment - international agreements: *party to:* Air Pollution, Air Pollution-Nitrogen Oxides, Air Pollution-Persistent Organic Pollutants, Air Pollution-Sulfur 85, Air Pollution-Sulfur 94, Antarctic-Environmental Protocol, Antarctic-Marine Living Resources, Antarctic Seals, Antarctic Treaty, Biodiversity, Climate Change, Climate Change-Kyoto Protocol, Desertification, Endangered Species, Environmental Modification, Hazardous

2

Wastes, Law of the Sea, Marine Dumping, Ozone Layer Protection, Ship Pollution, Tropical Timber 83, Tropical Timber 94, Wetlands *signed, but not ratified:* Air Pollution-Volatile Organic Compounds, Marine Life Conservation

Geography - note: second-largest country in world (after Russia); strategic location between Russia and US via north polar route; approximately 90% of the population is concentrated within 300 km of the US border

PEOPLE

Population: 32,507,874 (July 2004 est.)

Age structure:
0-14 years: 18.2% (male 3,038,800; female 2,890,579)
15-64 years: 68.7% (male 11,225,686; female 11,111,941)
65 years and over: 13% (male 1,807,472; female 2,433,396) (2004 est.)

Median age:
total: 38.2 years
male: 37.2 years
female: 39.2 years (2004 est.)

Population growth rate: 0.92% (2004 est.)

Birth rate: 10.91 births/1,000 population (2004 est.)

Death rate: 7.67 deaths/1,000 population (2004 est.)

Net migration rate: 5.96 migrant(s)/1,000 population (2004 est.)

Sex ratio: *at birth:* 1.05 male(s)/female

under 15 years: 1.05 male(s)/female

15-64 years: 1.01 male(s)/female

65 years and over: 0.74 male(s)/female

total population: 0.98 male(s)/female (2004 est.)

Infant mortality rate:
total: 4.82 deaths/1,000 live births
female: 4.33 deaths/1,000 live births (2004 est.)
male: 5.28 deaths/1,000 live births

Life expectancy at birth:
total population: 79.96 years
male: 76.59 years
female: 83.5 years (2004 est.)

4

Total fertility rate:
1.61 children born/woman (2004 est.)

HIV/AIDS - adult prevalence rate: 0.3% (2001 est.)

HIV/AIDS - people living with HIV/AIDS: 55,000 (2001 est.)

HIV/AIDS - deaths: less than 500 (2001 est.)

Nationality: *noun:* Canadian(s)
                   adjective: Canadian

Ethnic groups: British Isles origin 28%, French origin 23%, other European 15%, Amerindian 2%, other, mostly Asian, African, Arab 6%, mixed background 26%

Religions: Roman Catholic 46%, Protestant 36%, other 18%
note: based on the 1991 census

Languages: English 59.3% (official), French 23.2% (official), other 17.5%

Literacy: *definition:* age 15 and over can read and write
total population: 97% (1986 est.)
male: NA%
female: NA%

GOVERNMENT

Country name:
conventional long form: none
conventional short form: Canada

Government type: confederation with parliamentary democracy

Capital: Ottawa

Administrative divisions: 10 provinces and 3 territories*; Alberta, British Columbia, Manitoba, New Brunswick, Newfoundland and Labrador, Northwest Territories*, Nova Scotia, Nunavut*, Ontario, Prince Edward Island, Quebec, Saskatchewan, Yukon Territory*

Independence: 1 July 1867 (from UK)

National holiday: Canada Day, 1 July (1867)

Constitution: 17 April 1982 (Constitution Act); originally, the machinery of the government was set up in the British North America Act of 1867; charter of rights and unwritten customs

Legal system: based on English common law, except in Quebec, where civil law system based on French law prevails; accepts compulsory ICJ jurisdiction, with reservations

Suffrage: 18 years of age; universal (Right to vote)

Executive branch: *chief of state:* Queen ELIZABETH II (since 6 February 1952), represented by Governor General Adrienne CLARKSON (since 7 October 1999)

elections: none; the monarchy is hereditary; governor general appointed by the monarch on the advice of the prime minister for a five-year term; following legislative elections, the leader of the majority party or the leader of the majority coalition in the House of Commons is automatically designated prime minister by the governor general *head of government:* Prime Minister Paul MARTIN (since 12 December 2003); Deputy Prime Minister Anne MCLELLAN (since 12 December 2003)

cabinet: Federal Ministry chosen by the prime minister from among the members of his own party sitting in Parliament

Legislative branch: bicameral Parliament or Parlement consists of the Senate or Senat (members appointed by the governor general with the advice of the prime minister and serve until reaching 75 years of age; its normal limit is 105 senators) and the House of Commons or Chambre des Communes (301 seats; members elected by direct, popular vote to serve for up to five-year terms)

elections: House of Commons - last held at June 28, 2004

election results: **House of Commons - percent of vote by party -** Liberal Party 36.71%, Progressive Conservative Party 29.61% Bloc Quebecois 12.4%, New Democratic Party 15.6%; Other 5.6%

seats by party: as of July 2004 - Liberal Party 135, Conservative Party 29, Bloc Quebecois 54, New Democratic Party 19 , Others 1.

Judicialbranch: Supreme Court of Canada (judges are appointed by the prime minister through the governor general); Federal Court of Canada; Federal Court of Appeal; Provincial Courts (these are named variously Court of Appeal, Court of Queens Bench, Superior Court, Supreme Court, and Court of Justice)

Political parties and leaders: Bloc Quebecois [Gilles DUCEPPE]; Conservative Party of Canada (a merger of the Canadian Alliance and the Progressive Conservative Party) [Stephen HARPER]; Liberal Party [Paul MARTIN]; New Democratic Party [Jack LAYTON]

Political pressure groups and leaders: NA

International organization participation: ACCT, AfDB, APEC, ARF, AsDB , ASEAN (dialogue partner), Australia Group, BIS, C, CDB, CE (observer), EAPC, EBRD, ESA (cooperating state), FAO, G-7, G-8, G-10, IADB, IAEA, IBRD, ICAO, ICC, ICCt, ICFTU, ICRM, IDA, IEA, IFAD, IFC, IFRCS, IHO, ILO, IMF, IMO, Interpol, IOC, IOM, ISO, ITU, MICAH, MONUC, NAM (guest), NATO, NEA, NSG, OAS, OECD, OPCW, OSCE, Paris Club, PCA, UN, UNAMSIL, UNCTAD, UNDOF, UNESCO, UNFICYP, UNHCR, UNMIK, UNMOVIC, UNTSO, UPU, WCL, WCO, WFTU, WHO, WIPO, WMO, WTO, WTrO, ZC

Diplomatic representation in the US:
chief of mission: Ambassador Michael F. KERGIN
chancery: 501 Pennsylvania Avenue NW, Washington, DC 20001
FAX: [1] (202) 682-7726
telephone: [1] (202) 682-1740
consulate(s) general: Atlanta, Boston, Buffalo, Chicago, Dallas, Detroit, Los Angeles, Miami, Minneapolis, New York, and Seattle

consulate(s): Houston, Princeton, Raleigh-Durham, San Diego, San Francisco, and San Jose

Diplomatic representation from the US:
chief of mission: Ambassador Paul CELLUCCI
embassy: 490 Sussex Drive, Ottawa, Ontario K1N 1G8
mailing address: P. O. Box 5000, Ogdensburgh, NY 13669-0430
telephone: [1] (613) 238-5335, 4470
FAX: [1] (613) 688-3097

consulate(s) general: Calgary, Halifax, Montreal, Quebec, Toronto, and Vancouver

ECONOMY

Flag description: two vertical bands of red (hoist and fly side, half width), with white square between them; an 11-pointed red maple leaf is centered in the white square; the official colors of Canada are red and white

Economy – overview : As an affluent, high-tech industrial society, Canada today closely resembles the US in its market-oriented economic system, pattern of production, and high living standards. Since World War II, the impressive growth of the manufacturing, mining, and service sectors has transformed the nation from a largely rural economy into one primarily industrial and urban. The 1989 US-Canada Free Trade Agreement (FTA) and the 1994 North American Free Trade Agreement (NAFTA) (which includes Mexico) touched off a dramatic increase in trade and economic integration with the US. As a result of the close cross-border relationship, the economic sluggishness in the United States in 2001-02 had a negative impact on the Canadian economy. Real growth averaged nearly 3% during 1993-2000, but declined in 2001, with moderate recovery in 2002-03. Unemployment is up, with contraction in the manufacturing and natural resource sectors. Nevertheless, given its great natural resources, skilled labor force, and modern capital plant Canada enjoys solid economic prospects. Two shadows loom, the first being the continuing constitutional impasse between English- and French-speaking areas, which has been raising the specter of a split in the federation. Another long-term concern is the flow south to the US of professionals lured by higher pay, lower taxes, and the immense high-tech infrastructure. A key strength in the economy is the substantial trade surplus. Roughly 90% of the population lives within 160 kilometers of the US border.

GDP: purchasing power parity - $957.7 billion (2003 est.)

GDP - real growth rate:1.6% (2003 est.)

GDP - per capita: purchasing power parity - $29,700 (2003 est.)

GDP - composition by sector: *agriculture:* 2.2%

industry: 26%

9

services: 71.8% (2002 est.)

Population below poverty line: NA% (1998 est.)

Household income or consumption by percentage share:

lowest 10%: 2.8%

highest 10%: 23.8% (1994)

Distribution of family income - Gini index: 31.5 (1994)

Inflation rate (consumer prices): 2.8% (2003 est.)

Labor force: 16.4 million (2001 est.)

Labor force - by occupation: services 74%, manufacturing 15%, construction 5%, agriculture 3%, other 3% (2000)

Unemployment rate: 7.7% (2003 est.)

Budget: *revenues:* $178.6 billion

expenditures: $161.4 billion, including capital expenditures of $NA (FY00/01 est.)

Industries: transportation equipment, chemicals, processed and unprocessed minerals, food products; wood and paper products; fish products, petroleum and natural gas

Industrial production growth rate: 0% (2003 est.)

Electricity - production: 566.3 billion kWh (2001)

Electricity - production by source:

fossil fuel: 28%
hydro: 57.9%
other: 1.3% (2001)
nuclear: 12.9%

Electricity - consumption: 504.4 billion kWh (2001)

Electricity - exports: 38.4 billion kWh (2001)

Electricity - imports: 16.11 billion kWh (2001)

Oil - production: 2.738 million bbl/day (2001 est.)

Oil - consumption: 1.703 million bbl/day (2001 est.)

Oil - exports: 2.008 million bbl/day (2001)

Oil - imports: 1.145 million bbl/day (2001)

Oil - proved reserves: 5.112 billion bbl (1 January 2002)

Natural gas - production: 186.8 billion cu m (2001 est.)

Natural gas - consumption: 82.25 billion cu m (2001 est.)

Natural gas - exports: 109 billion cu m (2001 est.)

Natural gas - imports: 4.46 billion cu m (2001 est.)

Natural gas - proved reserves: 1.691 trillion cu m (1 Jan. 2002)

Agriculture - products: wheat, barley, oilseed, tobacco, fruits, vegetables; dairy products; forest products; fish

Exports: $279.3 billion f.o.b. (2003 est.)

Exports - commodities: motor vehicles and parts, industrial machinery, aircraft, telecommunications equipment; chemicals, plastics, fertilizers; wood pulp, timber, crude petroleum, natural gas, electricity, aluminum

Exports - partners: US 87.7%, Japan 2%, UK 1.1% (2002)

Imports: $240.4 billion f.o.b. (2003 est.)

Imports - commodities: machinery and equipment, motor vehicles and parts, crude oil, chemicals, electricity, durable consumer goods

Imports - partners: US 62.6%, China 4.6%, Japan 4.4% (2002)

Debt - external: $1.9 billion (2000)

Economic aid - donor: ODA, $1.3 billion (1999)

Currency: Canadian dollar (CAD)

Currency code: CAD

Exchange rates: Canadian dollars per US dollar - 1.4 (2003), 1.57 (2002), 1.55 (2001), 1.49 (2000), 1.49 (1999)

Fiscal year: 1 April - 31 March

COMMUNICATIONS

Telephones - main lines in use: 19,962,100 (2002)

Telephones - mobile cellular: 11.849 million (2002)

Telephone system: *general assessment:* excellent service provided by modern technology

domestic: domestic satellite system with about 300 earth stations
international: country code - 1; 5 coaxial submarine cables; satellite earth stations - 5 Intelsat (4 Atlantic Ocean and 1 Pacific Ocean) and 2 Intersputnik (Atlantic Ocean region)

Radio broadcast stations: AM 535, FM 53, shortwave 6 (1998)

Radios: 32.3 million (1997)

Television broadcast stations: 80 (plus many repeaters) (1997)

Televisions: 21.5 million (1997)

Internet country code: .ca

Internet hosts: 2,993,982 (2002)

Internet Service Providers (ISPs): 760 (2000 est.)

Internet users: 16.11 million (2002)

TRANSPORTAION

Railways: *total:* 73,301 km
standard gauge: 73,301 km 1.435-m gauge (129 km electrified) (2001)

Highways: *total:* 1,408,800 km
paved: 497,306 km (including 16,900 km of expressways)
unpaved: 911,494 km (2002)

Waterways: 3,000 km (including Saint Lawrence Seaway)

Pipelines: crude and refined oil 23,564 km; natural gas 74,980 km

Ports and harbors: Becancour (Quebec), Churchill, Halifax, Hamilton, Montreal, New Westminster, Prince Rupert, Quebec,

Saint John (New Brunswick), St. John's (Newfoundland), Sept Isles, Sydney, Trois-Rivieres, Thunder Bay, Toronto, Vancouver, Windsor

Merchant marine: *total:* 119 ships (1,000 GRT or over) 1,784,229 GRT/2,657,499 DWT

by type: barge carrier 1, bulk 59, cargo 13, chemical tanker 6, combination bulk 2, combination ore/oil 1, passenger 2, passenger/cargo 1, petroleum tanker 18, rail car carrier 1, roll on/roll off 11, short-sea/passenger 3, specialized tanker 1
registered in other countries: 43 (2003 est.)
foreign-owned: Germany 3, Hong Kong 2, Monaco 18, United Kingdom 3, United States 2

Airports: 1,357 (2003 est.)

Airports - with paved runways:

total: 505
over 3,047 m: 18
2,438 to 3,047 m: 16
914 to 1,523 m: 246
under 914 m: 75 (2003 est.)
1,524 to 2,437 m: 150

Airports - with unpaved runways:
total: 852
1,524 to 2,437 m: 69
914 to 1,523 m: 359
under 914 m: 424 (2003 est.)

Heliports: 12 (2003 est.)

MILITARY

Military branches: Canadian Armed Forces: Land Forces Command, Maritime Command, Air Command

Military manpower - military age: 17 years of age (2004 est.)

Military manpower-availability: *males age 15-49:* 8,417,314 (2004 est.)

Military manpower - fit for military service:

males age 15-49: 7,176,642 (2004 est.)

Military manpower - reaching military age annually: *males:* 214,623 (2004 est.)

Military expenditures - dollar figure:$9,801.7 million (2003)

Military expenditures - percent of GDP:1.1% (2003)

TRANSNATIONAL ISSUES

Disputes - international:

managed maritime boundary disputes with the US at Dixon Entrance, Beaufort Sea, Strait of Juan de Fuca, and around the disputed Machias Seal Island and North Rock; uncontested dispute with Denmark over Hans Island sovereignty in the Kennedy Channel between Ellesmere Island and Greenland

Illicit drugs: illicit producer of cannabis for the domestic drug market and export to US; use of hydroponics technology permits growers to plant large quantities of high-quality marijuana indoors; transit point for heroin and cocaine entering the US market; vulnerable to narcotics money laundering because of its mature financial services sector

Source The World Factbook

14

Population of census metropolitan areas, 2001 Census boundaries

	1999	2000	2001	2002	2003
	persons (thousands)				
Total census metropolitan areas	19,060.1	19,330.4	19,957.4	20,262.1	20,497.4
Toronto (Ontario)	4,645.6	4,746.1	4,882.5	5,011.9	5,101.6
Montréal (Quebec)	3,437.5	3,471.1	3,507.2	3,542.5	3,574.5
Vancouver (British Columbia)	2,012.6	2,040.3	2,076.1	2,110.6	2,134.3
Ottawa–Gatineau (Ontario–Quebec)	1,059.0	1,080.7	1,105.7	1,119.8	1,132.2
Calgary (Alberta)	928.4	952.5	976.7	1,000.2	1,016.6
Edmonton (Alberta)	931.1	946.8	961.4	978.6	990.5
Quebec (Quebec)	689.8	692.6	696.4	701.0	705.9
Hamilton (Ontario)	669.2	678.7	689.1	696.9	702.9
Winnipeg (Manitoba)	682.3	686.4	690.1	693.2	698.2
London (Ontario)	439.8	445.0	449.5	454.0	457.2
Kitchener (Ontario)	414.9	423.3	431.3	438.4	444.1
St. Catharines–Niagara (Ontario)	388.1	390.3	391.6	393.0	393.6
Halifax (Nova Scotia)	363.2	366.3	369.1	373.7	377.9
Windsor (Ontario)	307.4	313.7	320.7	325.5	329.0
Victoria (British Columbia)	320.4	321.8	325.4	326.8	326.7
Oshawa (Ontario)	292.6	299.4	305.4	312.6	319.3
Saskatoon (Saskatchewan)	230.0	230.3	230.8	231.9	233.9
Regina (Saskatchewan)	198.6	198.0	196.8	196.6	197.0
St. John's (Newfoundland and Labrador)	175.2	175.9	176.1	177.5	179.7
Sherbrooke (Quebec)	154.4	155.6	157.0	158.6	160.9
Greater Sudbury (Ontario)	163.8	162.2	161.5	161.0	160.3
Abbotsford (British Columbia)[1]	..	..	153.7	155.2	158.2
Kingston (Ontario)[1]	..	..	152.7	154.3	155.5
Saguenay (Quebec)	161.0	159.4	157.8	156.2	155.1
Trois–Rivières (Quebec)	140.9	140.6	140.1	139.9	140.6
Saint John (New Brunswick)	126.8	126.6	126.0	126.1	126.2
Thunder Bay (Ontario)	127.7	126.8	126.6	126.2	125.5

Note: Population as of July 1.

1. Abbotsford and Kingston became census metropolitan areas in 2001.

Source: Statistics Canada, CANSIM, table 051–0034 and Catalogue nos. 91–213-XIB and 91–213-XPB.

Last modified: 2004-05-06.

http://www.statcan.ca/english/Pgdb/demo05a.htm

Exchange rates, interest rates, money supply and stock prices

	1999	2000	2001	2002	2003
	US$ per $ Canadian				
Exchange rate	0.6731	0.6732	0.6456	0.6368	0.7138
	%				
Selected interest rates					
Bank rate (last Wednesday of the month)	4.92	5.77	4.31	2.71	3.19
Prime business loan rate	6.44	7.27	5.81	4.21	4.69
Chartered bank typical mortgage rate					
1 year	6.80	7.85	6.14	5.17	4.84
3 years	7.37	8.17	6.88	6.28	5.82
5 years	7.56	8.35	7.40	7.02	6.39
Consumer loan rate	10.25	11.71	10.06	9.36	9.51
90 day prime corporate paper rate	4.94	5.71	3.87	2.66	2.94
	$ millions				
Money supply					
Gross M1	92,557	106,155	119,001	133,265	144,137
M2	459,083	491,645	517,448	550,030	581,721
M3	617,661	666,880	702,436	744,492	788,196
	1975 = 1000				
Toronto Stock Exchange 300 index	7,059.11	9,607.74	7,731.72	7,036.18	7,161.60

Source: Statistics Canada, CANSIM, tables 176-0036, 176-0043, 176-0047 and 176-0064; Bank of Canada, *Bank of Canada Review*, Ottawa.

Last modified: 2004-07-09.

http://www.statcan.ca/english/Pgdb/econ07.htm

Private And Public Capital Expenditures

	2000	2001	2002	2003	2004[1]
	$ millions				
Canada	185,957.1	200,311.9	209,266.1	217,182.3	223,819.3
Newfoundland and Labrador	3,298.4	3,296.7	3,712.6	3,794.7	4,191.6
Prince Edward Island	555.0	596.2	639.2	656.5	665.7
Nova Scotia	4,535.4	4,992.2	5,755.1	5,436.2	5,480.8
New Brunswick	3,941.8	3,425.9	3,465.5	3,926.0	4,301.3
Quebec	34,683.3	36,193.2	39,876.9	42,079.9	44,272.0
Ontario	69,061.7	73,913.0	76,949.2	80,565.9	82,659.8
Manitoba	5,197.9	5,591.1	5,962.8	6,004.6	6,327.2
Saskatchewan	6,634.0	6,823.8	6,530.4	6,567.6	6,278.7
Alberta	35,908.0	40,914.4	41,452.7	42,159.7	42,341.9
British Columbia	20,846.7	22,625.1	23,026.9	24,422.9	25,723.1
Yukon	247.7	291.6	303.1	292.3	309.1
Northwest Territories	817.3	1,386.3	1,331.0	907.6	930.9
Nunavut	229.9	262.6	260.6	368.5	337.3

1. Data for the latest year shown are intentions.

Source: Statistics Canada, CANSIM, tables 029-0005 and 029-0009 and Catalogue no. 61-205-XIB (intentions).
http://www.statcan.ca/english/Pgdb/econ17.htm

17

CHOOSING A CITY FOR BUSINESS

Choosing a city to do business in, can largely be a numbers game. What city has the lowest costs? Highest growth rates? And even better prospects?

The cost of doing business rules the site selection process. But this process is also really dependent on local human capital.

Overall Canadian cities continually outperform the US when it comes to the cost of doing business, and there's no doubt that Canada is blessed with the highly skilled workforce mainly due to Canadian immigration policy under skilled worker class. Employer can find a production worker or general labour with international experience possessing a Bachelor or Master degree in Engineering, Science or Technology @ Can$ 9-12 per hour. Smart employers hire them on absolutely low wages. They train them according to their needs and save approximately more then 50% on wages in comparison, if they hire a locally educated engineer or technologist. These foreign trained professionals do posses the necessary education, skills and experience and all they need is just a brush-up or an orientation to fit in any small, medium or large enterprise.

According to Statistics Canada , people who migrated to Canada in last 10-20 years are more educated then the local born Canadians especially from Pakistan, India, China, Philippines and Bangladesh.

Toronto, Montreal and Vancouver are considered to be the best cities in terms of availability of human capital as most of the immigrants choose to settle in these cities or within the surrounding areas.

18

Top 20 Most Expensive Cities For Office Rents.

JAN.2004	CITY	PER SQ. FOOT
1	London (West end) U.K.	$ 194.70
2.	Tokyo (inner central), Japan	154.10
3.	London (city), UK	150.66
4.	Tokyo (outer Central)	137.66
5.	Paris, France	123.21
6.	Birmingham, UK	93.87
7.	Dublin, Ireland	90.88
8.	Milan, Italy	89.09
9.	Edinburgh, Scotland	87.50
10.	Manchester, UK	86.92
11.	Moscow, Russia	84.88
12.	Zurich, Switzerland	82.40
13.	Glasgow, Scotland	81.13
14.	Frankfurt, Germany	78.89
15.	Luxembourg (city), Luxembourg	78.50
16.	Rome, Italy	77.14
17.	Mumbai (Bombay), India	74.23
18.	Geneva, Switzerland	72.71
19.	Munich, Germany	70.87
20.	Stockholm, Sweden	69.08
32.	Toronto (downtown)	54.41

Source: Toronto Star

19

FEDERAL BUDGET 2004

An Introduction

Canadians are united by a belief in equality of opportunity. It is a principle that defines Canadians as a nation.

In the Speech from the Throne, the Government set out an ambitious agenda to improve the standard of living and quality of life of all Canadians. Its three themes are to strengthen Canada's social foundations, build a dynamic 21st century economy and restore Canada's influence in the world.

Just as Canadians are united by the belief in equality of opportunity, so too are the three themes of the current Government's (Libral Party) agenda. For it is by giving all Canadians the opportunity to succeed, to reach their potential, and to build a better life for themselves, their families and their communities that Canada will succeed and be a model for the world.

At the core of this budget is the recognition that to achieve our goal of better lives for all Canadians, our social and economic policies must be mutually reinforcing. Quite simply, there can be no strong economy without a secure society, and no secure society without a strong economy to support it. And underlying this must be the prudence of balanced budgets that comes with living within our means.

Therefore, this budget is built on the foundation of creating opportunity for individuals. It recognizes that opportunity has many dimensions and can be defined in many ways.

The measures in this budget have been designed to meet the test of what Canadians believe are our priorities as a nation. They focus on the importance of health care, learning, communities, the economy and our place in the world, each of which is crucial to the creation of opportunity for each and every Canadian. Each is a step down the path towards a Canada of opportunity and achievement.

This budget lays the foundation for that greater Canada, a nation where individual opportunity translates into economic achievement and social justice.

21

HIGHLIGHTS

Economic Developments and Prospects

- During 2003 economic activity in Canada slowed because of a series of unforeseen shocks. As a result, real gross domestic product (GDP) expanded only 1.7 per cent for the year, well below the 3.2 per cent expected by private sector economists at the time of the 2003 budget.

- Nevertheless, strength in domestic demand through most of the year, supported by low interest rates, helped offset the weakness in exports.

- Canada's labour market strengthened in the latter part of 2003. Since December 2002 the economy has created 271,900 new jobs, all full-time.

- Solid domestic fundamentals, low interest rates and a more favourable global environment, particularly a stronger U.S. economy, are expected to support more robust Canadian economic growth this year.

- Private sector economists expect the Canadian economy to grow by an average of 2.7 per cent in 2004, significantly better than last year but still well below the 3.5 per cent forecast at the time of the 2003 budget.

- Private sector economists expect a further pickup in growth to 3.3 per cent in 2005.

- There are two main risks to the Canadian economic outlook:

  - The uncertainty surrounding the economic impact of the rapid rise of the Canadian dollar.

  - The sustainability of the U.S. economic recovery.

Sound Financial Management

- The seventh consecutive balanced budget is projected for 2003–04, the first time since Confederation, and balanced budgets or better are forecast for 2004–05 and 2005–06.

- The $3-billion Contingency Reserve is maintained and $1 billion in economic prudence restored, for 2004–05 and 2005–06.

- The federal debt-to-GDP ratio is expected to fall to 42 per cent in 2003–04, down from its peak of 68.4 per cent in 1995–96. The ratio is forecast to decline to 38 per cent by 2005–06.

- To be in a better position to deal with pressures related to an aging population, the Government has set a new objective of reducing the federal debt-to-GDP ratio to 25 per cent within 10 years.

- In this budget program expenses are projected to grow an average of 4.4 per cent in 2004–05 and 2005–06, roughly in line with projected growth in the economy.

- As part of instituting a new management approach in government, the budget implements $1 billion in annual reallocation from existing spending in 2004–05 and beyond to meet Budget 2003 commitments.

- As well, the Cabinet Committee on Expenditure Review is examining all programs to identify at least $3 billion annually in savings within four years for reinvestment in the priorities of Canadians while improving government management.

- Furthermore, a new plan for better spending management and oversight is being introduced under the leadership of the President of the Treasury Board, which includes re-establishing the Office of the Comptroller General of Canada, strengthening departmental comptrollers and internal audits.

  - The Government intends to sell its remaining shares in Petro-Canada in 2004–05.

Moving Forward on the Priorities of Canadians

The Importance of Health

- Confirmation of an additional $2 billion for the provinces and territories for health, bringing to $36.8 billion the funding provided under the February 2003 First Ministers' Accord on Health Care Renewal.

- Establishment of a new Canada Public Health Agency as a focal point for disease control and emergency response.

- Immediate funding of $665 million in this fiscal year and over the next two years to improve Canada's readiness to deal with public health emergencies. This is in addition to the approximately $400 million to be transferred from Health Canada to the new Canada Public Health Agency.

- Improved tax fairness for Canadians with disabilities and caregivers.

- Increased funding of $30 million annually to support employment assistance programming delivered by provinces and territories for Canadians with disabilities.

The Importance of Learning

- Introduction of a new Canada Learning Bond, which will provide up to $2,000 for children in low-income families born after 2003 for post-secondary education.

- Enhancement of the Canada Education Savings Grant matching rate for low- and middle-income families.

- Introduction of a new grant of up to $3,000 for first-year, post-secondary dependent students from low-income families.

- Introduction of an up-front annual grant of up to $2,000 for post-secondary students with disabilities.

- Increase in the ceiling for Canada Student Loans to $210 a week from $165.

24

- Increase in the income thresholds used for determining eligibility for student loan interest relief.

- Increase in the maximum amount of debt reduction for students facing financial difficulty to $26,000 from $20,000.

- Extension of the education tax credit to employees who pursue career-related studies at their own expense.

- Investment of $125 million over five years for the Aboriginal Human Resources Development Strategy.

- Doubling to $50 million support for the Urban Aboriginal Strategy.

The Importance of Knowledge and Commercialization

- Annual increase of $90 million to Canada's three federal granting councils.

- Increase of $20 million annually to help offset the indirect costs of research by universities and research hospitals.

- An additional $60 million to Genome Canada to strengthen its research.

- Additional funding to improve the capacity for commercialization at universities, hospitals and other research facilities.

- New funding of $270 million set aside to enhance access to venture capital financing for companies turning promising research into new products and services.

- Acceleration by one year, from 2006 to 2005, of the increase in the small business deduction limit to $300,000.

- Increase in the capital cost allowance rate for computer equipment to 45 per cent from 30 per cent, and in the rate for broadband, Internet and other data network infrastructure equipment to 30 per cent from 20 per cent.

The Importance of Communities

- $7 billion in GST/HST relief for municipalities of all sizes over the next 10 years.

- Acceleration of the $1-billion Municipal Rural Infrastructure Fund, with spending over the next 5 years instead of 10.

- A stronger voice for municipalities in the federal decisions that affect them.

- New funding of $15 million a year in support of enhanced language training to reduce labour market barriers faced by immigrants.

- Increased funding for the Urban Aboriginal Strategy.

- Funding of $4 billion over 10 years to clean up contaminated sites.

- New funding ($1 billion over 7 years) to support the development and commercialization of new environmental technologies, reflecting the sale of Petro-Canada.

- More effective tax rules for registered charities and ongoing support for the Voluntary Sector Initiative.

- Increased support for community-based economic development and the social economy.

The Importance of Canada's Relationship to the World

- An additional $250 million to cover the costs of Canada's participation in peacekeeping missions in Afghanistan and the fight against terrorism.

- An additional $50 million for Canada's participation in the peacekeeping force in Haiti.

- Additional capital funding in 2005–06 to advance priority capital investments.

- Exemption from tax of the income earned by Canadian Forces personnel and police on high-risk international missions.

- Commitment of a further $605 million to address security issues.

- A reduction in the Air Travellers Security Charge.

- An increase of $248 million, or 8 per cent, in international assistance in 2005–06.

Spending and Revenue Initiatives: 2004 Budget

	2003–04	2004–05	2005–06
	(millions of dollars)		
Importance of Health			
Canada Health and Social Transfer cash supplement	2,000		
Strengthening Canada's public health system	500	80	85
Inclusion of persons with disabilities		50.5	57.9
Total	**2,500**	**131**	**143**
Importance of Learning			
Caring for Canada's children		91	93
Helping families plan ahead for post-secondary education		105	302
Encouraging lifelong learning		25	40
Economic opportunities for Aboriginal Canadians		30	31
Total		**251**	**466**
Importance of Knowledge and Commercialization			
Building research foundations		170	115
Commercialization of research		20	20
Venture capital financing[1]		(255)	(15)
Investing in offshore development		7	7
Small business and entrepreneurship		1	24.5
Strengthening the Canadian tax advantage		95	200
Total		**293**	**367**
Importance of Communities			
New Deal for communities: first steps	100	605	655
The community-based and non-profit sector		15	15
Supporting the social economy		35	43
Environment and sustainable		205	10

28

development			
Other initiatives in support of communities		52.5	53
Total	**100**	**913**	**776**
Importance of Canada's Relationship to the World			
Defence		277	85
Security reserve		115	115
International assistance[2]			248
Canada Corps		5	10
Total		**397**	**458**
Other			
Agriculture assistance	1,000		
Equalization and Territorial Formula Financing renewal		195	202
Other		37.5	100
Total	**1,000**	**233**	**302**
Total: spending and revenue initiatives	3,600	2,216	2,511
of which:			
Spending initiatives	3,500	1,486	1,621
Revenue initiatives	100	730	890

[1] Federal support will be in the form of an equity injection, i.e. the purchase of shares. As a result, there will be no budgetary impact.

[2] In the 2003 budget, the International Assistance Envelope was increased by 8 per cent in both 2003–04 and 2004–05.

Summary Statement of Transactions
(Including March 2004 Budget Measures)

	Actual			
	2002–03	2003–04	2004–05	2005–06
		(billions of dollars)		
Budgetary transactions				
Budgetary revenues	177.6	181.1	187.2	195.8
Total expenses				
Program expenses	−133.3	−143.4	−147.9	−156.1
Public debt charges	−37.3	−35.8	−35.4	−35.7
Total expenses	−170.6	−179.2	−183.3	−191.8
Underlying budgetary surplus	7.0	1.9	4.0	4.0
Prudence				
Contingency Reserve		1.9	3.0	3.0
Economic prudence			1.0	1.0
Total		1.9	4.0	4.0
Budgetary balance	7.0	0.0	0.0	0.0
Federal debt (accumulated deficit)				
Balanced budget (no debt reduction)	510.6	510.6	510.6	510.6
Apply Contingency Reserve to debt	510.6	508.7	505.7	502.7
Non−budgetary transactions	0.7	2.0	−4.5	−4.0
Financial source/requirement	7.6	2.0	−4.5	−4.0
Per cent of GDP				
Budgetary revenues	15.4	14.9	14.8	14.7
Program expenses	11.5	11.8	11.7	11.7
Public debt charges	3.2	2.9	2.8	2.7
Budgetary balance	0.6	0.2	0.3	0.3
Federal debt (accumulated deficit)				
Balanced budget (no debt reduction)	44.2	42.0	40.4	38.4
Apply Contingency Reserve to debt	44.2	41.9	40.0	37.8

30

Other

Public debt charges as a share of revenues	21.0	19.8	18.9	18.2
Annual per cent change				
Budgetary revenues	3.4	2.0	3.4	4.6
Program expenses	6.6	7.6	3.1	5.6
Total expenses	3.6	5.0	2.3	4.7

Note: Numbers may not add due to rounding.

Source: http://www.fin.gc.ca/budget04/brief/briefe.htm

Chapter 2

REASONS FOR INVESTING IN CANADA

Wherever you see a successful business,
someone once made a courageous decision.

(Peter Drucker)
A teacher, writer, and adviser to senior executives for more than 50 years. Author of 31 books

Why Should Invest or Start a Small Business in Canada

Invest for Success -- In Canada!

There are many reasons that make Canada a competitive investment destination. Find out why Canada is the country of choice for international business.

COMPETITIVE ECONOMY

From our sound economic fundamentals to our highly skilled work force, our low start-up costs to our high-tech infrastructure -- there are many reasons why Canada's competitive economy is an unsurpassed place to do business.

Strong Fiscal Situation

In the past ten years, Canada has taken decisive and successful action to put itself on a sound fiscal foundation. The Institute for Management Development ranked Canada as the best fiscally managed country in the G-7 in 2000. Federal government spending, as a percentage of GDP, is at a 50-year low. This is the key source of the Canadian fiscal turn-around.

In 1997, Canada became the first G-7 country to post a surplus in the 1990s. After six consecutive annual surpluses, balanced budget has announced for 2004 and better are expected each of the next five fiscal years.

Into the Future

Government in Canada has been in a surplus position since 1999, and is projected to remain so well into the future. *In terms of this key economic indicator, Canada significantly outperforms the U.S.*

A Balanced Budget plus Low Spending -- Sound Fiscal Management

The Institute for Management Development ranked Canada as the best fiscally-managed country in the G-7 in 2000.

Low Inflation and Low Interest Rates

Canada's government has created winning conditions for the private sector to operate in. And a fundamental part of Canada's attractiveness to the international business community is our low inflation, low interest rate environment. Canada's low inflation and low interest rates mean that companies can do business in a stable, predictable and low-cost business environment.

- With low inflation over the past decade, Canada is considered among low inflation countries. Over the past five years, Canadian inflation averaged 2.4% -- that's lower than the U.S.
- Canada´s targeted inflation rate is locked between 1% to 3% and has been extended until 2006.

GROWING DOMESTIC ECONOMY

Canada led the G-7 in terms of growth over the 2000-2003 period. Consensus Economics forecast the Canadian economy to be among growth leaders over the 2004-2005 period

Canada Welcomes Foreign Direct Investment

- Foreign direct investment in Canada has more than doubled since 1990.
- Increasingly more investment goes to knowledge-based industries in high-tech manufacturing such as electronics, communications and chemicals.

36

Tax Advantages

Very Competitive Tax Treatment:

Contrary to popular misconceptions, when it comes to business Canada is a low tax country. In 2000, the Canadian government announced the most progressive tax changes the country has seen in decades—and corporate tax rates will decline dramatically through 2008.

- Canadian locations compare well internationally in terms of statutory corporate income tax rates.
- Firms in Canada have a growing income tax rate advantage over U.S. firms.
- Elimination of capital tax helps increase tax advantage to 3.4 percentage points by 2008.

Low R&D Costs

Canada offers the most favorable tax treatment for R&D among the G-7:

- Canada provides a system of tax credits and accelerated tax deductions for a wide-variety of R&D expenditures. Eligible costs include salaries, overhead, capital equipment, and materials.

- These federal and provincial tax-based incentives permit firms to significantly reduce R&D costs through direct investment or sub-contracting in Canada.

SUPERIOR WORKFORCE

Most Important Asset - The Canadian People

For any corporation, the quality of its personnel — workers and managers alike — is a key consideration.

In Canada, the people are perhaps the most important asset. The Canadian workforce is unrivalled in terms of knowledge, education and skill level, and is also loyal and stable — Canadian labour turnover rates are quite low.

Moreover, Canada is always seeking to make its labour force even better! Canada made it easier for skilled people to come from abroad and put their talents to work in Canada.

Highly Skilled Labour Pool

It's impossible to build a great company without great people, and Canada has the human resources necessary to build success! The Canadian workforce is highly skilled:

- The overall skill level of Canada's workforce ranks high among competing countries.
- According to 2001 Census figures, Canada has the highest percentage of individuals, among OECD member countries, achieving at least college or university education.
- Canada also leads its major competitors in terms of the share of GDP that is devoted to public education.

High-Class Management Training

Management steers the corporate ship, and good management is essential for success in the business world. The quality of Canadian corporate management is outstanding.

- Canada ranks third among the G-7 and third overall in a 102-country study of locally available management education in first-class business schools.

- Seven Canadian business schools are ranked among the top 100 Management Schools in the world according to the Financial Times (UK) Global MBA rankings for 2004.

- In the October 21, 2002 edition of BusinessWeek magazine, four Canadian business schools ranked among the top ten non-U.S. schools.

- In a report by Forbes Magazine in September 2003, three Canadian business schools ranked among the top thirteen non-U.S. schools

Top Ten Non-U.S. Business Schools

Institution	Country	Rank
INSEAD	France	1
Queen's University	Canada	2
IMD	France.	3
London Business School	U.K.	4
University of Toronto	Canada	5
University of Westren Ontario	Canada	6
Rotterdam	Netherlands	7
IESE	Spain	8
HEC	France	9
York University	Canada	10

Source: BusinessWeek, Oct 21, 2002

Simplified Entry and Immigration

Immigration plays a significant role in the make-up of Canadian society, and skilled workers make up the biggest category by far of all immigrants to Canada. Independent immigrants are selected for the knowledge, skills and experience needed in Canada's labour markets. Canada also welcomes business immigrants who have the experience and resources to contribute to the Canadian economy.

EASY ACCESS TO MARKETS

Canadian companies have entry to the world's largest markets through the North American Free Trade Agreement (NAFTA) -- and are a vital presence in Asia, Europe and around the world as well.

In Canada, your company will have the world at its doorstep! Through the North American Free Trade Agreement (NAFTA), Canada is a vital part of the huge integrated North American market of almost 400 million consumers.

39

The Free Trade Area of the Americas (FTAA), poised to become the world's largest free trade area, will provide Canada:

- greater access to markets,
- fair and efficient dispute settlement,
- stability for Canadian businesses.

Canada also has strong historical trade ties with Europe, and unique access to Asian economies.

Streamlined Border Flows

The North American market is serviced through a well integrated transportation system which is among the world's best. Automated permit ports, transponder identification systems and joint processing centres are being tested and deployed.

Canada-U.S. Trade: Seamless, Integrated and Interdependent

Since the North American Free Trade Agreement (NAFTA) of 1994, Canada provides long-term assured access to the entire North America market — nearly 400 million people, with a combined GDP of over US$11.4 trillion.
In addition to eliminating tariffs, NAFTA provides procedures for:

- border facilitation;
- movement of personnel;
- investment and intellectual property protection; and
- product certification.

NAFTA facilitates the cross-border movement of certain business persons who are citizens of Canada, Mexico, or the United States

Smarter Borders

Improving the secure flow of goods and people at the border is a key priority for both Canada and the United States.

In December 2001, Canada and the USA signed a declaration to build a Smart Border for the 21st Century to accommodate the growth in trade and commerce.

The Declaration outlined a 30-Point Action Plan which provides for ongoing collaboration in identifying and addressing security risks, while efficiently expediting the legitimate flow of people and goods across the Canada-U.S. border.

FAST lanes for pre-approved low-risk commercial traffic opened at Windsor-Detroit, Sarnia-Port Huron, and Fort Erie-Buffalo.
Today, border wait times average less than 10 minutes, one of the most efficient systems in the world.

Short Distances to Markets

Ninety percent of Canada's population lives within 200 kilometres of the Canada/U.S. border, and many Canadian production centres are actually closer to their U.S. markets than U.S-based manufacturers.

Direct Access to the NAFTA Market

Canada offers ideal access to the huge U.S. market—tariff-free trade under North American Free Trade Agreement (NAFTA), and very short distances to major U.S. centres. From Canada, it's easy to ship anywhere in the U.S.

- The signing of NAFTA integrated the Canadian and U.S. economies for nearly all business purposes.

- As a result, Canadian-based business have access to one market of over 400 million consumers with a combined GDP of over US$11.4 trillion.

- Many Canadian production hubs are actually closer to U.S. markets than American production sites - of Canada's 20 largest cities, 17 are within an hour and half's drive of the U.S.

- Direct air service between major cities in Canada and the U.S. has nearly doubled in 6 years.

Major U.S. Trading Partner

Canada and the U.S. are separate political entities that are virtually intertwined in the marketplace. Canadian economies are closely integrated, and both nations are economically interdependent.

- Canada and the U.S. have the world's largest trade partnership, with two-way trade amounting to C$645 billion in 2003. In fact, this averages to more than C$1.2 million dollars a minute in trade.

- The U.S. trades more with Canada than with any other country - the U.S. trades more with Canada than with all of the countries of the E.U. combined!

Trade Links with the Americas

The Free Trade Area of the Americas (FTAA), poised to become the world's largest free trade area, will provide Canada with greater access to markets, fair and efficient dispute settlement, and stability for Canadian businesses.

Total Trade in Top Sectors – 2003
($CDN billions)

Transportation Equipment	158.9
Oil and Gas Extraction	49.8
Chemicals	40.9
Machinery	37.5
Computer & Electronics Products	33.8
Other Sectors	394.7
Total Trade	*715.6*

Strong Historical Trade Ties to Europe

Canada's links with Europe are strong, and European markets continue to provide tremendous trade opportunities for Canada.

Unique Access to Asian Economies

With its geographic location, its immigration links and its active participation in the Asia-Pacific Economic Cooperation, Canada is uniquely positioned to benefit from long-term growth in Asia.

BUSINESS ENVIRONMENT

Canada's Cost-Competitive Business Environment

Canada is a great place to do business! It's underlying fundamentals are extremely strong—and its exceptionally competitive business environment offers a number of significant and concrete cost advantages.

Here are some of the ways in which Canada can give your company a significant competitive cost advantage—and could end up being the best place in the world for you to do business!

Low Production Costs

The cost of production in Canada is extremely competitive with G-7 countries in general, and the U.S. in particular. Their productivity, skilled workers and low production costs all combine to create a very favourable — and cost-competitive — business environment. Canada's competitive position vis-a-vis the U.S. has improved substantially in the past 10 years.

The evidence of Canada's low cost of doing business is seen in many areas:

- In a recent study, "Competitive Alternatives" conducted by the management consulting firm KPMG, Canada is the overall cost leader for 2004 with a 9 percent cost advantage over the United States

43

- Canada ranks first in nine major industry sectors, including biomedical research, pharmaceuticals and aerospace.

- Canadian labour costs are lowest among G-7 nations. Total payments for Canadian statutory and other benefits are 29% of salary and wages compared to 32% in the U.S.

- Annual electricity costs for the average manufacturer are 22% lower in Canada than they are in the U.S., and the lowest of all G-7 nations

- In the advanced manufacturing sector, land and building costs are 8% lower in Canada than in the U.S.

- The value of the Canadian dollar provides major leverage, when compared to the U.S. dollar.

Internationally, Canadian locations compare favourably in terms of statutory corporate income taxes.

Competitive Corporate Taxes

Think Canada's taxes are high? Think again! Recent reforms to Canadian tax regime have made Canada a very attractive place for starting and growing a business.

- Canadian locations compare well internationally in terms of statutory corporate income tax rates.
- Firms in Canada have a growing income tax rate advantage over U.S. firms.
- Elimination of capital tax helps increases tax advantage to 3.4 percentage points by 2008.

LOW LABOUR COSTS

Employee Benefits

According to a <u>recent survey</u> by the consulting firm KPMG:

- Labour costs - the single most important location-sensitive cost factor - are the lowest in Canada.
- Total payments for Canadian statutory and other benefits are 29% of salary and wages compared to 32% in the U.S. Lower medical insurance premiums are an important reason for this.

CONSTRUCTION, LAND, OFFICE SPACE AND LEASES

Canadian business-cost advantages extend far beyond their competitive tax environment and low production costs. Expenses in virtually every key business area are lower in Canada.

- Canada has abundant oil, gas, coal and hydro-electric resources.
- Electricity costs for industrial users are significantly lower in Canada than in the U.S.: the annual electrical costs for an average manufacturer are 22% lower in Canada than in the U.S.
- Building construction costs in Canada are roughly 8% lower than those in the U.S. even after accounting for additional materials for climatic conditions.

Low Overall Cost of Doing Business

Lowest Business Costs Among Major North American Cities

The overall cost of doing business is considerably lower in Canada than in other industrialized nations.

Major Canadian cities, such as Toronto and Montreal, have lower business costs than any other major city of comparable size in North America. In comparison to U.S. cities, the Canadian cost advantage is highest vis-à-vis San Jose and New York.

POSITIVE BUSINESS CLIMATE

Canada enjoys a strong fiscal situation, low inflation and low interest rates, growing domestic economy and superior tax advantages.

And in addition, there are many other sound reasons that also help account for the positive business climate that Canada has created — and its great reputation as a dynamic yet stable and predictable business environment.

- Canada understands the importance of its business community and has created an environment to encourage its success

- Canada ranks **1st** in the Economic Intelligence Unit's global business rankings for the forecast period (2003-07), up from 4th place for the historical period (1998-2002).

- Regulations pertaining to the creation of new businesses are considerably more flexible in Canada than those in the rest of the G-7.

- Canada ranks highest among the G-7 and OECD countries in terms of the number of procedures in establishing new businesses.

- Canada ranks highest among the G-7 with regard to the number of days required in establishing new businesses.

First-Class Infrastructure

High-tech or low-tech -- whether it's access to broadband and the digital economy, Canada's sound and trustworthy banking system, or reliable municipal services, Canada offers a business infrastructure unmatched anywhere in the world.

Canada's business infrastructure is among the best in the world!
In the contemporary business and economic world, infrastructure must encompass far more than the "old economy" basics. *Canada's technological and marketplace infrastructure is designed with the 21st century in mind!*

Canada has all the state-of-the-art infrastructure you need to do business in a stable, predictable and hassle-free environment:

- first-class communications
- world standard research and development capabilities
- reliable financial institutions, wired and responsive to the needs of businesses
- fair, dependable and transparent marketplace rules

CANADA'S COST ADVANTAGES

Internet Usage

Canada is one of the most wired, computer literate nations in the world, and is first among all G-7 countries in the percentage of its population that uses the Internet. Canada is second only to the U.S. in the number of computers per 1,000 people.

Internet and Wireless Affordability

Communications are key to any company's ability to compete and do business — and in Canada, the cost of communicating is reasonable! Canada ranks first among the G-7 in terms of wireless communications costs and among leaders in terms of internet access charges.

Telephone Affordability

Business telephone charges are lower in Canada than in any other G-7 country. Canada ranks among leaders in residential telephone charges.

47

Telephone and Cable Penetration
Among Leaders in Household Penetration Rates:
Canadian households lead the G-7 in terms of cable penetration rates and rank a close 2nd behind Germany in telephone penetration.

Connectedness
A World Leader in Overall Connectedness:
Overall connectedness is one of the very best indicators of the degree to which a society and/or economy are participating in the contemporary world of high tech innovation. And Canada is a world leader in terms of overall connectedness!

Connectedness Rankings 2003*
Conference Board of Canada

10 Country Comparison

	Overall Connectedness	Availability	Price	Reach	Usage
U.S.	1	1	2	2	1
Canada	2	2	1	2	2
Sweden	2	3	2	1	3
Finland	4	4	5	5	5
U.K.	5	5	7	5	5
Australia	5	7	9	8	4
Germany	5	5	6	4	7
Japan	8	8	8	7	8
France	9	9	4	9	9
Italy	10	10	10	10	10

Source: The Conference Board of Canada, April 2004

* The four components are defined as follows:

1. Availability is the supply, reflecting the potential to be connected.
2. Reach is the demand. It refers to those people who already subscribe to the network.

3. Use measures such factors as actual hours online, number of transactions and dollars of revenue generated on the internet.
4. Price also comes into play insofar as it influences reach and availability.

Canada's technological infrastructure is also first class!

Canada's technological infrastructure is second only to the U.S. among G-7 nations—and it rank above or very close to the U.S. in terms of

- Internet users and Internet hosts
- Computers per capita

Building a universal, competitive, leading-edge Information Highway is a government of Canada priority.

Technological Infrastructure* World Ranking

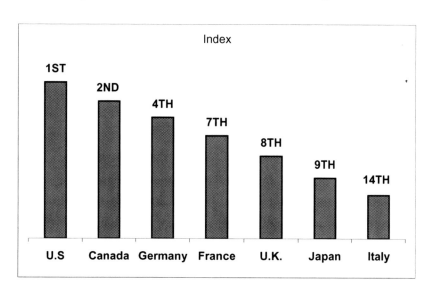

Sound Financial Institutions

In May 2002, Moody's Investors Services raised Canada's credit rating to AAA (the highest rating) in response to Canada's improved fiscal balance sheet and excellent long-term growth prospects.

49

Similarly in July 2002, Standard & Poor's raised Canada's long-term foreign sovereign credit rating to AAA.

According to Moody's Financial Strength ratings, Canadian banks rank first among the G-7, in terms of their intrinsic credit-worthiness.

Marketplace Rules
Fair and Transparent Marketplace Framework

Canada's marketplace framework laws are the standards for its innovative and vibrant economy. They set the rules of the game. The conditions for building a competitive and prosperous nation, where innovation is rewarded, investment encouraged, capital raised and international trade maximized.

Sound, coherent marketplace rules and services are essential for a dynamic business climate and a strong economy. They:

- govern corporate behaviour
- ensure that competition is brisk
- ensure that transactions are fair
- assure consumer protection
- make information—essential for informed choices and innovation—available
- set policy directions for sustainable growth

Fair, Dependable, Transparent

Marketplace services are essential to business. Companies need ground rules for everything from incorporation rules to competition policy, bankruptcy procedures to the protection of intellectual property so that they can operate in a predictable environment.

- For example, more than 200,000 Canadian businesses have chosen the *Canada Business Corporations Act* as their framework law to protect their corporate name and give them the right to carry on business across the country.

- Canada's marketplace frameworks and services are benchmarked against the best in the world, so that Canada can provide the world's best business environment.

Canada's fair, dependable and transparent marketplace rules ensure that business competes on a level playing field.

Research & Development
Cutting Edge Canadian Innovation

Canada is committed to innovation, and the basis of innovation is ground-breaking R&D.
The proof of Canada's commitment is the vast amount of top notch research and development work that is being carried out across the nation. In virtually every field—photonics, medicine, genetics, nanotechnology, wireless—Canadian researchers are helping lead the way, with the full support of the Canadian government.

- Making Canada the most connected Government to its citizens by 2005.

- Making high-speed broadband access available to Canadians in all communities by 2005.

- The Government of Canada has undertaken to double its investment in research and development by 2010.

- Canada's goal is to become one of the five most "research intensive" nations in the world.

Government Policies/Programs Aimed at Building the Knowledge Infrastructure

- 21st Century Chairs for Research Excellence
- Network Centres of Excellence
- Canadian Foundation for Innovation
- Canadian Institute for Health Research
- Telecommunications Policy
- Technology Partnerships Canada
- Granting Councils (NSERC, MRC, SSHRC)
- Communications Research Centre
- Industrial Research Assistance Programme (NRC)

51

- Co-operative sectoral research programs (PAPRICAN)
- Canadian Network for the Advancements of Research, Industry and Education (CANARIE)
- SE&ED (Scientific Research and Experimental Development) tax credit for private sector research and development
- Leading Edge information systems:
  - Strategis
  - CISTI (NRC)
  - Canadian Technology Network
  - Sector Competitive Frameworks

EXCELLENT PLACE TO LIVE

Canada offers a superb quality of life: a safe, just and equitable society, excellent health and social programs, a reasonable cost of living, a world-renowned natural environment, dynamic cities and a rich cultural life!

Yes, there are a multitude of sound business reasons for setting up shop in Canada:, its low corporate taxes, access to North American markets, unparalleled infrastructure, low costs ... the list goes on. But there's another powerful reason to come to Canada as well: quality of life.

Outstanding Quality of Life

For executives, management and workforce alike, Canada is a great place to live – an important factor when it comes to corporate morale and stability.

According to a recent annual quality-of-life ranking of 205 world cities by Mercer Human Resources Consulting, five Canadian cities ranked among the top 25.

Rapidly Improving Living Standards

- Canada's productivity rate has strongly improved and the employment rate has increased sizably.

- These factors have contributed to an increase in Canada's standard of living, as commonly measured by real GDP per capita.
- In fact, Canada's standard of living grew faster than any other G-7 country over the 1997-2003 period marking a major turnaround over the 1980-1986 period.

Reasonable Cost of Living

Canada is a very affordable place to live; in fact, it's less expensive to live in Canada than in any other G7 nation!

- The cost of living in most large Canadian cities is better than or comparable to similar U.S. cities.
- And, Canadian cities rank better than U.S. cities in terms of the level of crime, pollution, environment and leisure facilities.

Good Environment

Canada is renowned for its unspoiled environment but sustainability is what counts for long-term economic security, as well as environmental health.

Canada is famous world-wide for the quality and beauty of its environment: plentiful fresh water, an amazing variety of scenic ecosystems, abundant wildlife and flora, and so on.

But environmental quality and economic sustainability are also intimately linked, and here too Canada out-performs: as measured by the environmental sustainability index, Canada ranks highest among the G-7 in addressing environmental concerns such as air and water pollution, land protection, and greenhouse emissions.

Safe and Just Society

Canada has a well-deserved reputation as a stable, civil and equitable society, which fosters an environment of opportunity for all.

Canada tops the G-7 as a safe place to live and conduct business with the most fairly administered judicial system.

Equal Opportunity and Multiculturalism

- Canada ranks first among the G-7 in providing equal opportunities for individuals.
- Canada has one of the world's most multilingual societies with over 100 languages identified as the mother tongue.

Major Metropolitan Areas of Canada

City		Labour Force 2002 **	Unemployment Rate 2002 **
Toronto (region)	1	2 985.1	7.2
Montreal	2	1 922.4	8.3
Vancouver	3	1 163.1	7.7
Ottawa-Gatineau	4	618.7	7.1
Calgary	5	612.2	5.6
Edmonton	6	546.1	4.9
Quebec (city)	7	381.1	6.2
Hamilton-Wentworth	8	370.	6.5
Winnipeg	9	380.3	5.2
Kitchener-Waterloo	10	240.7	5.6
London	11	228.6	6.8
St. Catharines-Niagara	12	206.5	7.0
Halifax	13	197.4	7.4
Windsor-Essex	14	171.6	8.0
Victoria	15	161.5	6.9
Saskatoon	16	126.1	5.9
Regina	17	113.1	5.3
St. John's	18	96.	9.0
Saguenay	19	78.9	11.4
Sherbrooke	20	82.8	7.6
Sudbury	21	80.1	8.9
Barrie	22	75.2	5.6
Kelowna	23	77.1	9.6
Abbotsford	24	80.5	7.5
Kingston	25	58.1	7.1
Trois-Rivières	26	71.4	9.9
P.E.I	27	75.5	11.9
Saint John	28	66.7	8.1
Thunder Bay	29	64.8	6.3
Moncton	30	67.8	6.5
Guelph	31	71.4	4.3
Peterborough	32	34.9	9.2
Brantford	33	58.2	6.4

* Source : Adapted from Statistics Canada, 2001 Census. Reference Cat.# 97C0001. Telephone: (613) 951-8116 GeneralEnquiry.
** Source : Adapted from Labour Force Survey. Reference Cat.# 71543. Telephone: (613) 951-4168 J Ouellet.

55

Chapter 3

ARE YOU READY
TO TAKE THE CHALLENGE

Minding Your Own Business: Becoming an Entrepreneur

"Just do what you do best."

(*Red Auerbach, Hall of Fame Basketball Coach)*

SELF-EVALUATION

Do These Statements Apply To You ?

- I want my work to be more meaningful.
- I want work that is new, exciting and challenging.
- I need a change. I want a new start.
- I am not interested in my career the way I used to be.
- I'm out of work and I want something more than just another job.
- I often think about starting my own business.

If these statements describe you, you may be changing — inside. Perhaps the things that used to be important to you don't matter as much. Maybe you are beginning to define success differently than you once did. You may have taken on new priorities, values and interests. Or perhaps you need to change because of other circumstances. Your career may have been going smoothly when you were suddenly laid off. Your job loss may have been because of company downsizing, corporate restructuring, plant closure, or the introduction of new technology. Or maybe you have just graduated and have been unsuccessful in finding a good job.

Whatever the changes that are occurring in your life, you feel that it's time to make a career change, and you are wondering about starting your own business.

The Time Is Right

Even though the Canadian economy is going through some difficult changes, there are reasons why now is a good time to think about starting your own small business.

Shifting consumer demands, increasing global competition, and the introduction of new technologies have hit some industries hard. Many large companies have been forced to cut back on operations and to downsize their work forces. But small companies have proved to be more resilient. In fact, small businesses — not large corporations — are creating most of the new jobs in Canada. Why? Because a small business has more flexibility than a large one. It can

59

respond more quickly to changes in the economy and take advantage more easily of new opportunities.

Governments are now encouraging Canadians to consider starting small businesses. If you are interested, you will find support from all levels of government and many financial institutions.

You Won't Be Alone

A growing number of Canadians are starting their own businesses. Some find that they have a skill or talent that is in demand. Others find a product or service to sell that people need or want.

Most entrepreneurs find that their new ventures require careful research, sound planning, determination and energy. But those who are successful believe that the personal rewards are worth it. They like the independence of being self-employed. They like the flexibility of choosing their working hours. And they like the potential to earn more than they might in a job working for someone else. Successful business owners are often among the most satisfied members of the work force.

This Book Can Help You

This book is designed to help you decide if running your own business is a realistic career choice. It will:

- help you determine whether or not you have the right qualities and skills;
- offer advice on different approaches to starting a business and writing a business plan;
- provide information on different business structures;
- give you a better understanding of the challenges and problems you might face; and
- point you in the right direction to the next step.

COULD YOU SUCCEED IN SMALL BUSINESS?

You may have many reasons for wanting to start a business. They may include wanting to make money, having personal independence and self-fulfillment, or escaping the frustrations of employment — and unemployment. Your reasons may be good ones, but your decision must be based on more than simply a desire to change your situation. A new venture is risky. It may make heavy demands, financially and time-wise, on you and on those close to you. It might not provide you with security such as a regular pay cheque, medical and dental benefits, and a pension plan.

One of the first steps you should take in making the decision to start a small business is to determine if you have the right skills and temperament. You have to be as honest with yourself as possible.

A REALITY CHECK FOR SMALL BUSINESS OWNERS

The following checklist will suggest what to look for in yourself to improve your chances for success.

1. Do I have a burning desire to be "on my own"?
  Yes ___   No ___

Most entrepreneurs have a strong inner drive to strike out on their own. They like the idea of being their own boss and not having to report to anyone.

> *"I've always had an independent streak even when I was working in a large federal agency. I'm sure it was that independence that helped me decide to take the plunge and start my own business when I was let go. After three years, I still like the feeling of being in control."*
>
> *- K.T., Ottawa, Ontario*

61

2. Am I confident that I can succeed?
Yes ____ No ____

Successful entrepreneurs believe in themselves. They are optimistic about projects they undertake, and are good at motivating others and sharing their enthusiasm when pursuing goals. They are likely to say, "When I set my mind to it, I usually do well. I expect to succeed." or "I've succeeded in the past and I'll succeed now. I won't let a setback stop me."

3. Am I willing to take calculated and moderate risks?
Yes ____ No ____

Going into business involves taking a chance. You may have to push yourself beyond what is comfortable for you and try new things. Successful business people are willing to take risks, but they are also realistic. They gather as much information and support as possible before making a move. In this way, they build a safety net for themselves and decrease the amount of risk involved.

> *"The point about being in business is that you can't make an omelette without breaking some eggs. Buying inventory, signing a lease, hiring employees — you've got to be willing to handle some risk if you want to be in business for yourself. You can't be reckless, but you have to be willing to take calculated risks now and then."*
>
> *- S.D., Whitehorse, Yukon*

4. Am I a self-starter?
Yes ____ No ____

Successful entrepreneurs believe that what happens in life usually depends on themselves. They are often described as "internal" — people who choose to do something based on their own interests and views. Because they believe that they control their own destiny, they refuse to be at the mercy of others or of events. As a result, they take the initiative in starting projects and getting ideas off the ground.

5. Am I able to set long-term goals? Can I stick with them? Even if I'm faced with a difficult problem or situation?
Yes ___ *No* ___

Successful business people are patient and determined. They have the ability to work toward a goal, delaying rewards until a future time, and persist even in difficult times. They understand that it takes time to build success — sometimes years.

> *"At first, it was frightening to realize that everything about the business — the problems, the solutions, my staff of two, its ultimate success or failure — depended on me. But I was determined to take anything on and to make the business work. My hard work and determination got me through the low points to where I am now. It was worth it."*
> -   *V.B., Winnipeg, Manitoba*

6. Do I believe that money is the best measure of success?
Yes ___ *No* ___

If your only reason for going into business is to make money, it may not be enough to make you a success. The desire for money is not a prime motivation for most successful business people. Rather, they want personal fulfillment and enjoy doing their best. While money is important to them, it is a means to do more and not simply a way to gain wealth and prestige.

7. Am I creative? Am I always looking for new approaches and ideas? Am I innovative?
Yes ___ *No* ___

Entrepreneurs often have many ideas and a great capacity to dream up and carry out projects. They are highly motivated by their desire to innovate or to bring their own approach to doing things. Never satisfied or content, they believe there is always a better way to get a job done.

63

8. Am I good at making decisions? Are my decisions generally sound?   Yes ___ No ___

Successful business people tend to be comfortable making their own decisions. They say, "When I decide to do something, I carry it through to the end, overcome any obstacles and face all the issues."

9. Am I willing to market my product or service? Yes ___ No ___

Successful business people do not believe the old saying: "Build a better mousetrap and the world will beat a path to your door." They know that proper marketing is critical to business performance. They advise: "You must sell, sell, sell."

> *"I never imagined how hard it would be to sell myself — and I used to be in marketing. It was daunting the first year I was on my own. I was no longer selling the company product. I was selling myself and what I knew. I called every possible contact I could think of and sent out information packages. There were so many rejections, so many no-replies. I had to change my strategy. Instead of cold calls and mailings, I started using referrals to get new clients. Once I got a few good*
> *ones, the others followed."*
> *- L.S., Ottawa, Ontario*

10. Am I a good organizer? Do I pay attention to details? Yes ___ No ___

Conducting a successful business requires organizational skills and competence. As a small business owner, you *are* your own boss. Since there is no one looking over your shoulder to make sure you are doing your job well, you will need self-discipline. Your ability to pay attention to details can make the difference between success or failure.

11. *Am I flexible? Do I adapt to change? Can I handle surprises?*
Yes ___ No ___

Change is a fact of life. To succeed in business, you must accept this fact and use it to your advantage. Successful business people monitor social trends, adopt new technologies, compare themselves to the competition, and listen and watch with an open mind.

Do You Have What It Takes?

By now, you will be able to put together a good picture of the qualities and skills required to succeed in your own business. You are likely to be happy and successful in your own business if you:

- possess an inner drive to be independent;
- are able to set and achieve goals;
- are flexible and adaptable;
- are willing to work hard;
- have confidence in your ability to succeed;
- possess self-discipline, leadership abilities and organizational skills; and
- have the confidence to make decisions and take calculated risks.

If you don't have all these qualities, you might need to develop some additional skills, or perhaps you might require an associate, partner, or employee whose strong qualities can counterbalance your weaknesses.

If you don't have at least some of these qualities, you will have to decide if a small business is the right career option for you. If it isn't, and you are already employed, you might be better off staying in your current job and creating new possibilities there. If that doesn't work, you might consider other jobs that could interest you either with your current employer or with a new one. If you do not have a job, perhaps you should look for new employment in your area of expertise.

65

If you are still having difficulty deciding if starting a business is the best career option for you, go through the reality check again with a friend or someone you trust to be honest with you. Ask them for their opinion. Compare notes. The exercise can be very revealing — and worthwhile.

CHOOSING THE RIGHT BUSINESS

Going With What You Know

Barry was working as an electrician with a large company before he decided to start his own electrical contracting business. Since he was a licensed electrician and knew the construction business, he didn't find the transition too difficult.

In starting a business in an area in which you already have expertise, you have many advantages:

- a proven track record;
- basic talents, skills and abilities;
- additional skills and knowledge acquired through experience; and
- contacts who will either be customers or can make referrals.

Whether you call yourself a consultant, free-lancer or independent contractor, you are taking your expertise and building a new career with it. If you are like most Canadians who have made this choice, you are off to a good start. Many experts say that the best chance for success in running a business is to offer a product or service that you know well already.

Going in A New Direction

Maria had worked as a property manager for 12 years when she decided that it was time for change. She had always loved reading and after researching the market she opened a bookstore in a local mall. The start-up costs were high and Maria couldn't afford to pay herself until she had been in business for three years. For her, it was all worth it.

Starting your own business from scratch is riskier than building one based on your existing expertise and experience. It usually requires more effort to establish and develop regular customers. Financing may also be more difficult to obtain. You should expect a period of low income and possibly even losses in the early stages of your business.

If you are determined to have a complete career change when starting your own business, you have to come up with an idea for a new venture. This is how to start:

1. *Learn about yourself*

Think hard about what you like to do, including your hobbies and studies. You are more likely to be successful if you do something that really interests you. Typically, successful business people have found their life's passion. They often say that there is very little difference between their work and their play — in fact, both are the same thing to them.

> *"I have always enjoyed making pasta dishes. So after I was given the pink slip, I decided that a small gourmet shop specializing in pasta seemed the right thing for me to try. It was what I loved to do and my research showed that the demand was there because people are looking for low-fat, nutritional food that's delicious. At the time, the financial lenders were starting to encourage women in business. It was that encouragement that got me started."*
>
> *- E.C., Québec, Quebec*

2. *Study the marketplace*

Are there products or services lacking in your community, or ones that could be improved? Be alert for the signals: "Why don't they...?" or "I wish that...!". Think about problems you encounter in everyday living. If it's a problem for you, it's bound to be a problem for others.

Environmental concerns, the growth and decline of specific industries, new developments in research, changing consumer expectations — this type of information may lead you to business opportunities. Many successful business people say, "There was a niche in the market and I filled it."

68

3. Put your ideas to the test

You may like the idea of providing a service in your community or selling a product that you have either manufactured yourself or purchased from someone else. It's a good step at this point to test your ideas. Inexperienced business people often make decisions about services or products based only on what they like or want, while ignoring the needs of their potential customers.

Try an informal survey. Take a description of your services or a sample of your products to several people who will provide you with an honest and objective evaluation. Ask them the following questions:

- Would you be interested in buying my product or service?
- What do you like and dislike about my product or service?
- If you dislike my product or service, is there some way I can improve it so that it appeals more to you? What would make you more likely to buy it?
- Do you buy something similar to my product or service now? Are you satisfied with it?
- Is there anything about my product or service that makes it stand out from the others?
- How much do you pay for the other product or service?
- How much would you pay for my product or service?

If more of them like the idea or product and respond positively, you are probably on the right track. At this point, you may consider a more formal marketing or research survey.

In summary, start with what you like to do and take a good look at what the market needs. See if there is any area where your interests and market needs intersect. With this information, you can start narrowing down the types of business that appeal to you. Once you have chosen a product or service that you want to sell, do some more research by talking to people whose opinions are honest and reliable.

SETTING UP A BUSINESS

No business opportunity is ever lost — if you fumble it, your competitor will find it.

Most successful entrepreneurs begin their new ventures by writing a business plan. A good business plan can be useful in organizing your thoughts and giving you a clear idea of where you're headed. Also, if you need financing from a bank or other financial institution, you will have to prepare a business plan to apply for a loan.

A sound business plan profiles your business, outlines your financing needs and sets out your assets and liabilities. It should be realistic and achievable and have well-defined milestones by which to evaluate your progress. It must include:

- the business proposal, its goals and how you plan to achieve them;
- market analysis — who are your suppliers, customers and competitors;
- your budget and financing, cash flow and anticipated profits; and
- time lines and schedules.

If you're uncertain about how to write up a business plan, there are many places you can go for information, including libraries, university courses, government agencies and financial institutions.

What Type of Business Will You Have?

There are four basic types of business structures recognized under Canadian law. They are:

1. Sole Proprietorship

A sole proprietorship is the simplest of the business structures.

- It usually involves one person and can be operated under that person's name.
- The owner owns the business entirely, and there is no legal separation between the owner's personal assets and those of the business.
- The business is taxed through the owner's personal income tax, and losses can be used to reduce taxes on other sources of personal income.

2. Partnership

A partnership is created when two or more people agree to carry on a business for profit.

- A partnership, whether there is a written agreement or not, is a legally binding relationship in which each partner is liable for the actions of the other partners.
- There is no difference legally between a proprietorship and a partnership, except that in a partnership, the partners share the profits and the liabilities.
- Partners are taxed on all the earnings of the business in proportion to their share in the business.

3. Limited Company (Corporation)

Corporations are identified by the use of such words as Limited, Incorporated or Corporation — or appropriate abbreviations of these words — after the company name.

- A limited company is a separate entity in law, distinct and separate from its shareholders, officers and directors.
- The assets of the company belong to the company, not the owner(s). Similarly, the owner(s) of a limited company cannot be held personally responsible for any debts of the company unless such debts have been guaranteed personally.
- A limited company may be incorporated federally or provincially.

4. Business Co-operatives (Co-op)

The business co-op is a special form of an incorporated structure.

- The start-up capital of a co-op is raised by members' shares.
- The liability of each member is limited to the amount of share capital she or he owns.
- Co-op members provide mutual support and pool skills.

Franchise

A franchise is not a unique business structure. Rather it is a technique for marketing goods and services.

- A company, the Franchiser, grants to another person, known as the Franchisee, the privilege, right, or license to carry on a business in a certain manner for a limited period of time in a designated location.
- The Franchisee is permitted to sell the goods or services of the Franchiser and use its methods and know-how, its trademarks and image, or a combination of these.
- In return for the right to sell the Franchiser's goods or services, the Franchisee must pay an initial fee and ongoing royalties.

There are advantages and disadvantages of each type of business structure or marketing technique. It is important that you find out which would be best for you by researching further and discussing your choice with an accountant or lawyer.

THOSE WHO HAVE TAKEN THE CHALLENGE

Running a business is one of the most difficult and demanding of career options. However, many people who have made that choice are successful. This section of the book provides you with comments and profiles of some entrepreneurs and will give you a glimpse of the challenges and rewards that they faced.

Building A Business On What They Knew

Some people started up their businesses based on their training and work experience. Although it wasn't easy for any of them, their expertise helped them get their businesses off the ground. They were able to find customers from an established clientele that needed their services.

Mike and Gloria's Story

Mike and Gloria were working as translators with a large government agency when they decided to run a free-lance translation business out of their home. It was a difficult decision at the time.

Mike recalls, "We were both ready for a change. We had the skills and we knew there was a good market for our services. But I was terrified of the unknown. Now that I look back, it was the best decision we ever made. We wouldn't trade the flexibility of our work for anything."

Gloria adds, "For me, the biggest worry was not having a pay cheque every two weeks. In the first six months on our own, we certainly found out what cash flow was all about. It's something that never crossed our minds when we were employed."

They were lucky because they did not have to do a lot of marketing. "We placed ourselves on several source lists and the calls just started coming in," Gloria says. "At first, we took every job and treated each one as though it were our last," Mike adds. "We ended up working way more hours than we ever had at the office because we couldn't refuse anything. Now we've learned how to pace ourselves better." Professional advice from their accountant was very helpful. Mike says, "Because we are working at home, we are entitled to a number of tax deductions. He advised us about them and helped us to set up detailed records."

Paul's Story

After Paul completed his horticulture program at a community college, the only work he could find was a part-time job with the local landscaping company where he had worked as a summer student. "I wasn't all that thrilled about it," he recalls. "The company hadn't kept up with environmental trends and was still using chemical herbicides and pesticides. I wanted to be a guardian of nature, not a polluter."

Paul had often thought about starting his own nature-friendly gardening business. "It's strange how things just seem to fall into place sometimes. One of my instructors at the college called me one day and asked if I would be interested in buying an already established gardening business — a two-man operation that had a loyal clientele. The owner wanted to retire and was looking for 'a young go-getter with new-fangled ideas, but who wouldn't throw out all the old ways either.'"

As soon as they met, Paul and the owner knew they had found the right match. "I started with him the very next day, even though we hadn't even discussed the details of the purchase. I guess you could say he was satisfied that he found the type of person he was looking for."

Since the business had an established clientele, Paul had little difficulty getting financing and his cash flow has never been a problem. Now he is cautiously expanding his client base, always with the goal of maintaining the high quality of personal service set by his mentor. And recently, he started hosting a local cable show on traditional gardening.

Starting From Scratch

Some people decide to start completely new ventures. Without training or experience in their choice for a small business, they usually find that they have to take courses, research their market and develop their clientele.

Bill's Story

"I love university life," Bill says. "After graduating, I dreamed of opening a magazine and coffee shop in a university town. I felt the two things would really go well together." His plan was to attract students with a large magazine selection, and by providing a cosy café-type area at the back, entice them to stay for a coffee and inexpensive dessert. "I saw it as a place for them to get away from campus for awhile and just relax by themselves or with their friends."

Bill's layoff from a computer company gave him the incentive to put his dream into action. "It was now or never," he recalls. "I believed in my idea, but I also knew I needed heavy foot traffic and good volume to pull it off."

Bill feels that the smartest thing he ever did was to have a thorough market research study done. It confirmed his belief that a magazine-and-coffee/dessert combination had real potential. The next step was to find the right town and the right location. Bill found a place halfway between two universities and he was a success in his first year. Students come in droves to browse at the magazines and to sip coffee. On many days, it seems that the whole town has made his shop a part of their weekly routine. Magazines and newspapers are selling as Bill anticipated, but the café has flourished beyond his expectations. He plans to extend it into a walled-in courtyard for the summer.

Marie-Claire's Story

After 12 years of working as an administrative clerk at a large insurance company, Marie-Claire became increasingly dissatisfied with her job. "I remember feeling so guilty," she says. "Here I was in a secure, well-paying job when a lot of people I knew were losing theirs. But I was unhappy with my work. I used to think that there had to be a better way to make a living — that life was just passing me by."

The turning point for Marie-Claire was when she read an article on the growing demand for personal image consultants. The more she thought about it, the more she liked the idea. "I've been fascinated by the fashion world as long as I can remember. It probably runs in the family. My father is a clothing manufacturer and I was always reading fashion magazines."

Marie-Claire knew she had the necessary administrative skills to go on her own, but not the expertise in fashion sketching and make-up application. "I decided not to leave my job right away. I wanted to move slowly and get the skills I needed while I was still working. It wasn't easy taking courses and working full time. It took several years, but I stuck with it."

Today, Marie-Claire runs a successful personal image consulting service in a downtown shopping centre. "I just love what I'm doing," she says. "For the first time in my life I'm really me. I'm truly living my dream."

Buying A Franchise

Other people make the decision to buy a franchise business. They feel that a franchise would be less risky than starting a business on their own because the franchising company usually has successful experience in selling its goods or services at other locations. Statistics show that this is true. Franchisees have an 80 percent chance of success compared with 20 percent if they start a completely new venture

Ron and Bob's Story

Ron and his partner Bob saw franchising as a way of starting a career in business. Ron had worked for 20 years as a property manager. Bob had 19 years' experience as an accountant. Both were ready for a career change and had built up a sound financial base.

"We knew we wanted to do something different," Ron says, "but we didn't want the stress of starting a business from scratch. We wanted to go into a business with a solid track record." For more than a year, Ron and Bob researched franchise opportunities. "We're both cautious by nature," Bob explains. "We wanted to be sure we selected the right franchise for us. We had read about people who rushed into signing an agreement and then discovered that the franchiser didn't come through with the promises — and that included some well-known franchisers."

They finally decided to buy a travel franchise. As successful franchisees, Ron and Bob have to follow strict guidelines. As Ron points out, "The franchisee must be willing to work as part of a team, be flexible and work with the head office 100 percent. In return, the franchisee gets to share in the overall success of the whole franchise network. This way, many of the unknowns can be eliminated, especially for people like us who are new to the business world."

Other franchisees say:

"My wife and I have been franchisees for five years now. It was hard work at the beginning because running a business was so new to us. But our franchiser was always there to help. That's crucial. Head office gave a great training session, and the field representative always came whenever we needed advice and consultation. Knowing we're part of a team has given us confidence. We're treated as partners and business people, not as employees."

- V.T., Sarnia, Ontario

"As a franchisee, I have the best of both worlds. In a sense, I'm independent. It's my initiative and hard work that determines how successful the business will be. But I can't be completely independent — nor would I want to be — since I'm part of a bigger system."

V.F., Rimouski, Quebec

"Investing in a franchise can be an expensive venture. Your one-time franchise fee can be $15,000 or more. And the long-term investment for construction or leasehold improvements, fixtures, equipment and inventory can be over $100,000 for even a modest franchise. So you have to know exactly what you're getting into. Do the running around, find out the details and get the advice of your accountant, lawyer, and financial adviser — right away. Don't sign anything until you've done that."

W.M., Saint John, New Brunswick

"One of the most helpful things we did at the start was talk to other people associated with the franchise. We got first-hand accounts of their experiences in the business, and we were able to evaluate the product and find out how well-organized and managed the franchiser was."

C.M., Summerside, Prince Edward Island

WORKING OUT OF THE HOME

Today more than two million Canadian households are involved in home-based businesses. As the cost of personal computers, modems and fax machines has gone down, working out of the home has become more practical. People who once required office staff to complete tasks such as typing reports and filing material can now easily perform this type of work at home. Traditional home-based workers such as plumbers, electricians, contractors, writers and craftspeople can also perform many of their office tasks more effectively and efficiently than in the past.

Types Of Home-Based Businesses

Construction: general contracting, painting, decorating

Manufacturing and processing: picture framing, furniture upholstery, sewing, crafts

Retail: mail order, crafts, silk flowers, wood products

Financial services: insurance, real estate, accounting

Personal services: hairstyling, manicure and massage, tutoring, music lessons

Business services: computer programming, desktop editing, bookkeeping

Health services: physiotherapy, psychotherapy, herbalism

Entertainment: disk jockey, music recording

Other services: catering, automotive repair, writing, equipment rentals

Most people who started businesses in their homes found that the positive aspects of running a home-based business — such as not commuting, increased quality time with family, and stress reduction — far outweighed any negatives.

Linda's Story

Linda was the manager of an income tax preparation agency when the company downsized and she lost her job. "I've always enjoyed helping clients with their tax returns," she says, "so when I had to strike out on my own, it was easy to decide what I was good at — selling my tax expertise to clients. Only this time, it was on my own and out of my home."

She used some of her savings to buy a computer and software, a fax machine and a copier. She also bought stationery and business cards. "I didn't want to spend the money," she recalls, "but I felt that I had to appear as professional as possible."

Linda wasn't able to bring her previous clients with her or even tell them she was going into business for herself. She recalls vividly how hard it was at the beginning. "It was in November. I had business cards made and over the holidays I handed them out to practically everyone I met. I remember many nail-biting days in January when the telephone never rang once. Those were the longest days of my life."

In February, Linda began to get calls as people started to think about their taxes. "More clients, including some of my old ones, began calling as word of mouth spread. It has really worked out well."

Although Linda found she enjoyed working out of her home — especially not having to commute to an office — her business is now too big for a single person. "This spring, I plan to move out of my home and into a small office space downtown. I've even convinced my former secretary to join me."

Linda took courses on running a small business and found them very useful. "I attended several weekend seminars at a local university about home-based businesses. And now I'm taking evening courses offered by the Federal Business Development Bank. They're just what I need to strengthen my weak areas."

Others who are successfully running home-based businesses say:

"Getting to work was a job in itself — waking at 6:00 a.m., dressing for the day, making breakfast, battling rush-hour traffic. Half my energy was gone by the time I reached the office at 8:30. Now I can get up as late as 7:30, and still be at my desk by 8:30, coffee in hand, relaxed and ready to go."

- C.M., Mississauga, Ontario

"Isolation was one of the things about working at home that I hadn't bargained for. At first, I felt cut off both as a person and as a professional. Then I started to build a small network of like-minded people who were also working out of their homes. I have closer friends and colleagues now than I ever had at the office."

- J.G., Victoria, British Columbia

"I find that I am more productive at home than I could ever have been at the office. Without telephone interruptions and colleagues dropping by with their coffee, I can do in one morning what used to take a day or more to get done at the office."

- O.E., Fredericton, New Brunswick

"The neighbours may say, "What a life!" when they see you coming and going throughout the day. What they don't realize is that you end up putting in longer hours when you're working for yourself. You're doing all kinds of work your neighbours aren't aware of — marketing, accounting, income tax and GST. Then, after finishing those tasks, you end up working most of the night to keep up the quality of your product."

- R.S., Dorval, Quebec

"I've been in business for four years, and it has really been an eye-opener. I was prepared for the usual costs such as rent, heat, lights and wages for my two employees. What I wasn't prepared for were all the other employee costs — Employment Insurance, medical coverage, Canada Pension Plan. I wish I'd taken a course about that before I started. The knowledge would have helped."

- M.M., Arnprior, Ontario

FINDING OUT MORE

Most successful entrepreneurs research and plan carefully before they start up their businesses. There are many places you can get information.

Libraries

There are many books on small business. Check your local library or the library of a nearby university or community college for recent listings. Introduce yourself to the librarians. They are a very knowledgeable resource and can help you use the library to your best advantage. As well as recommending specific books, librarians can also guide you to relevant periodicals, government documents, research studies, newspaper clippings, magazines and directories.

Canada Business Service Centres

A Canada Business Service Centre might be your entry point to the full range of business-related programs and services available from federal, provincial and municipal government departments and agencies. Canada Business Service Centres are located in most metropolitan areas. Consult the blue pages of your local telephone directory and call for further information.

Canada Employment Centres

A Canada Employment Centre (CEC) can advise you on a number of business-related programs. For example, its Self-Employment Assistance (SEA) program provides income support, training and technical advice to Employment Insurance claimants and social assistance recipients interested in starting their own business. The CEC is also the contact point for Business Development Centres (BDCs) in designated "Community Futures" areas. BDCs provide loans and technical advice to persons wishing to start their own business. They also work closely with local organizations and can refer you to other services.

Instructional Materials And Courses

Many universities and community colleges offer excellent full- and part-time programs in small business management as well as weekend or one-day seminars. Call the educational facilities in your area for details.

The National Film Board (NFB) is a useful contact for business films and videos. Write or call the NFB to inquire about its latest catalogue. Also, your public library or your local video store may have business videos.

Finally, you might want to check with your local television network for business courses. Some television networks now offer instructional programming on how to start your own business.

Professional Advice

The right professional can help you make important decisions about starting your own business. If you don't already have a working relationship with the type of professionals you need, talk to other small business people to obtain the names of those people who can provide the service you want.

Accountants and bookkeepers can help you to set up systems for tracking revenues and expenses, provide advice on personal and business tax problems, and assist you in completing tax returns. Many accounting firms also have publications on starting and running a small business.

Lawyers can help with the legal matters associated with establishing a business as well as advise you on what form or structure your business should take.

Financial institutions such as banks, trust companies, credit unions and caisses populaires provide financial advice and support and often have a wide range of publications on starting a small business.

Insurance agents and brokers can advise you on standard insurance needs such as fire and theft, and other types of insurance specific to your business needs such as disability, business interruption (loss of income), partnership and product or service.

Business consultants can advise you on all aspects of your business — from developing a business plan to ongoing consultation once your business is underway. Fees charged by business consultants will vary. You might want to start by contacting your local university or community college to see if they provide student consultants through their business programs.

Chapter 4

BUSINESS ESSENTIALS

The only way to success is failure, no failure, no success
(*Lesley Heylen*)

FEASIBILITY CHECKLIST FOR STARTING A SMALL BUSINESS

This checklist is for the owner-manager of a small business enterprise or for one contemplating going into business for the first time. The questions concentrate on areas you must seriously consider to determine if your idea represents a real business opportunity and if you really know what you are getting into. You can use the checklist to evaluate a completely new venture proposal or an apparent opportunity in your existing business.

Perhaps the most crucial problem you will face after expressing an interest in starting a new business or capitalizing on an apparent opportunity in your existing business will be determining the feasibility of your idea. Getting into the right business at the right time is simple advice, but advice that is extremely difficult to implement. The high failure rate of new businesses and products indicates that very few ideas result in successful business ventures, even when introduced by well established firms. Too many entrepreneurs strike out on a business venture so convinced of its merits that they fail to thoroughly evaluate its potential.

This checklist should be useful in evaluating your business idea. It is designed to help you screen out ideas that are likely to fail before you invest extensive time, money and effort in them

Preliminary Analysis

A feasibility study involves gathering, analyzing and evaluating information with the purpose of answering the question: "Should I go into this business?" Answering this question involves a preliminary assessment of both personal and project considerations.

General Personal Considerations

The first seven questions ask you to do a little introspection. Are your personality characteristics such that you can both adapt to and enjoy small business ownership/management?

	Yes	No
Do you like to make your own decision?	____	____
Do you enjoy competition?	____	____
Do you have will power and self-discipline?	____	____
Do you plan ahead?	____	____
Do you get things done on time?	____	____
Can you take advice from others?	____	____
Are you adaptable to changing conditions?	____	____

The next series of questions stress the physical, emotional and financial strains of a new business.

	Yes	No
Do you understand that owning your own business may entail working 12 to 16 hours a day, probably six days a week, and maybe on holidays?	____	____
Do you have the physical stamina to handle a business?	____	____
Do you have the emotional strength to withstand the strain?	____	____
Are you prepared to lower your standard of living for several months or years?	____	____
Are you prepared to lose your savings?	____	____

Specific Personal Considerations

	Yes	No
Do you know which skills and areas of expertise are critical to the success of your project?	____	____
Do you have these skills?	____	____
Does your idea effectively utilize your own skills and abilities?	____	____
Can you find personnel that have the expertise you	____	____

lack?

Do you know why you are considering this project? ____ ____

Will your project effectively meet your career____ ____ aspirations?

The next three questions emphasize the point that very few people can claim expertise in all phases of a feasibility study. You should realize your personal limitations and seek appropriate assistance where necessary (i.e. marketing, legal, financial).

                                                      Yes   **No**

Do you have the ability to perform the feasibility____ ____ study?

Do you have the time to perform the feasibility____ ____ study?

Do you have the money needed to have the____ ____ feasibility study done?

General Project Description

Briefly describe the business you want to enter.

_____

List the products and/or services you want to sell.

_____

Describe who will use your products/services.

_____

Why would someone buy your product/service?

_____

What kind of location do you need in terms of type of neighbourhood, traffic count, nearby firms, etc.

_____

List your products/services suppliers.

_____

List your major competitors - those who sell or provide similar products/services.

List the labour and staff you require to provide your products/services.

Requirements for Success

To determine whether your idea meets the basic requirements for a successful new project, you must be able to answer at least one of the following questions with a "yes."

	Yes	No
Does the product/service/business serve a presently unserved need?	____	____
Does the product/service/business serve an existing market in which demand exceeds supply?	____	____
Can the product/service/business successfully compete with existing competition because of an "advantageous situation", such as better price, location, etc.?	____	____

Major Flaws

A "Yes" response to questions such as the following would indicate that the idea has little chance for success.

	Yes	No
Are there any causes (i.e. restrictions, monopolies, shortages) that make any of the required factors of production unavailable (i.e. unreasonable cost, scarce skills, energy, material, equipment, processes, technology, or personnel)?	____	____
Are capital requirements for entry or continuing operations excessive?	____	____
Is adequate financing hard to obtain?	____	____
Are there potential detrimental environmental effects?	____	____

Are there factors that prevent effective marketing? _____ _____

Desired Income

The following questions should remind you that you must seek both a return on your investment in your own business as well as a reasonable salary for the time you spend in operating that business.

How much income do you desire?

_____

Are you prepared to earn less income in the 1st - 3rd years?

_____

What minimum income do you require?

_____

What financial investment will be required for your business?

_____

How much could you earn by investing this money? (A)

_____

How much could you earn by working for someone else? (B)

_____

Add the amounts in (A) and (B). If this income is greater than what you can realistically expect from your business, are you prepared to forego this additional income to be your own boss with the prospects of more substantial profit/income in future years?

Supply

	Yes	No
Can you make a list of every item of inventory and operating supplies needed?	_____	_____
Do you know the quantity, quality, technical specifications, and price ranges desired?	_____	_____

Do you know the name and location of each
potential source of supply? ____ ____

Do you know the price ranges available for each ____ ____
product from each supplier?

Do you know about the delivery schedules for each ____ ____
supplier?

Do you know the sales terms of each supplier? ____ ____

Do you know the credit terms of each supplier? ____ ____

Do you know the financial condition of each ____ ____
supplier?

Is there a risk of shortage for any critical materials ____ ____
or merchandise?

Are you aware of which suppliers have an ____ ____
advantage relative to transportation costs?

Will the price available allow you to achieve an ____ ____
adequate markup?

Expenses

	Yes	**No**
Do you know what your expenses will be for: rent, wages, insurance, utilities, advertising, interest, etc.?	____	____
Do you need to know which expenses are direct, indirect, or fixed?	____	____
Do you know how much your overhead will be?	____	____

Do you know how much your selling expenses will____ ____
be?

Miscellaneous

	Yes	No
Are you aware of any major risks associated with your product, service and/or business?	____	____
Can you minimize any of these major risks?	____	____
Are there major risks beyond your control?	____	____
Can these risks bankrupt you?	____	____

Venture Feasibility

	Yes	No
Are there any major questions remaining about your proposed venture?	____	____
Do the above questions arise because of a lack of data?	____	____
Do the above questions arise because of a lack of management skills?	____	____
Do the above questions arise because of a "fatal flaw" in your idea?	____	____
Can you obtain the additional data needed?	____	____
Can you obtain the additional managerial skills needed?	____	____
Are you aware that there is less than a 50-50 chance that you will be in business two years from now?		

BUSINESS PLAN GUIDE

This outline is intended to assist an entrepreneur in writing a BUSINESS PLAN for the establishment, the purchase or the expansion of an existing business.

What is a Business Plan?

A business plan is a recognized management tool used by successful and/or prospective businesses of all sizes to document business objectives and to propose how these objectives will be attained within a specific period of time. It is a written document which describes who you are, what you plan to achieve, where your business will be located, when you expect to get under way, and how you will overcome the risks involved and provide the returns anticipated.

Why Do You Need a Business Plan?

A business plan will provide information of your proposed venture to lenders, investors, and suppliers to demonstrate how you plan to use their money, and to establish a basis for credibility of your project

When Should a Business Plan Be Prepared?

The sooner you develop your business plan, the better. You will find that the final copy of your business plan may differ from the original draft, as you will be updating, revising and refining it as you go. It is important that you examine all the relevant factors now. Therefore, you will be able to anticipate any surprises after your business has opened its doors.

Who Should Prepare a Business Plan?

The business plan should be prepared by those persons who will be implementing it. Outside assistance from consultants, accountants, bookkeepers, and experienced business people can definitely help, but you must draft the initial plan. After all, you are the one that is going to run the business once it is open.

Think through each element of your business plan thoroughly so you have a good understanding of the overall picture and all of the details.

Present your plan to others for constructive criticism and advice, and try to profit from their experience. Modify your plan if necessary.

What's in this for Me?

If you have never drawn up a business plan before, you may be curious as to what the benefits are for you. First and most important, your plan gives you a guide to follow. Second, it gives your lending agency insight into your business opportunity therefore, positively affects your loan application. Finally, your plan will help you develop as a manager by giving you practice in thinking about competitive conditions, promotional opportunities, sources of finance, etc. Your goal is to put the plan into action.

1. Executive Summary/Business Description

Briefly describe:

- if this is a new business venture, expansion of an existing business or the purchase of an existing business;
- the type of business activity in which you are engaged (manufacturing, wholesale, retail, food processing, service, high technology, etc.);
- your product or service and its uniqueness;
- the market to be served;
- your advantage over the competition;
- the main objectives of your organization;
- your management background;
- the project time frames involved.
  (This should be no more than a **one** page summary of your business plan.)

In addition, briefly describe what form of business structure you have chosen:

- sole proprietorship;
- partnership (enclose agreement);
- corporation (enclose shareholders agreement);
- cooperative (enclose membership agreement).

Include:

- date the business was registered/incorporated;
- the business name and address;
- the business phone number;
- the principal(s) name(s) and telephone number(s);
- the percentage of business or number of shares held by each (in partnership or corporation);
- the Web site address and relevant E-mail addresses.

2. Project Costs and Project Funding

Identify the costs of the proposed business venture and the sources of the project funding.

Project Cost Summary

Land and Buildings   _____

Leasehold Improvements   _____
(renovations)

Equipment/Furniture   _____

Other Assets (goodwill, franchise,   _____
etc.)

Vehicles (if used in the business)   _____

Inventory (opening cost)   _____

Other Start Up Expenses as per Cash   _____
Flow (accounting, taxes and
licenses, insurance, rent, supplies,
etc.)

Working Capital   _____

Total Project Cost   _____

Project Funding

Equity

- cash   _____

- contributed assets   _____

Land and Building Mortgage   _____

Equipment Loan   _____

Other Loan   _____

Line of Credit (L/C)   _____

Grant/Subsidy   _____

Total Project Funding   _____

*

TOTAL PROJECT COSTS AND PROJECT FUNDING MUST BE EQUAL

3. Product/Service

- Describe the products to be produced or the services/good to be provided.
- What makes your product/service unique, or, how is your business different from others in the industry?
- What are the features/advantages that will entice customers to buy from you (i.e.., convenience, service, performance)?
- Will you offer any product or service guarantees/warranties?
- Provide information on any patents, trade secrets, or other technical advantages over the competition.

4. Marketing

- Identify the total market for your product or service.
- To whom are you targeting your product or service?
- Identify your competition detailing their strengths and weaknesses and your opportunities and threats relative to them.
- How will your competition react to you entering the market?
- What are your past sales (if applicable) and future projections?

- What price (manufacture, wholesale, retail, etc.) do you intend to charge for you product/service and how does it compare to the competition?
- What are your selling terms (cash or credit)?
- Identify promotional campaigns that will be used.

5. Operating Requirements

- Identify your facility requirements as to the size, location, and type of premises. Include drawings of the proposed building layout. Attach the most recent real estate appraisal, offers to purchase or lease agreement, supplier quotations, etc. Indicate why you have selected this location.
- Provide details relating to special requirements as to water, power, compressed air, ventilation, heat, air conditioning, drainage, disposal, Department of Health requirements, etc. Attach most recent approvals from Public Health, Liquor Licensing, City zoning, etc.
- Provide a detailed listing (including legal descriptions) of the land and building(s), leasehold improvements, equipment and furniture, vehicles, inventory and other assets. The listing should include the proposed purchase price of each asset.
- Provide a general description of the day-to-day operations of the business (include hours of business, days open, seasonality of business, suppliers and their credit terms, etc.).
- Provide product/manufactured cost estimates (if applicable).

6. Management

- What is the proposed organization chart of the company (i.e. who does what)? Include a brief job description for each position.
- Provide brief management biographies of the key personnel (include their ages and backgrounds in this type of business). State the compensation package (salary, bonus, profit sharing, etc.) for each member of management.

7. Personnel

- List employees (not owner or manager) using the following headings:
  - position: full-time, part-time, seasonal, temporary; and
  - method of payment: hourly, monthly, commission, etc.
- Provide a job description for each position, identifying the responsibilities and duties involved. Include what skill level is needed.
- If job training is required, identify the duration and the cost of the training.

8. References

Identify your:

	Name	Phone Number	E-mail
Accountant			
Banker			
Consultant			
Insurance Company			
Lawyer			

9. Financial Projections

Provide a projected (pro-forma) Three Year Cash Flow, Balance Sheet and Profit or Loss Statement.

10. Additional Information

It is common for a financial institution to request that the principal(s) submit, with a loan application, a statement of personal net worth. This form is usually provided by the financial institution. If applicable, historical financial statements on the business venture may also be requested. Other supplementary and supporting documents for your business plan should be included in appendices

The following Web sites may assist you in preparing your business plan:

- Interactive Business Planner -
  http://www.cbsc.org/ibp/home_en.cfm
  (see the document Interactive Business Planner - IBP)

- Royal Bank - Tools for Business -
  http://www.royalbank.com/business/tools/bigidea.html

- TD Business Planner -
  http://www.tdcanadatrust.com/smallbusiness/planner.jsp

Business Plan for Retailers

A good business plan gives the small retail firm a pathway to profit. This publication is designed to help an owner-manager work up a sound business plan.

To profit in business, you need to consider the following questions: What business am I in? What goods do I sell? Where is my market? Who will buy? Who is my competition? What is my sales strategy? What merchandising methods will I use? How much money is needed to operate my store? How will I get the work done? What management controls are needed? How can they be carried out? When should I revise my plan? Where can I go for help?

As the owner-manager, you have to answer these questions to draw up your business plan. The pages of this publication are a combination of text and suggested analysis so that you can organize the information you gather for research to develop your plan, giving you a progression from a common sense starting point to a profitable ending point.

What is a Business Plan?

The success of your business depends largely upon the decisions you make. A business plan allocates resources and measures the results of your actions, helping you set realistic goals and make logical decisions.

You may be thinking, "Why should I spend my time drawing up a business plan? What's in it for me?" If you've never worked out a plan, you are right in wanting to hear about the possible benefits before you do the work. Remember first that the lack of planning leaves you poorly equipped to anticipate future decisions and actions you must make or take to run your business successfully. A business plan:

- Gives you a path to follow. A plan with goals and action steps allows you to guide your business through turbulent often unforeseen economic conditions.
- A plan shows your banker the condition and direction of your business so that your business can be more favourably considered for a loan because of the banker's insight into your situation.
- A plan can tell your sales personnel, suppliers, and others about your operations and goals.
- A plan can help you develop as a manager. It can give you practice in thinking and figuring out problems about competitive conditions, promotional opportunities and situations that are good or bad for your business. Such practice over a period of time can help increase an owner-manager's ability to make judgements.
- A sound plan tells you what to do and how to do it to achieve the goals you have set for your business.

What Business Am I in?

In making your business plan, the first question to consider is: What business am I really in? At the first reading, this question may seem silly. "If there is one thing I know," you say to yourself, "it is what business I'm in." Hold on and think. Some owner-managers have gone broke and others have wasted their savings because they did not define their business in detail. Actually they were confused about what business they were in.

Look at an example. Mr. Jet on the East Coast maintained a dock and sold and rented boats. He thought he was in the marina business. But when he got into trouble and asked for outside help, he learned that he was not necessarily in the marina business. He was in several businesses. He was in the restaurant business with a dockside cafe, serving meals to boating parties. He was in the real estate business, buying and selling lots. He was in the boat repair business, buying parts and hiring a mechanic as demand arose. Mr. Jet was trying to be too many things and couldn't decide which venture to put money into and how much return to expect. What slim resources he had were fragmented.

Before he could make a profit on his sales and a return on his investment, Mr. Jet had to decide what business he really was in and concentrate on it. After much study, he realized that he should stick to the marina format, buying, selling, and servicing boats.

Decide what business you are in and write it down - define your business. To help you decide, think of answers to questions like: What do you buy? What do you sell? Which of your lines of goods yields the greatest profit? What do people ask you for? What is it that you are trying to do better or more of or differently from your competitors? Write it down in detail.

Marketing

When you have decided what business you are in, you are ready to consider another important part of your business plan. Marketing. Successful marketing starts with the owner-manager. You have to know the merchandise you sell and the wishes and wants of your customers you can appeal to. The objective is to move the stock off the shelves and display racks at the right price and bring in sales dollars.

The text and suggested working papers that follow are designed to help you work out a marketing plan for your store. Determining the Sales Potential

In retail business, your sales potential depends on location. Like a tree, a store has to draw its nourishment from the area around it. The following questions should help you to work through the problem of selecting a profitable location.

- In what part of the city or town will you locate?
- In the downtown business section?
- In the area right next to the downtown business area?
- In a residential section of the town?
- On the highway outside of town?
- In the suburbs?
- In a suburban shopping centre?

On a worksheet, write where you plan to locate and give your reasons why you chose that particular location.

Now consider these questions that will help you narrow down a place in your location area.

- What is the competition in the area you have picked?
- How many of the stores look prosperous?
- How many look as though they are barely getting by?
- How many similar stores went out of business in this area last year?
- How many new stores opened up last year?
- What price line does the competition carry?
- Which store or stores in the area will be your biggest competitor(s)?

Again, write down the reasons for your opinions. Also write out an analysis of the area's economic base and give the reason for your opinion. Is the area in which you plan to locate supported by a strong economic base? For example, are nearby industries working full time? Only part time? Did any industries go out of business in the past several months? Are new industries scheduled to open in the next several months?

When you find a store building that seems to be what you need, answer the following questions:

- Is the neighbourhood starting to get run down?
- Is the neighbourhood new and on the way up?

- Are any super highways or throughways planned for the neighbourhood?
- Is street traffic fairly heavy all day?
- Do pedestrians look like prospective customers?
- How close is the building to bus lines and other transportation?
- Are there adequate parking spaces convenient to your store?
- Are the sidewalks in good repair (you may have to repair them)?
- Is the street lighting good?
- Is your store on the sunny side of the street?
- What is the occupancy history of this store building? Does the store have a reputation for failures? (Have stores opened and closed after a short time)?
- Why have other businesses failed in this location?
- What is the physical condition of the store?
- What service does the landlord provide?
- What are the terms of the lease?
- How much rent must you pay each month?

Estimate the gross annual sales you expect in this location.When you think you have finally solved the site location question, ask your banker to recommend people who know most about locations in your line of business. Contact these people and listen to their advice and opinions, weigh what they say, then decide.

Attracting Customers

When you have a location in mind, you should work through another aspect of marketing. How will you attract customers to your store? How will you pull business away from your competition?

It is in working with this aspect of marketing that many small retailers find competitive advantages. The ideas that they develop are as good as and often better than those that large companies develop. The work blocks that follow are designed to help you think about image, pricing, customer service policies, and advertising.

109

Image

A store has an image whether or not the owner is aware of it. For example, throw some merchandise onto shelves and onto display tables in a dirty, dimly lit store and you've got an image. Shoppers think of it as a dirty, junky store and avoid coming into it. Your image should be concrete enough to promote in your advertising and other promotional activities. For example, "home-style cooked" food might be the image of a small restaurant.

Write out on a worksheet the image that you want shoppers and customers to have of your store.

Pricing

Value received is the key to pricing. The only way a store can have low prices is to sell low-priced merchandise. Thus, what you do about the prices you charge depends on the lines of merchandise you buy and sell. It depends also on what your competition charges for these lines of merchandise. Your answers to the following questions should help you to decide what to do about pricing.

In what price ranges are your line of merchandise sold:

High _____   Medium _____   Low _____

Will you sell for cash only?

What services will you offer to justify your prices if they are higher than your competitor's prices?

If you offer credit, will your price have to be higher than if all sales are for cash? The credit costs have to come from somewhere. Plan for them.

If you use credit card systems, what will it cost you? Will you have to add to your prices to absorb this cost?

Customer Service Policies

The service you provide your customers may be free to them, but you pay for it. For example, if you provide free parking, you pay for your own parking lot or pick up your part of the cost of a lot you share with other retailers

Make a list of the services that your competitors offer and estimate the cost of each service. How many of these services will you have to provide just to be competitive? Are there other services that would attract customers but that competitors are not offering? If so, what are your estimates of the cost of such services? Now list all the services you plan to offer and the estimated costs. Total this expense and figure out how you can include those added costs in your prices without pricing your merchandise out of the market.

Advertising

Advertising was saved until the last because you have to have something to say before advertising can be effective. When you have an image, price range, and customer services, you are ready to tell prospective customers why they should shop in your store.

When the money you can spend for advertising is limited, it is vital that your advertising be on target. Before you think about how much money you can afford for advertising, take time to determine what jobs you want to do for your store.

List the strong points of your store. List what makes your store different from your competitors. List the facts about your store and its merchandise that your advertising should tell shoppers and prospective customers.

When you have these facts listed and in hand, you are ready to think about the form your advertising should take and its cost. Ask the local media (newspapers, radio and television, and printers of direct mail pieces) for information about the services and results they offer for your money.

How you spend advertising money is your decision, but don't fall into the trap that snares many advertisers who have little or no experience with advertising copy and media selection. Advertising is a profession. Don't spend a lot of money on advertising without getting professional advice on what kind and how much advertising your store needs.

When you have a figure on what your advertising for the next twelve months will cost, check it against what similar stores spend. Advertising expense is one of the operating ratios (expenses as a percentage of sales) that trade associations and other organizations gather.

If your estimated cost for advertising is substantially higher than this average for your line of merchandise, take a second look. No single expense item should get out of line if you want to make a profit. Your task in determining how much to spend for advertising comes down to the question, "How much can I afford to spend and still do the job that needs to be done?"

In-Store Sales Promotion

To complete your work on marketing, you need to think about what you want to happen after prospects get inside your store. Your goal is to move stock off your shelves and displays at a profit and to satisfy your customers. You want repeat customers and money in your cash register.

At this point, if you have decided to sell for cash only, take a second look at your decision. Don't overlook the fact that people like to buy on credit. Often a credit card, or other system of credit and collections, is needed to attract and hold customers. Customers will have more buying confidence and be more comfortable in your store if they know they can afford to buy. Credit makes this possible.

To encourage people to buy, self-service stores rely on layout, attractive displays, signs and clearly marked prices on the items offered for sale. Other stores combine these techniques with personal selling.

List the display counters, racks, special equipment (something peculiar to your business like a frozen food display bin or a machine to measure and cut cloth), and other fixtures. Figure the cost of all fixtures and equipment by listing them on a worksheet as follows:

Type of Equipment   Number x Unit Cost = Cost

Draw several layouts of your store and attach the layout that suits you to the cost worksheet. Determine how many signs you may need for a twelve month operation and estimate that cost also.

If your store is a combination of self-service and personal selling, how many sales persons and cashiers will you need? Estimate, I will need ___ sales persons at $____ each week (include payroll benefits in this salaries cost). In a year salaries will cost $____

Personal attention to customers is one strong point that a small store can use as a competitive tool. You want to emphasize in training employees that everyone has to pitch in and get the job done. Customers are not interested in job descriptions, but they are interested in being served promptly and courteously. Nothing is more frustrating to a customer than being ignored by an employee. Decide what training you will give your sales people in the techniques of how to greet customers, show merchandise, suggest other items, and handle customer needs and complaints.

Buying

When buying merchandise for resale, you need to answer questions such as:

- Who sells the line to retailers? Is it sold by the manufacturer directly or through wholesalers and distributors?
- What delivery service can you get and must you pay shipping charges?
- What are the terms of buying?
- Can you get credit?
- How quickly can the vendor deliver fill-in orders?

You should establish a source of supply on acceptable terms for each line of merchandise and estimate a plan for purchasing

Stock Control

Often shoppers leave without buying because the store did not have the items they wanted or the sizes and colours were wrong. Stock control, combined with suppliers whose policies on fill-in orders are favourable to you, provides a way to reduce "walkouts".

The type of system you use to keep informed about your stock, or inventory, depends on your line of merchandise and the delivery dates provided by your suppliers.

Your stock control system should enable you to determine what needs to be ordered on the basis of:

- What is on hand.
- What is on order.
- What has been sold.

Some trade associations and suppliers provide systems to members and customers, otherwise your accountant can set up a system that is best for your business. Inventory control is based upon either a perpetual or a periodic method of accounting that involves cost considerations as well as stock control. When you have decided what system you will use to control stock, estimate its cost.

You may not need an extensive (and expensive) control system because you do not need the detailed information such a system collects. The system must justify its costs or you will just waste money and time on a useless effort.

Stock Turn Over

When an owner-manager buys reasonably well, you can expect to turn over stock several times a year. For example, the stock in a small camera shop should turn over four times to four and a half times a year. What is the average stock turnover per year of your line of merchandise? How many times do you expect your stock to turn over? List the reasons for your estimate.

114

Behind-The-Scenes Work

In a retail store, behind-the-scenes work consists of the receiving of merchandise, preparing it for display, maintaining display counters and shelves, and keeping the store clean and attractive to customers. The following analytical list will help you decide what to do and the cost of those actions.

First list the equipment (for example a marking machine for pricing, shelves, a cash register) you will need for:

- receiving merchandise;
- preparing merchandise for display;
- maintaining display counters and shelves;
- keeping the store clean.

Next list the supplies you will need for a year, for example, brooms, price tags, and business forms.

Who will do the backroom work and cleaning that is needed to make a smooth operation in a store? If you do it yourself, how many hours a week will it take? Will you do these chores after closing? If you use employees, what will they cost? On a worksheet describe how you plan to handle these tasks. For example:

- Backroom work will be done by one employee during the slack sales times of the day. I estimate that the employee will spend___ hours per week on these tasks and will cost $___ (number of hours times hourly wage) per week and $____ per year.

- I will need ____ square feet of space for the backroom operation. This space will cost $__ per square foot or a total of $____ per month.

- List and analyze all expense items in the same manner. Examples are utilities, office help, insurance, telephone, postage, accountant, payroll taxes, and licenses or other local taxes. If you plan to hire others to help you manage, analyze these salaries.

115

Put Your Plan into Dollars

At this point, take some time to think about what your business plan means in terms of dollars. This section is designed to help you put your plan into dollars.

The first question concerns the source of dollars. After your initial capital investments in a small retail store, the main source of money is sales. What sales volume do you expect to do in the first twelve months? Write your estimates here $_____ and justify your estimate.

Start-up Costs

List the following estimated start-up costs:

Fixtures and equipment	$_____
Starting inventory	$_____
Decorating and remodelling	$_____
Installation of equipment	$_____
Deposits for utilities	$_____
Legal and professional fees	$_____
Licenses and permits	$_____
Advertising for the opening	$_____
Accounts receivable	$_____
Other expenses	$_____
Operating cash	$_____
Total	$_____

Expenses

In connection with annual sales volume you need to think about expenses. If, for example, you plan to do sales amounting to $100,000, what will it cost you to do this amount of business? How much profit will you make? A business must make a profit or close.

A suggested list of expenses to consider is as follows:

- advertising;
- bad debts;
- delivery;
- depreciation (other than real estate);
- donations;
- dues and subscriptions;
- insurance;
- interest
- legal and accounting expenses;
- occupancy expenses;
- office supplies and postage;
- payroll and other employee expenses;
- supplies;
- taxes (other than real estate and payroll);
- telephone and fax;
- travel, buying and entertainment;
- unclassified expenses.

Cash Forecast

A budget helps you to see the dollar amount of your expected revenue and expenses each month. Then from month to month the question is: Will sales bring in enough money to pay the store's bills? The owner-manager must prepare for the financial peaks and valleys of the business cycle. A cash forecast is a management tool that can eliminate much of the anxiety that can plague you if your sales go through lean months.

Is additional money needed? Suppose at this point that your business needs more money than can be generated by present sales. What do you do? If your business has great potential or is in good financial condition, as shown by its bank balance sheet, you will borrow money (from a bank most likely) to keep the business operating during start-up and slow sales periods.

The loan can be repaid during the fat sales months when sales are greater than expenses. Adequate working capital is needed for success and survival: but cash on hand (or the lack of it) is not necessarily an indication that the business is in bad financial shape. A lender will look at your balance sheet to see the business' Net Worth of which cash and cash flow are only a part. The sample balance sheet statement format shows a business' Net Worth (financial position) at a given point in time, say as of the close of business at the end of the month or at the end of the year.

Even if you do not need to borrow money, you may want to show your plan and balance sheet to your banker. It is never too early to build good relations and credibility (trust) with your banker. Let your banker know that you are a manager who knows where you want to go rather than someone who merely hopes to succeed.

Control and Feedback

To make your plan work you need feedback. For example, the year-end profit and loss (income) statement shows whether your business made a profit or took a loss for the past twelve months

Don't wait twelve months for the score. To keep your plan on target you need readings at frequent intervals. An income statement compiled at the end of each month or at the end of each quarter is one type of frequent feedback. Also you must set up management controls that help you insure that the right things are done each day and week. Organization is needed because you as the owner-manager cannot do all the work. You must delegate work, responsibility, and authority. The record keeping systems should be set up before the store opens. After you're in business it is too late.

The control system that you set up should give you information about stock, sales, receipts and disbursements. The simpler the accounting control system, the better. Its purpose is to give you current useful information. You need facts that expose trouble spots. Outside advisers, such as accountants, can help.

Stock Control

The purpose of controlling stock is to provide maximum service to your customers. Your aim should be to achieve a high turnover rate on your inventory. The fewer dollars you tie up in stock, the better. In a small store, stock control helps the owner-manager offer customers a balanced assortment and enables you to determine what needs ordering on the basis of:

- What is on hand.
- What is on order.
- What has been sold.

When setting up inventory controls, keep in mind that the cost of the stock is not your only cost. There are inventory costs, such as the cost of purchasing, the cost of keeping stock control records, and the cost of receiving and storing stock.

Sales

In a small store, sales slips and cash register tapes give the owner-manager feedback at the end of each day. To keep on top of sales, you need answers to questions such as:

- How many sales were made?
- What was the dollar amount?
- What were the best selling products?
- At what price?
- What credit terms were given to customers?

Receipts

Break out your receipts into receivables (money still owed such as a charge sale) and cash. You know how much credit you have given, how much more you can give, and how much cash you have with which to operate.

119

Disbursements

Your management controls should also give you information about the dollars your company pays out. In checking on your bills, you do not want to be penny-wise and pound-foolish. You should pay bills on time to take advantage of supplier discounts. Your review systems should also give you the opportunity to make judgements on the use of funds. In this manner, you can be on top of emergencies as well as routine situations. Your system should also keep you aware that tax monies, such as payroll income tax deductions, must be set aside and paid out at the proper time.

Break-Even

Break-even analysis is a management control device that approximates how much you must sell in order to cover your costs with NO profit and NO loss. Profit comes after break-even.

Profit depends on sales volume, selling price, and costs. Break-even analysis helps you to estimate what a change in one or more of these factors will do to your profit. To figure a break-even point, fixed costs (like rent) must be separated from variable costs (like to cost of goods sold.) The break-even formula is:

Break-even point = (in sales dollars)   Total fixed costs / (1 - total variable costs / corresponding sales volume)

Sample break-even calculations: Bill Mason plans to open a shoe store and estimates his fixed expenses at about $9,000 the first year. He estimates variable expenses of about $700 for every $1,000 of sales. How much must the store gross to break-even?

BE Point	=	$9,000 / (1 - 700 / 1,000)
	=	$9,000 / (1 - .70)
	=	$9,000 / .30
	=	$30,000

120

Is Your Plan Workable?

Stop when you have worked out your break-even point. Whether the break-even point looks realistic or way off base, it is time to make sure that your plan is workable.

Take time to re-examine your plan before you back it with money. If the plan is not workable, better to learn it now than to realize six months down the road that you are pouring money into a losing venture.

In reviewing your plan, look at the cost figures you drew up when you broke down your expenses for the year (operating ratios on the income statement). If any of your cost items are too high or too low, change them. You can write your changes above or below your original entries on the worksheet. When you finish making your adjustments, you will have a REVISED projected statement of sales and expenses.

With your revised figures, work out a revised break-even analysis. Whether the new break-even point looks good or bad, take one more precaution. Show your plan to someone who has not been involved in working out the details with you. Get an impartial, knowledgeable second opinion. Your banker, or other advisor may see weaknesses that failed to appear as you went over the plan details. These experts may see strong points that your plan should emphasize.

Put Your Plan into Action

When your plan is as thorough and accurate as possible, you are ready to put it into action. *Keep in mind that action is the difference between a plan and a dream. If a plan is not acted upon, it is of no more value than a wishful dream.* A successful owner-manager does not stop after gathering information and drawing up a business plan, as you have done in working through this publication. USE the plan.

At this point, look back over your plan. Look for things that must be done to put your plan into action. What needs to be done will depend on your situation and goals. For example, if your business plan calls for an increase in sales, you may have to provide more funds for this expansion. Have you more money to put into this

121

business? Do you borrow from friends and relatives? From your bank? From your suppliers (through credit terms)? If you are starting a new business, one action may be to get a loan for fixtures, stock, employee salaries, and other expenses. Another action will be to find and to hire capable employees.

Now make a list of things that must be done to put your plan into action. Give each item a date so that it can be done at the appropriate time. To put my plan into action, I must:

Do
(action)_____   by (date) _____

Etc.

Keep Your Plan Current

Once you put your plan into action, look out for changes. They can cripple the best business no matter how well planned. Stay on top of changing conditions and adjust your business plan accordingly. Sometimes the change is within your company. For example, several of your sales persons may quit. Sometimes the change is with customers whose desires and tastes shift and change or refuse to change. Sometimes the change is technological as when products are created and marketed.

In order to adjust your plan to account for such changes, you, the owner-manager, must:

- Be alert to the changes that come about in your line of business, in your market and in your customers.
- Check your plan against these changes.
- Determine what revisions, if any, are needed in the business plan.

The method you use to keep your plan current so that your business can weather the changing forces of the market place is up to you. Read trade and business papers and magazines and review your plan periodically. Once each month or every other month, go over your plan to see whether or not it needs adjusting. Certainly you will have been in business for a time. Make revisions and put them into action. You must be constantly updating and improving. A good business plan must evolve from experience and the best current information. A good business plan is good business.

Note: see the document **Interactive Business Planner - IBP** or visit the IBP Web site at http://www.cbsc.org/ibp//home_en.cfm

CHECKLISTS FOR FRANCHISEES

Franchising has become a major force in today's business environment. Franchising is a system of distribution used by companies to sell products or perform services. The company (franchisor) offers its technical expertise, established marketing system, symbols and trademarks, and ongoing operational support, in exchange for a continuing right to receive royalties from the operator (franchisee). The aim is to be mutually beneficial to both parties, by combining the marketing and technical strengths of the franchisor with the local market familiarity, energy and capital of the franchisee.

There are many opportunities available regarding franchised businesses. To add further complexity, there are many variations in the franchising methods offered. To ensure your success, you must be fully aware of and evaluate all available facts pertaining to your franchise opportunity.

The following checklist of questions should assist you in making a decision about acquiring a franchise. In addition, we strongly recommend that you consult with your lawyer and accountant before you sign any documents or contracts.

Self Evaluation

- Do you have the capital required for investment?
- Do you have the necessary management skills, education and work experience required?
- Are you fully aware of the work involved in running this franchise?
- What is the best franchise for you? (The answer is a combination of four things)
    - What types of businesses are succeeding these days, with every indication that they will continue to succeed?
    - What is the kind of business you would like to be in?

124

- Is someone offering a franchise in your area of interest, that you believe will help you to succeed, and that you can afford?
- Can you work within the limits of a franchise system? Franchisors are not looking for real entrepreneurs, but more entrepreneurial sergeants who can fit into the system.

The Franchise Operation

- What is the franchisor's background and how long has it been offering franchises?
- Is the franchise financially stable?
- How selective is the franchisor when choosing its franchisees? Did they ask your qualifications and financial standing?
- Who are the principals involved and are they experienced in business?
- How many franchises are operating now? Are new locations being opened on a regular basis? Have any locations failed?
- If the franchise is new, what is its record of accomplishment?
- What innovations has the franchisor introduced since first starting?
- Are you required to meet with existing franchise owners?
- Does the franchisor provide localised on-going training for franchisees for the length of the contract?

The Product or Service

- What makes the product or service unique?
- Is there a reasonable demand for it? Have sales been increasing or decreasing? Is it seasonal?
- Is it a product or service you would buy?
- Are you allowed to carry other product lines?
- Is it priced competitively with similar products or services?
- Can the franchisor guarantee continual supply at a fair price?
- Are there product warranties or guarantees? Whose responsibility?
- Is the product protected by a patent, trademark, or copyright?

- When your inventory levels become low, can you use other sources until the franchisor's products arrive?

Location and Sales Territory

- Is your territory clearly defined and exclusive? What guarantees do you have?
- What is the sales potential for the territory? Has the franchisor provided you with market information and statistics to support this?
- What is the future growth potential?
- Can you select your own location? Are there flexible standards for location and premises? Do you own or lease? Terms?
- What competition, both franchises and non-franchised is in the area?

Other Franchisee Experience

Have you been in contact with other franchisees? Get the franchisor to give you a list of those operating in your vicinity. These are some of the questions you should ask them when you visit or phone them.

- What was the total investment required by the franchisor?
- Were there any hidden or unexpected costs?
- Are you satisfied with the quality of goods supplied by the franchisor?
- How reliable is delivery from the franchisor?
- How long was it before your operating expenses were covered by revenue, and how long before you could draw a reasonable salary?
- Were the projected sales and profit figures provided by the franchisor accurate?
- Has your franchise been as profitable as you expected?
- What kind of management and staff training was provided? Did it meet your expectations? Where was it held?
- Have you ever had a serious disagreement with the franchisor? What about? Was it settled amicably?

- Does the franchisor respond promptly and helpfully to questions or advice you are seeking?
- Are you satisfied with the marketing, promotional, and advertising assistance that you receive from the franchisor?
- If you could change your contract, what would you change?
- Would you recommend starting a franchise with this particular franchisor?
- What have you done to make your franchise successful?

Franchise Contract

The franchise agreement is a business contract that should clearly indicate the terms and conditions relevant to the business operation. Have your lawyer and accountant carefully check out the agreement, particularly those areas dealing with bankruptcy, termination, renewal, transfer and sale of the franchise.

- Does the contract protect yourself as well as the franchisor?
- Are the rights and obligations of both parties clearly stated?
- Is the contract specific as to the type and size of operation you are expected to manage?
- Is the nature, duration, cost and extent of your training outlined in the contract?
- Are your payments to the franchisor clearly specified? Are the following shown?
  - the franchise fee;
  - any other fixed yearly payments the franchisor receives;
  - are royalty payments reasonable? Advertising payments;
  - fees for continuing services provided by the franchisor.
- Must you purchase your essential supplies from the franchisor or designated suppliers?
- Is there a minimum amount of merchandise you must purchase from the franchisor each year? If this merchandise cost is pricier than other comparable products, is this a hidden franchise cost?

- What happens if supplies are interrupted? Can you purchase goods from alternative suppliers?
- Have you the right to the franchisor's latest innovations?
- Is there an annual sales quota? Is it attainable?
- What types of reports are you expected to provide the franchisor?
- Does the contract cover in detail all the franchisor's verbal promises made during the interviews?
- Will the franchisor maintain any necessary federal and provincial registrations?
- Can the contract be renewed? If so, on what terms?
- When confronted with a monthly loss, can royalty payments be deferred to a later, more profitable month?
- Do you have to follow franchisor controls and policies exactly, or can you exercise some creativity regarding the product or service and its delivery?
- If leasing the location, will the lease be for the same term as the franchise agreement? Can the lease be renewed if you renew the franchise?
- Are you responsible for the construction or improvement of premises? If so, will the franchisor provide you with plans and specifications, and can these be changed or altered?
- To what extent can you choose your territory or location?
- Are you permitted to have multi-locations within your territory?
- Can you sell the franchise? What are the conditions?
- Can you keep any profits made from the sale? How is the sale price determined?
- Can you terminate the contract if, for some reason, you have to?
- If you terminate the contract, is there a penalty cost?
- When and how can the franchisor terminate your franchise?
- How will you be compensated for the goodwill you have built up in the business?
- If you default on the contract, how much time do you have to rectify the situation?
- Is there an arbitration clause regarding defaults?

- What happens to the business in the event of your prolonged illness or death? Have questions regarding succession been clearly addressed?
- Are you prevented from engaging in any other business activity for the duration of the contract?
- Does the contract prevent you from establishing, owning, or working in a competing business for a certain number of years after termination of the contract?
- Before you sign the contract, are you sure that the franchise can do something for you that you cannot do for yourself?

For more information on franchises, contact:

Canadian Franchise Association
Suite 300
2585 Skymark Avenue
Mississauga, Ontario L4W 4L5

Tel.: (905) 625-2896 or 1-800-665-4232
Fax: (905) 625-9076
E-mail: info@cfa.ca
Web site: http://www.cfa.ca

Entrepreneur Magazine
Entrepreneur Media Inc.
2392 Morse Avenue
Irvine, CA 92614

Tel.:(904) 261-2325
Fax: (714) 755-4211
Web site: http://www.entrepreneur.com

Franchise Annual On-Line
Info Franchise News Inc.
9 Duke Street
P.O. Box 755
St.Catherines, Ontario L2R 6W8

Tel.: (905) 688-2665
Fax: (905) 688-7728
E-mail: infopres@infonews.com
Web site: http://www.infonews.com/online.html

The Franchise Handbook On-Line
c/o Enterprise Magazines Inc.
Suite 111
1020 North Broadway
Milwaukee, WI 53202

Tel.: (414) 272-9977
Fax: (414) 272-9973
Web site: http://www.franchise1.com

Business Opportunities Classifieds Online
Web site: http://www.boconline.com

Franchise Market
Web site: http://www.entremkt.com/index.shtml

Entrepreneur Magazines Franchise Channel
Web site: http://www.entrepreneurmag.com

DEALING WITH YOUR BANKER & OTHER LENDERS

Your Financing

The success or failure of your business will depend on whether or not you have enough capital to:

- buy the equipment and inventory you need;
- pay overhead costs such as rent, salaries, etc.; and
- have a large enough reserve fund for extra working capital which could be used to take advantage of "specials"; and for surviving temporary setbacks.

What Funding Do You Need?

Your funding requirements can be broken down into two main categories:

1. Initial costs (i.e. land, building, fixture, machinery, supplies, vehicles, pre-opening expenses and opening inventory).

2. Daily operating costs, rising inventories, payroll, rent, taxes, advertising, accounts receivable, etc.

It is essential to know the sum of all these costs. You must prepare a cash flow forecast, which will give you a reasonable estimate of your cash requirements for the first 12 months. If you cannot do a cash flow forecast yourself, it would be best to hire someone to do it for you.

The money required to operate your business can come from several sources, including: your own savings or loans from friends, relatives, investors, charted banks, credit unions, or the Business Development Bank of Canada. Other financial assistance may include lines of credit from your various suppliers.

TWO TYPES OF BORROWED FUNDS:

Long term financing

Used to buy fixed assets such as buildings, machinery and fixtures; paid back in equal monthly installments.

Short term financing

Used to pay for current assets such as inventory, accounts receivable and other working capital requirements. Usually covered by a demand note at the bank, and fluctuating weekly or monthly depending on the need.

It is easier to borrow money by pledging fixed assets, so don't pull all your equity into machinery or buildings; instead save it for working capital needs.

What lenders need to see:

- you can repay the loan out of normal business activities;
- the loan is big enough to do the job;
- a description of your project(s) in writing;
- cash flow projections for the first 12 months, including repayment plans;

- projected profit or loss for the first and second year;
- list of stock and equipment;
- list of assets you can offer as collateral;
- short history of your business experience; and
- statement of your personal net worth.

Cash Flow Forecasting

A cash flow forecast is your most useful tool to help ensure financial solvency. With this forecast, you try to predict all the funds that you will receive and disburse, and the resulting surplus or deficit. You take into account not only the operating and capital budgets, but also the ratio of cash sales to credit sales and the paying habits of your customers. To estimate cash outflow, you must also consider the promptness you intend to pay for your materials and merchandise.

By making a cash flow analysis you can estimate:

- how much cash will be needed to operate your business each month;
- when you will need additional short term funds from the bank; and
- when you will have a surplus funds reduce your bank loans.

This information can assist you in timing your capital expenditures more appropriately, accelerate collection of accounts receivable, ward off a cash shortage, plan short term borrowing well in advance and perhaps invest a temporary surplus.

Finding a Source of Funds

The most common source of financing for small businesses is the chartered bank. To provide working capital, banks can provide short term loans, long term mortgage loans and loans against inventory or accounts receivable, etc.

Banks also offer a full range of banking services, including: personal and business deposit and loan accounts, buying and selling of foreign exchange, purchase and sale (or safekeeping) of securities and other valuables, letters of credit and the provision of market and credit information in Canada and other countries.

Other leading sources of finance are the insurance companies, trust companies, credit unions, commercial credit and acceptance companies, venture capital loan companies and factoring companies.

Equity capital represents the net value of the business since all other financing amounts to some form of borrowing which must ultimately be repaid. Also, business profits can be reinvested as additional financing once your business has started.

Leasing may also be considered as a source of funds. The interest rates are relatively high, but payments are deductible from income tax. Leasing arrangements are usually used for machinery, vehicles and office equipment, where it is desirable to avoid heavy capital cost outlays.

Getting the Most From Your Bank

Bank Loans

Your involvement with the banking world begins even before you start your business. Develop a good working relationship with the bank of your choice from the very beginning. Faster and better services are supplied when a bank is familiar with its customers and their business. In that environment, suggestions for keeping a business financially healthy are more readily given, crisis borrowing can be avoided and good loan planning can be developed.

Never surprise your banker with sudden or unplanned requests for funds.

Unless you are independently wealthy and insist on using your own money, you will require financial aid from the bank in the form of a term loan for any of the following purposes:

- to assist in establishing your new business;
- to purchase an existing business;
- to purchase new equipment;
- to provide additional working capital; and
- to provide funds to retire a bond issue or outstanding preferred stock.

Dealing With Your Banker

Points to Keep in Mind

- Bankers are impressed only by your standards of management excellence. Experience counts heavily in planning, organizing, supervision, directing, control, development and demonstrated success.

- Arrange your borrowing needs well in advance and keep time on your side. With time on your side and banks being in competition to attract top calibre business accounts, you may find the bank more willing to negotiate competitive terms, such as security margins, interest rates and collateral requirements.

134

- Risk-taking must be a calculated endeavour not a speculative gamble. Remember, bankers are risk avoiders, not risk-takers.

- Always put your loan request in writing and finalize all loan documents before making any other financial commitments.

- Do not borrow by way of overdraft unless your line of credit is established for such borrowing. Any verbal line of credit for recurring overdrafts should be formalized as soon as possible.

- Negotiate your fiscal credit needs at your year end while your financial statement is still correct. It may be tempting to anticipate that your next interim statement will improve six months later, only to find that you would have been better off with a reduced line of credit at the beginning of the year than to have none at all in the middle of a poor season.

- Keep yourself current on the prevailing lending attitudes so that you can adjust your own administration of receivables and collections accordingly.

- The only constant human element in your banking relationship is yourself. There is about an 80% chance the banker you are dealing with today will no longer be handling your account two years from now.

- There are countless instances where bank customers will casually sign just about anything while they are in the bank office. Read, understand and retain copies of all banking documents before you sign.

Developing Good Bank Relationships

To develop good bank relationships:

- find out the services your bank offers (location, hours, etc.) and, if practical, use the bank most of your customers and potential customers use;
- give the bank manager all the information he requires for head office approval of the loan;
- annually arrange a line of credit to meet peak requirements (but borrow only what is necessary, when necessary);
- adjust the loan level as actual requirements change;
- make realistic repayment commitments;
- avoid overdrafts; and
- be prepared to provide security for the loan.

What a Lender Needs to Know

The lender will require the following information:

- amount of loan and period for which is needed;
- reason for the loan;
- brief history of the company;
- financial statements of the business for the past three years;
- details of current financial position including specific data on:
  - accounts receivable;
  - accounts payable;
  - inventory;
  - fixed assets;
  - short and long term debt;
  - special accounts;
  - facts about company operations;
  - facts about management and officers;
  - details of the project to be financed;
  - cash flow statements for the next 12 months (perhaps indicating an operating line of credit);

136

- projected financial statements (indicating present requirements); and
- the security you're offering.

Evaluation by a Lender

Your application will be evaluated on:

- your debt paying record;
- ratio of debt to net worth;
- past earnings and potential future earnings of company;
- value and condition of the collateral for security;
- your character and management ability;
- the prospect that the business opportunity is too volatile; and
- the fact that you have prepared a business plan.

Collateral Accepted by a Lender

The lender will accept the following as collateral:

- granting of a floating charge debenture;
- personal guarantees of officers of limited companies;
- co-signers or guarantors;
- pledging of inventories;
- assignment of accounts receivable, leases, savings, warehouse receipts or securities;
- pledging of cash surrender value of life insurance; and
- agreement to restrict salaries, drawings and loan payments of proprietors, partners and principal shareholders.

Restrictions Imposed on the Borrower

- maintain working capital at a specified amount;
- furnish financial statements annually or semi-annually;
- share structure;
- limit dividends;
- sell the company or the assets;
- create no new debt except as agreed;
- provide no guarantees on behalf of others; and
- restrict drawings or benefits to shareholders.

Security for Term Loans

The following will serve as security for term loans:

- mortgage on property or chattel;
- floating charge debenture on other assets; and
- personal guarantees.

MARKETING PLAN

A marketing plan is designed to direct company activities towards the satisfaction of customer needs; determine what the customer wants, develop a product/service to meet those needs, get the product/service to the end user and communicate with the customer - at a profit!

Introduction

WHO	is the company, principals, employees, community?
WHAT	is the product/service, what is the company's goal?
WHERE	is the plant to be established
HOW	does the company intend to meet its objectives, production levels, sales volumes?
WHY	was the product/service developed, what are its attributes or qualities, and how is it superior to existing products?

Target Markets

- What is the company's initial proposed market?
    - local
    - provincial
    - western provinces
    - national

- How does the company fit in the chain of basic markets?
    - consumer
    - industrial
    - government
    - international
    - supplier
    - manufacturer

139

- wholesaler

- What are the target market boundaries?
    - by consumer group
    - geographically

- Define the dollar value of total potential sales within the proposed target market.

- Describe the targeted user groups by age, gender, lifestyle, values (major customer groups).

- Define the company's sales level objectives and what percentage of total market share they represent.

- Describe how planned production capability compares to proposed market demand.

- Outline any outside influencing factors which may affect the marketability of the product, and how they can be overcome:
    - packaging/labelling regulations
    - GST (effect on consumer price acceptance)
    - buyer preferences (health food vs. junk food)
    - technology changes to production (extrusion method)

- Describe when the product/service is usually purchased; on impulse or as a regular grocery shopping item. Does the proposed marketing strategy address these trends?

- Who usually does the purchasing of the product/service? Who makes the purchasing decision? Is the marketing strategy properly directed to this group?

- Describe the varieties of the product available:
    - by flavour
    - by size of package

- What are the markets for each of the above?

- Where is the product normally purchased?
    - supermarkets
    - grocery stores

- convenience stores
- snack bars
- gas bars
- vending machines
- schools
- Are the marketing efforts properly targeted to these locations?

Market Demands

- Who is the competition?

- What are their products/services?

- How does this product/service compare by quality, price, packaging and variety?

- What percentage of the total market does each competitor enjoy?

- What can this company realistically expect to obtain as market share (provide sales forecasts)?

- What does the public normally demand from this type of product/service? Does it meet these demands?

- Does the packaging (sales aids/point of purchase displays) emphasize the qualities of the product/service?

- What level of sales growth is anticipated over the next three years? Can the plan deliver the production levels necessary to support this growth?

- What are the company's long range plans?

Product Pricing

- What is the consumer acceptance price range for this type of product/service?

- How does the proposed product's/service's price compare?

- Is there sufficient margin between the manufacturer's cost and the consumer acceptance price level to provide for markups at the wholesale, distributor and retail level?

- Does the price allow for freight, projected profit, price fluctuations in the market place and consumer interpretation of value?

- Are coupons or discounts being considered to promote consumers to try other flavours, etc.? Product introduction.

- What is the product cost breakdown?

  - Costs of goods sold
    - direct labour
    - direct materials
  - Operating expenses
    - selling expenses
    - communications expense
    - general and administration expenses (including freight)

- What markups are allowed at each level of distribution (markup chain and channel pricing)?

For example:

Manufacturer		Wholesaler		Retailer	
Cost	90%	Cost	80%	Cost	60%
+		+		+	
Markup	10%	Markup	20%	Markup	40%
=		=		=	
Selling Price	100%	Selling Price	100%	Selling Price	100%

- Are the most economical/cost efficient methods of processing and packaging utilized (including raw materials inputs) to keep product/service costs down?

Distribution Channels

- How does the company plan to get the product/service to the end user?
- What channel of distribution is to be used?
  - direct - manufacturer to consumer
  - one stage - manufacturer to retailer to consumer
  - traditional - manufacturer to wholesaler to retailer to consumer
  - multi-stage - manufacturer to broker to wholesaler to retailer to consumer
- Who/what company will carry out the distribution?
- Are commissioned salespersons to be used?
- What are the costs associated with the proposed distribution channels?
- How do these channels effect delivery/production time frames?
- What are delivery terms?
- How are products to be packaged for shipping, end-user display? What physical handling is required?
- Are display aids (clip racks, bins, etc.) to be provided to retailers?
- Does packaging meet regulatory agency requirements (labelling, seals, etc.)?
- Is packaging eye appealing, complementary to product, portraying universal labelling, coded, priced?
- Is there a method for feedback on customer satisfaction, quality control?
- What minimum shipping orders are required? (cost efficient)

143

- What minimum inventory levels must be maintained to ensure no loss of sales due to late deliveries, back orders, split shipments?

- What system is to be used for processing orders, shipping, billing?

- What trade terms will be offered?

Promotions/Advertising

- Describe the company's "communications package".

For example:

- advertising
- selling
- sales promotion
- publicity

- How much is budgeted in Year 1 in each category?

- **Advertising**
  - What percentage of each media is to be used in your overall advertising package?
  - television
  - radio
  - newspapers
  - magazines
  - billboards
  - business cards
  - co-operative advertising with wholesalers/retailers
  - other

- **Selling**
  - What type of sales persons are to be used - food brokers, commissioned salespersons, etc.?
  - What tools are to be provided to salespersons to assist getting orders (volume discounts, purchasing shelf space, etc.)?
  - Will a sales training program be offered?

144

- How will sales effectiveness be measured?
- What incentives will be offered to salespersons for new accounts, achievements?

- **Sales Promotion**
    - What sales promotion activities are planned?
    - point of purchase displays/sales aids
    - samples
    - coupons
    - What costs are associated with each?

- **Publicity**
    - How does the company plan to "kick off" the introduction of the product using publicity?
    - endorsements (Sask-Made)
    - testimonials
    - referrals
    - truck signs
    - consistent visual theme

ARE YOU PLANNING TO IMPORT?

This section will help you to navigate through the federal and provincial government programs, services and regulations that may apply to individuals and businesses importing products into Ontario. Although many of your questions will be answered in this section, the list of resources given here is not exhaustive.

If you are **new to business**, you should visit the COBSC (Canada-Ontario Business Service Centre) Web site or review the document **Business Start-Up Info-Guide**, which provides a general overview of starting a business in Ontario.

A listing of other useful business resources can be found by visiting the Business Guides document:

- **Business Guides**

    The COBSC has two other Internet products that may be of particular interest to new entrepreneurs:

- The **Online Small Business Workshop**, at

    http://www.cbsc.org/osbw/workshop.cfm, which is a Web-based workshop designed to provide you with techniques for developing your business idea, starting a new venture and improving your existing small business.

- The **Interactive Business Planner** (IBP), at

    http://www.cbsc.org/ibp, which will assist you in preparing a 3-year business plan for a new or existing business. The IBP helps you write your business plan, provides a format for writing your business plan and creates financial projections based on the information you enter.

147

Further information on the programs, services and regulations listed in this section can be obtained through the following:

- calling the telephone numbers listed under each section;
- visiting the Web sites listed under each section;
- calling the COBSC at **1-800-567-2345** or **(416) 775-3456** and speaking with one of our Information Officers;
- visiting the COBSC Web site at http://www.cbsc.org/ontario; or
- visiting **Regional Access Sites**, which are located throughout Ontario.

AN OVERVIEW OF IMPORTING

1. Customs Brokers

Importers can clear their own goods (see the document **Accounting for Imported Goods and Payment of Duties** on CBSC Web site); but in the event they choose to have another party clear their goods, that party must be licensed by the Canada Border Services Agency (CBSA). Under section 32 of the ***Customs Act***, only a licensed customs broker may, on a commercial basis, account for goods and pay duties and taxes on behalf of an importer. An importer must authorize the broker to conduct business. The authorization can be specific to a particular brokerage firm or it can allow the initial brokerage firm to appoint one or more subagents to transact business at locations where the original broker is not licensed. To obtain more information on licensed customs brokers, see the document **Licensing of Customs Brokers**.

2. Market Research

Market research is an important aspect of any business venture. Importers especially need to conduct additional research given the risks associated with bringing a product into the domestic market from outside of Canada. Information on Canadian standards, current international trade data for the product(s) (including entry into Canada) and product origin is vital to any importer.

Statistics Canada collects and distributes a wide range of statistical information on commercial importing based on CBSA data. Using Customs reports, Statistics Canada maintains trade data according to the Harmonized System (HS). The HS is an internationally recognized system used to classify and describe commodities according to quantity, value, commodity and country of origin. Statistics Canada also maintains detailed trade data by commodity or industry and records related to exports and imports. There might be costs associated with obtaining the statistics produced by Statistics Canada.

For more information on Statistics Canada's products, contact the department at **1-800-263-1136**, visit the Statistics Canada Web site at http://www.statcan.ca or see the document **Trade Data and Statistics**. You can also search through the department's online products at http://www.statcan.ca/english/services/online.htm.

Strategis also offers importers several Internet-based databases on import and export statistics:

• **Trade Data Online** provides detailed information on Canadian and U.S. imports, exports and trade balances - in terms of dollars or percentages - with 200 countries for over 5,000 commodities (by HS codes) for the latest ten complete years and the current year to date. Monthly details are also available for the last two years. In a separate module, information is available on the imports, exports, trade balances, manufacturing shipments, apparent domestic markets and export intensities of Canadian industries (by NAICS and SIC codes). For further information on Trade Data Online, see the document **Trade Data Online** or visit the Web site at http://strategis.gc.ca/tdo .

• **Canadian Industry Statistics** presents statistical analyses of manufacturing industry trends for establishments, employment, wages, production, costs, investment, international trade and industry performance in Canada for the ten more recent years. Industries are defined according to the North American Industry Classification System (NAICS). For more information on Canadian

Industry Statistics, see the document **Canadian Industry Statistics** or visit the Web site at http://strategis.gc.ca/cis.

3. Regulations, Business Number - Importer/Exporter Account Number

Canadian businesses importing commercial goods must obtain a Business Number in order to account for their goods. The CRA uses this number to process customs release and accounting documents. Business Number application forms are available from all CRA offices that clear commercial shipments and from Business Window sites where you may also submit completed forms

To obtain further information on the Business Number for importers and exporters, please consult the document **Business Number - BN** and the document **Importer/Exporter Account Number** or visit the CRA's Web site at the following address: http://www.cra-arc.gc.ca/tax/business/topics/bn/menu-e.html.

To download the Business Number application, go to **http://www.cra-arc.gc.ca/E/pbg/tf/rc1c/README.html**. You can also contact a Business Window at **1-800-959-5525** for information

Import Restrictions Prohibited and Controlled Imports

Some government departments/agencies prohibit certain goods from entering Canada. Certain other goods are controlled, meaning that permits, certificates, labelling or authorizations from a federal department/agency are needed before the good(s) can be released by CBSA, which holds them until the importer meets all the requirements. For further information on prohibited and controlled goods, see the document **Requirements for Imports and Exports of Prohibited and Controlled Goods** on CBSC Website

Other Federal Governments Departments:

The **Export and Import Controls Bureau** of the Department of Foreign Affairs and International Trade (DFAIT) administers the ***Export and Import Permits Act*** and related regulations which allow for the imposition of restrictions and quotas on certain goods or countries. Importers should do some research to determine if the

150

product is restricted either through the_Import Control List_or the _Area Control List_ and contact the appropriate federal government agency for any permits and certificates that may apply. The Export and Import Controls Bureau's Web Site can be found at http://www.dfait-maeci.gc.ca/eicb/.

Import Quotas

Under the_**Export and Import Permits Act,**the Minister may place certain goods on the_Import Control List_ in order to implement an intergovernmental arrangement or commitment. Goods that are on this list may be subject to quotas or restrictions and require a permit for importation into Canada. The Minister may also determine a method for allocating a quantity of goods to residents of Canada who apply for an allocation. For more information on import quotas, see the document **Import Quotas**.

Import Permits

The Export and Import Controls Bureau of DFAIT is responsible for assisting importers to determine if import permits are required. Importing goods which are on the _Import Control List_ to Canada for commercial or personal purposes are controlled by a series of quotas and import licences. The following goods, in most cases, need an import permit: textiles and clothing; carbon and specialty steel; agriculture (chicken and turkey; egg products; beef and veal; cheese; dairy products; barley; wheat/wheat products). For other agriculture-related products, please contact the Canadian Food Inspection Agency Import Service Centre at **1-800-835-4486.** For further information on import permits, see the document **Import Permits**.

Import Certificates

The_**Export and Import Permits Act**_ places restrictions and quotas on certain goods or countries of origin. Regulations govern the considerations to be taken into account in the issuance of international import certificates under the Act. The import certificate is required by the exporting country (named on the application form) before it will allow the export of the goods to Canada. The importer will need to adequately describe the goods and certify that he or she

151

intends to import those goods into Canada. For more information on import certificates, see the document **International Import Certificates**.

4. Labelling

Most goods produced domestically or imported into Canada require some form of consumer package labelling. Importers should become aware of these requirements before offering goods for sale in Canada.

Textiles

Under federal legislation, most consumer textile articles offered for sale in Canada, including clothing, carpets and upholstered furniture must bear a label with information on fibre content and dealer identity. Fibre content information must be provided in English and French. Dealer identification may be provided in the form of a CA Number (for Canadian dealers only) or by listing the complete name and postal address of the responsible dealer. For additional information on textile labelling, please see the document **Labelling - Textiles** or visit the following Web site at

http://strategis.ic.gc.ca/epic/internet/incb-bc.nsf/vwGeneratedInterE/cp01145e.html.

For more information on CA Numbers, see the document

CA Number Registration and Database.

Upholstered and stuffed articles in Ontario must have labels regarding the quality of the filing materials. For more information on the requirements for upholstered and stuffed articles, visit the Web site of the Technical Standards and Safety Authority at http://www.tssa.org/usa/safety_regs_updates.asp.

Food

Imported foods are subject to the same labelling and composition requirements applied to domestic foods. The *__Food and Drugs Act__* prohibits the labelling, packaging, treating, processing, selling or advertising of any food (at all levels of trade) in a manner that would mislead or deceive consumers as to the character, value, quantity, composition, merit or safety of the product. As well, it prohibits health claims that might suggest that a food is a treatment, preventative or cure for specified diseases or health conditions. It also requires bilingual labelling. The Food and Drug Regulations prescribe the labelling of all prepackaged foods, including requirements for ingredient labelling, durable life dates, nutrient content claims, mandatory nutrients declarations and foods for special dietary needs.

The Canadian Food Inspection Agency (CFIA) is responsible for enforcing the *__Food and Drugs Act__* as it relates to food and administering the federal labelling requirements for prepackaged foods under the *__Consumer Packaging and Labelling Act.__* Some prepackaged foods are also subject to the labelling requirements of the regulations under the *__Canada Agricultural Products Act__*, the *__Meat Inspection Act__*, the *__Fish Inspection Act__*, the *__Weights and Measures Act__* and in a few cases, provincial acts and regulations. For information on food inspection and labelling, please see the document **Food Labelling** or visit the CFIA Web site at http://www.inspection.gc.ca. To see CFIA's Guide to Food Labelling and Advertising (including Nutrition Labelling), please visit the following address:

http://www.inspection.gc.ca/english/bureau/labeti/guide/guidee.shtml.

For information on alcoholic beverages, see the Guidelines on the Labelling of Alcoholic Beverages at this address:

http://www.inspection.gc.ca/english/fssa/labeti/guide/tab10e.shtml.

Import Service Centres (ISC) process import request documentation/ data sent electronically or by fax by the importing community across Canada. They review the information and return the decision either electronically to the CBSA, which then relays it to the client, or by fax directly to the broker/importer, who then submits the release package to the CBSA.

In addition, ISC staff handle telephone inquiries regarding import requirements for all commodities inspected by the CFIA and, when necessary, coordinate inspections for import shipments. For

153

additional information on these Centres, see the document **Import Services Centres**.

Health Canada is responsible for food safety policy, standard-setting, risk assessment, research and the assessment of the effectiveness of the Canadian Food Inspection Agency's programs and activities related to food safety and nutrition. Under the Food and Drug Regulations, Health Canada is responsible for the safety evaluation of submissions by industry regarding the use of a variety of foods and food ingredients and/or substances and processes used before, during and after the fabrication of food (e.g., veterinary drugs, agricultural chemicals, food additives and novel foods such as those derived from biotechnology), infant formula, and foods for special dietary use. For further information on food regulations and importing, see the document **Food.**

Consumer Products

Under the ***Consumer Packaging and Labelling Act,*** the Competition Bureau administers the packaging and labelling of prepackaged non-food products at all levels of trade. The Act defines three mandatory labelling requirements:

- product identity;
- product net quantity;
- dealer's name and principal place of business.

Information must be included in both official languages, except the dealer's name and address, which can appear in either language. The ***Consumer Packaging and Labelling Act*** is applicable to any person who is a retailer, manufacturer, processor or producer of a product, or a person who is engaged in the business of importing, packing or selling any product. For more information on labelling non-food consumer goods, see the document **Labelling - Packaging Consumer Products (Non-Food).**

Some consumer products such as cosmetics, toys, and children's clothing are regulated by Health Canada through the ***Hazardous Products Act***. The Regulations specify the requirements for

154

labelling and instructions for assembling, design, construction, finish, performance, flammability and toxicity. Businesses that manufacture, retail or import consumer goods should be aware of all labelling requirements regarding their product.

5. Duties and Tariffs

Products entering Canada for commercial sale may be subject to duty payments. These payments are based on the type of products(s) imported and the tariff classification.

To find out how much duty and tax to apply to an imported good, importers first have to know the value of the good. Generally, importers will use the purchase price (i.e. price paid or payable) as the basis for determining the customs value. Adjustments added to or deducted from the purchase price may be required to account for such elements as transportation, packaging, royalties, etc. The CBSA regional Customs Client Services officers applying the valuation for duty provisions of the ***Customs Act*** can assist importers in making this determination. For further information on Customs Client Services, see the document **Valuation of Imported Goods.**

Tariff Classification of Imported Goods

Canada uses the international Harmonized Coding System (HS) to classify imported goods. This classification is used for statistics and to see if any of the following apply: prohibitions; quotas; anti-dumping or countervailing duties; North American Free Trade Agreement (NAFTA) provisions; other preferential tariff treatments

Importers must provide a complete and accurate description of their goods so that the correct tariff classification can be assigned to them. The description may consist of a general description with detailed characteristics of the goods (e.g. textiles or gaskets), or it may include a commercial description (e.g. steel rods, plates, sheets and their size and dimensions). For further information on tariff classification, see the document **Tariff Classification of Imported Goods**.

Tariffs are applicable based on country of origin and trade agreements. Goods imported into Canada may be subject to one of 12 separate tariff treatments. These treatments have been established as the result of trade agreements (such as NAFTA) negotiated with Canada's trading partners. Some treatments have been established unilaterally for various reasons, such as granting preferential duty treatment to developing countries. For further information on tariff treatments, see the document **Tariff Treatment - Origin - Imported Goods**.

CBSA writes national customs rulings (NCRs) for importers or their agents to let them know, up front, how the CBSA applies customs legislation to an import shipment. NCRs are issued for tariff classification, origin, marking and value for duty. These rulings are binding on both the CBSA and the importer, and are honoured nationally, unless the NCR is modified or revoked. The importer has to advise the CBSA of any changes related to an NCR. For more information on national customs rulings, please see the document **National Customs Rulings Program**.

6. Free Trade Agreements

Canada has entered into free trade agreements with other countries to reduce or eliminate tariffs on products. Importers should be aware of any arrangements that Canada has with other countries in order to assess the impact such agreements may have on the products being imported.

North American Free Trade Agreement (NAFTA)

Under this agreement, as of January 1, 2003, virtually all trade between Canada, Mexico and the United States is tariff-free. NAFTA provides secure access for Canadian exports to the U.S. and Mexico. NAFTA's provisions include, among others, disciplines on the regulation of investment, services, intellectual property, competition and the temporary entry of business persons. For further information on NAFTA, see the document **North American Free Trade Agreement - NAFTA**.

Canada-Chile Free Trade Agreement (CCFTA)

This agreement provides for the elimination or reduction of customs duties on qualifying goods. For further information on CCFTA, see the document **Canada-Chile Free Trade Agreement - CCFTA** and the document **Canada-Chile Free Trade Agreement - Agriculture**.

Canada-Israel Free Trade Agreement (CIFTA)

This agreement improves market access for agri-food products of export interest to both Canada and Israel and eliminates tariffs on virtually all industrial goods. For further information on CIFTA, see the document **Canada-Israel Free Trade Agreement - CIFTA)** and the document **Canada-Israel Free Trade Agreement - Agriculture**.

Advance Ruling Program

CBSA issues advance rulings on a wide range of NAFTA, CIFTA or CCFTA related issues, including the following:

- whether or not an imported good qualifies as an originating good and thus qualifies for preferential tariff treatment under NAFTA, CIFTA or CCFTA;

- whether or not the good meets a specific regional value content requirement or tariff classification change requirement (these rules are collectively known as "rules of origin" and determine the eligibility of a good for preferential tariff treatment under NAFTA, CIFTA or CCFTA).;

- whether or not the proposed marking of a good satisfies country-of-origin marking requirements.

To get an advance ruling on future imports, a request in writing should be made to the Chief, Client Services in the region in which most of the importing will occur. CBSA will review all written applications and let the applicant know if any additional information is required. The agency aims to issue these rulings within 120 days of receiving the complete information. For further information on advanced rulings, see the document **Advance Rulings Program** or visit **http://www.cbsa-asfc.gc.ca/E/pub/cp/c-142/**. For information on tariffs and origin, see the document **Tariff Treatment - Origin - Imported Goods - NAFTA/CIFTA/CCFTA**.

7. Reporting and Recording Imports

The ***Customs Act***governs the administration and enforcement of customs laws, including reporting and record keeping. Under this Act, all goods imported into Canada must be reported to the nearest open Canada Customs office. The Reporting of Imported Goods Regulations specify how the reports must be made. For further information on import reporting, see the document **Reporting of Imported Goods.**

In addition, the Act also specifies that anyone importing goods for sale or for any industrial, occupational, commercial, institutional, or any other use must keep records of those goods at the place of business. The regulations specify how long importers must keep records, and the type of records they must keep. For further information on import record keeping, see the document **Record of Imported Goods**.

For more detailed information on reporting and records related to importing, call a Customs Client Service Office. For a list of the Customs Client Service Office numbers, please see document **Customs Offices - CBSA - Supplement**.

8. Customs

The CBSA offers an overview of the customs process for bringing your goods into Canada. To obtain additional information on customs, please visit the CBSA's Web site at the following address:http://www.cbsa-asfc.gc.ca/import/menu-e.html.

The CBSA provides importers with various automated methods of processing imported goods.

The **Customs Commercial System** (CCS) automates many of the processes used to control the import of commercial goods into Canada from the point of cargo release through the adjustment of historical data. This system applies to all importers or agents for importers of commercial goods into Canada. For further information on the CCS, see the document **Customs Automated Systems: Customs Commercial System - CCS**.

Customs Automated Data Exchange (CADEX) and **Customs Declaration** (CUSDEC) are **Electronic Data Interchange** (EDI) systems which the CBSA offers, allowing importers and brokers to file customs accounting documents (B3 forms) electronically. Importers or customs brokers able to transmit data electronically are eligible to use this system and must post security with CBSA. Users must also purchase application and communications software and pay for their own telecommunications costs.

CADEX and CUSDEC also offer centralized accounting privileges and can send accounting information to clients. Other features include data transmission for notification of customs release, overdue entries and classification. The system also includes information on tariffs, Goods and Services Tax (GST) and excise tax rate changes on commodities. For further information on filing customs documents with these systems, see the document **Customs Automated Data Exchange - CADEX - and Customs Declaration - CUSDEC**.

The **Accelerated Commercial Release Operations Support System** (ACROSS) lets the importer, broker or carrier use EDI technology to transmit customs release, cargo and conveyance data to any automated customs office for all modes of transport including rail, marine and highway. EDI lets you transmit information from one computer to another quickly, easily and accurately. For more information on the ACROSS system, see the document **Accelerated Commercial Release Operational Support System - ACROSS**.

The **Postal Import Control System** (PICS) and **Customs Refund System** (CRS) are computerized systems used to collect or refund duties and taxes. If the commercial package being mailed is worth $1600 CDN or more, PICS creates a letter to the importer asking for a completed Form B3, the Canada Customs Coding Form. This letter is also a cargo control document. The customs mail centre holds the package and keeps a record in the computer's inventory file until the importer presents a completed form and pays the duties and taxes to the nearest Canada customs office. Canada Post can then deliver the package.

Casual Refund Centres refund duties, excise taxes, Goods and Services Tax/Harmonized Services Tax, Provincial Sales Tax, specific provincial taxes, tobacco and alcohol provincial taxes and *Special Import Measures Act*taxes on non-commercial imports through the postal, traveller and courier streams. This process applies to claims submitted by brokers for mail order goods that have subsequently been returned to the exporter by the casual importer. For further information on PICS and CRS, see the document **Postal Import Control System and Casual Refund System.**

9. Duty Deferral Programs

The CBSA has two programs to assist companies that import goods in recovering duties paid.

The **Duty Drawbacks** program helps Canadian companies compete in export markets and certain domestic markets by allowing them to **recover** duties they paid on imported goods under certain circumstances (the export of Canadian manufactured goods; the import and subsequent export of goods; the destruction of obsolete or surplus goods, etc.). You cannot recover GST payments under this program. For further information on duty drawbacks, see the document **Duty Deferral Program - Duty Drawbacks** or visit the Web site at http://www.cbsa-asfc.gc.ca/import/drawbacks-e.html

The **Duties Relief** program **relieves** the payment of duties on imported goods that will eventually be re-exported either in the same condition or after being used, consumed or expended in the processing of other goods. Relief of the GST is also available under certain circumstances. The program is available to businesses that

160

import goods into Canada or receive goods that were imported into Canada which have been, or will be, exported from Canada. It may apply to importers, manufacturers, processors, exporters, customs brokers and manufacturing and trade associations with an interest in international trade.

For further information on duties relief, see the document **Duty Deferral Program - Duties Relief**. Duties relief administrators in the regional offices are also available to answer questions. For a list of Customs Client Services Offices, see the document **Customs Offices - Supplement** or contact the COBSC.

Protective Measures for Canadian Products against Unfair Foreign Competition

The CBSA and the Canadian International Trade Tribunal (CITT) are jointly responsible for administering the ***Special Import Measures Act***(SIMA), which has been put in place to protect Canadian industry from injury caused by the dumping or subsidizing of imported goods. Canadian producers are protected from unfair trade under SIMA and can lodge complaints alleging injury from product dumping or subsidizing. Trade associations can lodge a complaint on behalf of their members. For further information on SIMA, see the document **Protective Measures for Canadian Products Against Unfair Foreign Competition**.

Temporary Importation/Exportation Programs

All goods entering Canada, including those being imported temporarily or goods that have been temporarily exported, are subject to duty and tax on their full value, unless there is a provision in legislation or regulations to relieve the duties and taxes owing. For more information about these provisions, see the document **Temporary Importation/Exportation Programs**.

10. Automated Customs Information Service (ACIS)

The ACIS is a computerized, 24-hour telephone service that automatically answers all incoming calls and provides general customs information. With the help of a touch-tone telephone, clients can hear recorded information. Customs officers are available for specific questions during working hours. For more information on ACIS, see the document **Automated Customs Information Service (ACIS)** or visit the CBSA's Web site at **http://www.cbsa-asfc.gc.ca/E/pub/cp/rc4040/README.html**. To reach ACIS, call **1-800-461-9999** .

11. Publications

A number of import-related publications are available through the CRA and CBSA Web sites. The forms and publications can be viewed online and downloaded onto your computer or printed. You can also use the online order form to have printed forms and publications mailed to you. Or you can request a printed form or publication by phoning **1-800-959-2221** or by visiting a CRA office. Local tax services offices are listed in the blue pages of your telephone book under the "Canada Revenue Agency" or on the Web at http://www.cra-arc.gc.ca/contact/tso/ON-e.html:

- Guide for Canadian Small Business (RC 4070), available on the Internet at

  http://www.cra-arc.gc.ca/E/pub/tg/rc4070/rc4070eq.html

- Guide to Importing Commercial Goods (RC 4041), available on the Internet at

  http://www.cbsa-asfc.gc.ca/E/pub/cp/rc4041/

- Importing Commercial Goods into Canada, available on the Internet at **http://www.cbsa-asfc.gc.ca/E/pub/cp/rc4229/**

12. Personal Information Protection

Personal Information Protection - Privacy Commissioner of Canada

The Guide to Canada's *Personal Information Protection and Electronic Documents Act* (PIPEDA) helps businesses understand their obligations and comply to the Act. On January 1, 2004, the PIPED Act will cover the **collection, use** or **disclosure** of **personal information in the course of all commercial activities in Canada**, except in provinces which have enacted legislation that is deemed to be substantially similar to the federal law.

For more information, call **1-800-282-1376**, see the document **Protection of Personal Information: Your Responsibilities** or visit the Privacy Commissioner's Web site at http://www.privcom.gc.ca/information/guide_e.asp.

ARE YOU PLANNING TO EXPORT ?

1. Exporting?

Many companies see exporting as a way to expand their operations. The global marketplace is increasingly seen as having greater opportunities for Canadian entrepreneurs wishing to look beyond domestic sales, and begin to promote and sell their products and services in other countries.

There are a number of reasons to consider exporting:

- New and expanding markets may generate ideas for future product or service advancements;
- Exporting may reduce reliance on domestic markets;
- Exporting may increase sales and profits in the long-term;
- Exporting may open up the market base, particularly for niche or unique product types.

Whatever the reasons a business cites for wanting to export, the benefits are not a guarantee. There are always risks involved in any new venture. Businesses considering exporting need to take the time to assess their readiness and ability to move in this new direction.

Although this is not an exhaustive list, businesses preparing to export often take the following considerations into account :

- Is my firm prepared to devote the time and resources necessary to break into foreign markets?

- Does my business have the production capacity for new markets?

- Do I have sufficient cash flow to support export market demands?

- Is my product or service ready for international markets or are there modifications required to meet the needs of interested foreign customers?

164

- Where is the best place in the world to sell my product or service and why?

- Should my business look at hiring export professionals (e.g. export consultant, freight forwarder, customs broker)?

- Is exporting consistent with other company objectives?

- Can your goods and/or services be easily distributed abroad?

- Is your product and/or service cost competitive?

- Are you and/or your staff capable of conducting business in the appropriate language/time zone?

2. Helping Exporters Get Started

The **Team Canada Inc 1-888 Export Information Service** connects businesses to the full range of government export programs, services and expertise. This service is delivered by CBSCs across Canada on behalf of Team Canada Inc. Calls are automatically routed to the client's local CBSC, and answered by trained Information Officers. While general export information is provided directly, clients who require more expert advice or export counselling are referred to appropriate domestic export development services.

For additional information on Team Canada Inc services, see the document **Team Canada Inc 1-888 Export Information Service.** To speak with an Information Officer, call Team Canada Inc at **1-888-811-1119**, or visit http://exportsource.gc.ca.

The **Canada-Ontario Export Forum (COEF)** is a partnership dedicated to helping companies in Ontario achieve success in global markets. The key areas of focus are export preparation services; market information and intelligence; export counselling; and international financing. For more information on the Canada-Ontario Export Forum, see the document **Canada-Ontario Export Forum (COEF)** or visit the COEF Web site at http://www.ic.gc.ca/coef.

Through the **Department of Foreign Affairs and International Trade (DFAIT) Enquiries Services**, callers can request general information and publications on trade, foreign policy and consular services. For further information, please see the document **Enquiries Services**, or call **(613) 944-4000** (Ottawa) or **1-800-267-8376**, e-mail **enqserv@dfait-maeci.gc.ca**, or visit the Web site at http://www.dfait-maeci.gc.ca/.

3. Assessing Your Export Potential

The first step in the decision to export your product or service is to assess your ability to export. There are several online diagnostic tools available to "new to exporting" businesses that help determine export readiness:

The **Export Diagnostic** at http://www.exportdiagnostic.ca/ will give you an opportunity to test your export readiness and identify priorities as you prepare for a foreign market.

Take a World View at http://strategis.gc.ca/twv is an export preparation and information tool designed to assist service exporters become export-ready. For further information on Take a World View, see the document **Take a World View... Export Your Services**.

Services 2000 is a Government of Canada Web site containing interactive management and diagnostic tools to assist exporters. Steps to Competitiveness will present, in a modular format, information on competitiveness issues and gaps facing small and medium sized service firms. For more information, go to http://services2000.ic.gc.ca/, or consult the document **Services 2000**.

Another useful resource for assessing export preparedness is the **Export Business Plan** at

http://www.cbsc.org/alberta/search/display.cfm?Code=8016&coll= AB_PROVBIS_E. This tool, published by the Canada-Alberta Business Service Centre, takes you through the steps to developing your Export Business Plan.

The Interactive Export Planner uses the capabilities of the Internet to assist entrepreneurs in preparing an export plan or an export-focused business plan for their new or existing business by:

- guiding you through each section of your plan using a question and answer format;
- teaching definitions and tips, and showing sample plans to help you write your own plan;
- preparing financial projections for you, based upon the information you provide; and
- assisting you in researching your export plan or business plan.

For more information or to access the Interactive Export Planner, please visit the following Web site:

http://www.exportsource.gc.ca/iep.

The **ExportSource** Web site includes A Step-by-Step Guide to Exporters. This guide can help new exporters gather the appropriate information to ensure they are ready to export and know what is required to export products and services. Visit

http://exportsource.gc.ca/gol/exportsource/interface.nsf/engdocbasic/1.2.html.

4. Picking Your Target Market - Market Research

After deciding that you want to proceed with the export of your products or services, you need to identify potential export markets. Research on the most promising countries includes, but is not limited to:

- demographics;
- economic profiles;
- geography;
- political and legal aspects;
- trade practices and customs;
- literacy rates;
- culture and consumer patterns;
- attitudes toward foreign businesses;
- climate/weather conditions;
- transportation and communication systems;
- risk assessment;
- currency/inflation rates;

167

- intellectual property protection.

ExportSource is Canada's most comprehensive online source of export information. Exporters looking for market intelligence on either a specific geographic region or business sector should visit the Market Research section of ExportSource located at http://exportsource.ca/index_e.cfm.

Exporters of food products may wish to contact the **Agri-Food Trade Service (ATS)** online at http://ats-sea.agr.ca/. This service provides access to international trade and market information for Canadian agri-food exporters. Information includes:

- country and product reports;
- export assistance;
- market analysis;
- market trends and opportunities;
- global trade rules;
- trade shows and missions;
- international trade statistics;
- world trade news;
- exporting guides;
- federal government trade contacts;
- a database of international trade contacts including foreign buyers, Canadian suppliers, programs and services.

For more information, you may visit the ATS Web site at http://ats-sea.agr.ca or call Team Canada Inc's Export Information Service at **1-888-811-1119.**

Central Intelligence Agency World Factbook is the U.S. government's complete geographical handbook, featuring over 260 full-colour maps and flags of all nations and geographical entities. Each country profile tracks such demographics as population, ethnicity and literacy rates, as well as political, geographical and economic data. To access the World Factbook, please visit http://www.odci.gov/cia/publications/factbook/index.html.

Statistics Canada collects and distributes a wide range of statistical information on exporting based on Canada Border Services Agency

(CBSA) data. Statistics Canada maintains detailed trade data for anyone whose business depends on importing or exporting (costs are applicable). For more information, see the document **Trade Data and Statistics** or visit the Statistics Canada Web site at http://www.statcan.ca/.

Trade Data Online on Strategis provides annual information on the value of imports and domestic exports in terms of dollars or percentages. It targets more than 200 countries for over 5,000 commodities covering 500 industries for the latest five complete years and the current year to date. The data is obtained from Statistics Canada and the U.S. Department of Commerce. For further information on Trade Data Online, see the document **Trade Data Online** or visit the Web site at http://strategis.gc.ca/tdo.

Canadian Industry Statistics offers a comprehensive source of statistics on Canadian industrial sectors, including information on importing and exporting trends. For more information on Canadian Industry Statistics, please see the document **Canadian Industry Statistics** or visit http://strategis.gc.ca/cis.

5. Export Training

The **Forum for International Trade Training (FITT)** provides interested exporters with the training and skills necessary to compete in international markets:

- **FITTskills** is a comprehensive package of courses consisting of eight individual modules focusing on the day-to-day mechanics of international business, including entrepreneurship, marketing, finance, logistics, market entry and distribution, research, legal aspects and trade management. This program is available online or in classrooms at institutions across Canada.

- **Going Global Workshop Series** is designed to help companies, individuals and export service providers make the decision to "go global", by providing them with an understanding of the benefits and challenges of exporting. Developed and delivered in partnership with Team Canada

169

Inc, the three-hour workshops in the series include: Introduction to International Trade, Introduction to Market Research, Introduction to International Marketing, Introduction to International Finance, Introduction to International Trade Logistics & Distribution.

- **Enterprise FITT** is international trade training, individually tailored to meet the unique requirements of a business or organization. Learning objectives are defined with the client, based upon a careful needs analysis. Training can be delivered on or off-site through practical exercises and scenarios, presentations, workshops, or any mixture of approaches that best suit the learning style of the organization.

For further information on **FITT** programs, see the document **Forum for International Trade Training - FITT Inc.,**

contact **FITT** at **(613) 230-3553** (Ottawa) or **1-800-561-3488**, fax your request to **(613) 230-6808**, e-mail **corp@fitt.ca** or visit their Web site at http://www.fitt.ca.

ExportUSA is a group of programs that can assist exporters in developing or expanding their access to the U.S. market by giving them first-hand exposure to target American markets and export contacts.

- **New Exporters to Border States Program (NEBS),** focuses on export education. It introduces companies to the essentials of exporting and provides practical export information and first-hand exposure to markets in the United States.

- **Exporters to the United States program (EXTUS)** is a program similar to NEBS that serves Canadian companies already exporting to the U.S. border states. Formerly known as NEBS Plus, EXTUS focuses on expanding the markets of successful Canadian exporters to other regions of the United States.

- **Reverse NEBS** program serves Canadian companies not yet exporting to the United States by providing informative seminars in Canada on the essentials of exporting.

For additional information about the ExportUSA programs, see the document **ExportUSA** and visit the following Web site: http://www.infoexport.gc.ca/docs/view-e.asp?did=5272&gid=538. For the **Export USA Calendar**, which includes program dates, locations and contacts, please visit

http://www.dfait-maeci.gc.ca/can-am/export/menu.asp.

OMAF's **PROFIT Food Export Seminar** is a two-day seminar that addresses the basics of exporting to the U.S. market. For additional information, see the document **PROFIT Food Export Seminar** or visit OMAF's export services web site at:

http://www.gov.on.ca/OMAFRA/english/food/export/services.htm.

Seminars and Workshops Each event is organized in partnership with local industry associations, municipalities, businesses, non-profit (also known as not-for-profit) organizations and colleges and universities with international business programs. Workshop topics and areas of discussion at each event are developed with input from local participants and are specific to each community. Local partners, local sponsors and local facilitators help ensure that each event successfully meets the needs of the community. General export seminar topics covered are Export Financing; E-Commerce; E-Business; Internet Exposure Benefits; and Managing Export Growth.

For additional information, see the document **Seminars and Workshops**, or contact Ontario Exports Inc. at **1-877-468-7233**.

Note: Many community colleges and some boards of education offer courses in international marketing and import/export methods. Several universities operate Centres for International Business Studies or international business oriented MBA programs. Industry and trade associations also offer various seminars on trade. Visit the **Association of Universities and Colleges of Canada (AUCC)**, at

171

http://www.aucc.ca/can_uni/index_e.html, to search through a comprehensive list of international programs offered by some Canadian universities and colleges.

6. Regulations

There are various regulations that apply to exporting Canadian goods to other regions of the world. The Canada Border Services Agency's (CBSA) publication **Exporting Goods from Canada** provides an overview of the rules involved in exporting a product. This publication is available on the Internet at **http://www.cbsa-asfc.gc.ca/E/pub/cp/rc4116/rc4116-e.html**

Business Number - Importer/Exporter Account Number

All Canadian individuals or businesses exporting on a commercial basis must obtain a Business Number in order to account for their goods. CRA uses this number to identify a business and to process customs accounting documents. Application forms are available from all CRA offices that clear commercial shipments, and from Business Window offices.

For further information on Business Numbers, see the documents **Business Number - BN** and **Importer/Exporter Account Number**, visit CRA's Web site at http://www.cra-arc.gc.ca/E/pbg/tf/rc1c/README.html or contact the CRA at **1-800-959-5525**.

Automated Customs Information Service (ACIS) is an automated telephone service providing information on customs-related topics such as personal importing; travellers' exemptions; Visitor Rebate Program; commercial importing and exporting; currency exchange rates; postal importing and refunds; CANPASS; Free Trade Agreements (North American, Israel, and Chile); customs news and current events specific to each calling area. Callers may access ACIS throughout Canada by calling **1-800-461-9999**.

For additional information on ACIS, see the document **Automated Customs Information Services - ACIS** or visit the CBSA's Web site at http://www.cbsa-asfc.gc.ca/import/acisintro-e.html.

Reporting Exports

Exporters must report to CBSA commercial shipments valued at more than $2,000 (CDN) exported to a country other than the United

States, as well as any goods being shipped through the United States to another country.

Canadian Automated Export Declaration (CAED) is a Windows-based software application that has been jointly developed by CBSA and Statistics Canada. The CAED is available free of charge and has been designed to offer flexibility and convenience, to streamline the export reporting process by automating the preparation of CBSA's B13A Export Declaration. It provides exporters or their agents the ability to transmit completed Export Declarations directly to the Federal Government of Canada via the Internet.

For more information on the CAED, please visit the Statistics Canada Web site at

http://www.statcan.ca/english/exports/index.htm. Exporters who do not use the CAED must report their exports by completing form B13A Export Declaration. For further information on reporting exports, see the document **Reporting of Exports** or contact your nearest CBSA Trade Administration Services Office (listed in the document **Customs Office - Supplement**).

Exports of Prohibited and Controlled Goods

Some government departments prohibit certain goods from entering or leaving Canada. Certain other goods are controlled, meaning that permits, certificates, labelling or authorizations from a federal department are needed before CBSA will release the goods. Exporters must submit a permit or certificate when shipping controlled, regulated or prohibited goods.

For additional information, please see the document **Requirements for Imports and Exports of Prohibited and Controlled Goods : Other Federal Government Departments**, visit the CBSA's Web site at **http://www.cbsa-asfc.gc.ca/menu/D-e.html** or call **1-800-461-9999** for a list of federal departments and the goods they control.

Export Permits

Export Permits are required when the export destination is a country on the **Area Control List** or when the goods are on the **Export**

Control List. The Export and Import Controls Bureau of the Department of Foreign Affairs and International Trade (DFAIT) provides assistance to exporters in determining if export permits are required, and publishes brochures and Notices to Exporters that are available free on request.

For further information on Export Permits, see the document **Export Permits**, contact the Export and Import Controls Bureau of DFAIT at **(613) 996-2387**, fax your request to **(613) 996-9933** or visit their Web site at http://www.dfait-maeci.gc.ca/~eicb/epd_home.htm

7. Export Financing

There are several sources of financing to help businesses export their products or services.

Export Development Canada (EDC) offers a range of risk reduction financial services, including export financing, where EDC extends financing to a foreign buyer so that it can purchase your Canadian goods or services. EDC's **Export Receivables Insurance** covers your company against 90 percent of losses if your foreign buyer does not pay. Export contracts can be insured against a wide range of commercial and political risks.

For more information on EDC, see the documents **Export Development Canada - Mandate**, **Export Receivables Insurance** and **Financing Services for Smaller Capital Goods Exporter**, or visit the EDC Web site at http://www.edc.ca.

The **Canadian Commercial Corporation (CCC)** is a federal Crown Corporation providing Canadian exporters with a range of export sales, consulting, contract management services, and access to pre-shipment financing services to help win sales on better terms, in a variety of market sectors around the world. For further information on CCC, see the document **Canadian Commercial Corporation - Mandate**, or visit the CCC Web site at http://www.ccc.ca.

8. Sources of Export Assistance

One of the keys to exporting success is to find accurate and up-to-date information on the regions of the world where you plan to export your product or services. Listed below are some valuable sources of information for new exporters.

ExportSource, Team Canada Inc's online resource, provides a one-stop shop for new and experienced exporters, with access to multiple sources of export-related information. Trade information from more than 800 government and private sources is brought directly to your work space to help you find the information you need on foreign markets, trade statistics and export financing, logistics of delivery, trade shows, export missions and sources of assistance.

For further information on ExportSource, see the **ExportSource**, or visit http://exportsource.ca.

InfoExport is the Web site of the Trade Commissioner Service (TCS). Through this site, Canadian companies have free access to over 600 sectoral market studies and country-specific reports prepared by the Market Research Centre of the Trade Commissioner Service and by the many offices abroad. A section of the site is also dedicated to other DFAIT trade-related programs and initiatives. For further information on InfoExport, see the document **InfoExport** or visit http://www.infoexport.gc.ca.

The **Business Women in Trade** Web site was created by InfoExport to support businesswomen with information relevant to exporting and export activities. It provides an entry point to a wealth of information on how to prepare for, and to succeed in, the export marketplace, including direct links to other useful Internet resources. For further information, see the document **Businesswomen in Trade** or visit http://www.infoexport.gc.ca/businesswomen.

The **DFAIT Web site** offers valuable country information to exporters. Statistics on trade with Canada, the economy, demographics, and political structure are all available on this site. You can see country market reports by visiting this Web site at http://www.dfait-maeci.gc.ca/geo/menu-e.asp.

Strategis is the largest business information Web site in Canada. Within Strategis, Canadian businesses have access to a vast array of management resources, perspectives and data that can help them further develop and expand their markets, create alliances and find new clients. The **Trade and Investment section** has valuable information to assist exporters.

For additional information on Strategis, please see the document **Strategis** or visit the Web site at http://strategis.gc.ca.

Canadian Company Capabilities is an online Strategis database which profiles thousands of Canadian companies. It offers free registration, and company information is available globally. This database contains vital company information that can be searched to locate Canadian suppliers and distribution channels, to determine competition, to form partnerships and to uncover export opportunities.

For further information on Canadian Company Capabilities, see the document **Canadian Company Capabilities** or visit the Strategis Web site at http://strategis.gc.ca/cdncc.

COBSC Regional Access Sites (and many libraries) offer public access to the Internet. To obtain a list of Regional Access Sites in Ontario, see the document **Regional Access Program** or contact the COBSC.

The **Agri-Food Trade Service (ATS)** of Agriculture and Agri-Food Canada provides simplified centralized access to international market information and intelligence, export trade counselling and export support activities, which will take the exporter from initial enquiry to foreign market. To obtain information on ATS, please see the document **Agri-Food Trade Services - ATS**.

The Export Marketing Unit of the **Ontario Ministry of Agriculture and Food (OMAF)** offers a number of services to new and experienced exporters of food, beverage and agricultural products. These services include counselling, seminars, outgoing and incoming missions, international trade shows, sourcing and market intelligence. For further information on the Ontario Ministry of Agriculture and Food, see the document **Export Marketing Unit**.

177

Ontario Exports Inc., the lead trade agency of the Ontario Government, can help Ontario firms begin to export or expand markets and can assist foreign buyers in finding Ontario suppliers. For more information, please contact a Trade Information Officer at **1-877-468-7233**, or visit http://www.ontarioexportsinc.com/.

Non-governmental Trade Organizations

There are many trade organizations that have a strong export focus. Many of these organizations offer seminars and export information on foreign markets.

- Canadian Manufacturers and Exporters (CME) at http://www.cme-mec.ca/home.asp?l=EN;

- the Canadian Boards of Trade and Chambers of Commerce; http://www.chamber.ca/;

- Ontario Chamber of Commerce; **http://www.occ.on.ca/**;

- the Chambre économique de l'Ontario**; http://www.ceo-on.com/** (services are offered to both French and English exporters, but site is in French only);

- the Canadian Council for International Business; **http://www.ccib.org/**;

- Municipal Boards of Trade and Chambers of Commerce;

- most local Economic Development Offices;

- numerous industry associations;

- international business councils (e.g. Canada-Japan Trade Council, Canada-India Business Council).

The main branches of Canadian Chartered Banks have Trade Finance Sections that will provide you with information and advice on their export services. Your local library can also be a valuable resource when doing your market research.

9. Additional Resources and Publications

Once your business has made the decision to export there are two other Info-Guides that could be examined for additional information:

- **Researching World Markets**; and
- **Entering World Markets**.

The resources listed below will provide additional information to help your business prepare, research and plan to export to world markets:

- International Business Opportunities Centre, at http://www.iboc.gc.ca/;

- Ontario Exports Inc.; http://www.ontarioexportsinc.com/;

- **Getting Ready to Export**, from Ontario Exports Inc.;

- **Ontario E-Commerce Export Guide**, from Ontario Exports Inc.;

- World Trade Organization, at http://www.wto.org/;

- Worldwide Governments on WWW, at http://www.gksoft.com/govt/;

- Trade Team Canada Sectors, at http://ttcs.ic.gc.ca/;

- **Virtual Trade Commissioner - VTC**;

- Smallbiz Xpress, at http://smallbizxpress.tpl.toronto.on.ca/servlet/HomePage.

MUNICIPAL REQUIREMENTS TO START A BUSINESS

Municipal Licences

Each municipal government has the authority to issue its own business licences within its jurisdiction. Many but not all types of businesses require a municipal licence. The fees can vary from a few dollars to a thousand or more, but in most cases the fees are nominal. Since there is no uniformity throughout the province regarding municipal licences for businesses, you should consult with the appropriate local official to determine if your business will be affected by local regulations and licences.

Where city business licences are required, they are usually intended to control businesses which pose special problems regarding health, safety, and the general well-being of the community. The local municipality is also responsible for the administration of certain provincial laws like the ***Health Protection and Promotion Act***, which governs community health standards.

For more information on business licences, check with the municipal licensing board, commission or bylaw officer.

Zoning Bylaws

Zoning bylaws are used by the city or town to regulate the use of land. They state exactly what land uses are permitted in the community and provide information such as where buildings may be located, the types of uses and dwellings permitted, and standards for lot size, parking requirements and building height. Most municipalities have a planning board to designate areas within the municipality as residential, commercial, light industry, heavy industry, noxious industry, green belt or parkland. Construction, reconstruction, alterations or additions to a building require approval of the designs by the building department.

If you propose using your property in a way that does comply with the existing bylaw you will have to apply for a zoning change. Before you apply for rezoning, you should discuss your proposal with the planning staff in the municipality or with the municipal clerk. They can offer preliminary advice on how to proceed with a formal application and on the fees that may be required.

If you have a proposal that meets the main requirements of the zoning by-law, but does not conform exactly, you can apply for a minor variance. As long as the general purpose and intent of the bylaw can be maintained, a change of minor variance can be considered by the municipality. Obtaining a minor variance involves an application to your local Committee of Adjustment followed by a public hearing and full consideration of your proposal. The public is involved in the process of evaluating your application for zoning amendments or variances.

For details on fees and other requirements, contact the municipal clerk or zoning officer of the city in which the business will be located.

Ontario Building Code and Municipal Building Department

A business location is subject to inspection by the Municipal Building Department to make sure that it meets local safety requirements, such as those designated by the **Ontario Building Code** and the **Ontario Fire Code**. Most municipalities require a building permit before alterations or new construction begins. It is extremely important, therefore, that you check zoning regulations before signing a lease, and obtain the necessary building permit before beginning alterations or new construction.

"Starting a Small Business in Ontario" contains some useful tips on purchasing and leasing premises. The Municipal Building Department may also have some valuable information for you.

Note: The print version of "Starting a Small Business in Ontario" can be picked up free of charge at Small Business Self-Help Offices and Enterprise Centres across the province (listed in the blue pages of your telephone directory) or purchased from Publications Ontario at **(416) 326-5300** or **1-800-668-9938**.

Municipal Business Taxes

Many cities and towns charge business taxes to businesses within their jurisdiction. For more information on these taxes, you should contact the taxation office of the city or town where your business will be located.

Additional Web Sites of Interest

- Ontario Municipal Board, at http://www.omb.gov.on.ca/

- Municipal Property Assessment Corporation, at http://www.assessmentontario.com/

- Your Local Government, at http://www.yourlocalgovernment.com

- Association of Municipalities of Ontario, at http://www.amo.on.ca

- document **Questions to Ask Before You Sign a Lease,**

- Starting a Small Business in Ontario, at http://www.ontariocanada.com

Other Contact(s):

Please contact the local government of the city, town, etc. in which you will operate your business, listed in the blue pages of the telephone book. Ministry of Economic Development and Trade - MEDT

Your Canada Wide CBSC Contacts

Alberta Contact(s):
The Business Link Business Service Centre
Suite 100
10237 - 104 Street North West
Edmonton, Alberta
T5J 1B1
Toll-free: 1-800-272-9675
Telephone: (780) 422-7722
Fax: (780) 422-0055
E-mail: buslink@cbsc.ic.gc.ca
Web site: http://www.cbsc.org/alberta
Voice Web: http://vweb.cbsc.org/english/forms/ab/talktous.jsp

British Columbia Contact(s):
Canada / British Columbia Business Services Society
601 West Cordova Street
Vancouver, British Columbia
V6B 1G1
Toll-free: 1-800-667-2272 (in B.C. only)
Telephone: (604) 775-5525
Fax: (604) 775-5520
E-mail: comments@cbsc.ic.gc.ca
Web site: http://www.smallbusinessbc.ca
Voice Web: http://vweb.cbsc.org/english/forms/bc/talktous.jsp

Manitoba Contact(s):
Canada/Manitoba Business Service Centre
P.O. Box 2609
Room 250
240 Graham Avenue
Winnipeg, Manitoba
R3C 4B3
Toll-free: 1-800-665-2019
Toll-free TTY: 1-800-457-8466
Voice Web: http://vweb.cbsc.org/english/forms/mb/talktous.jsp
Telephone: (204) 984-2272
Fax: (204) 983-3852
E-mail: manitoba@cbsc.ic.gc.ca
Web site: http://www.cbsc.org/manitoba

New Brunswick Contact(s):
Canada / New Brunswick Business Service Centre
Atlantic Canada Opportunities Agency
Ground Floor, Barker House
570 Queen Street
Fredericton, New Brunswick
E3B 6Z6
Toll-free: 1-800-668-1010 (Atlantic region only)
Toll-free TTY: 1-800-887-6550 (Atlantic region only)
Telephone: (506) 444-6140
Fax: (506) 444-6172
TTY: (506) 444-6166
E-mail: cbscnb@cbsc.ic.gc.ca
Web site: http://www.cbsc.org/nb
Voice Web: http://vweb.cbsc.org/english/forms/nb/talktous.jsp

183

Newfoundland and Labrador Contact(s):
Canada/Newfoundland & Labrador Business Service Centre
P.O. Box 8687, Station A
Room 101
90 O'Leary Avenue
St. John's, Newfoundland and Labrador
A1B 3T1
Toll-free: 1-800-668-1010 (Atlantic region only)
Telephone: (709) 772-6022
Fax: (709) 772-6090
E-mail: info@cbsc.ic.gc.ca
Web site: http://www.cbsc.org/nl

Northwest Territories Contact(s):
Canada/NWT Business Service Centre
P.O. Box 1320
8th Floor
Scotia Centre
Yellowknife, Northwest Territories
X1A 2L9
Toll-free: 1-800-661-0599
Telephone: (867) 873-7958
Fax: (867) 873-0101
E-mail: yel@cbsc.ic.gc.ca
Web site: http://www.cbsc.org/nwt

Nova Scotia Contact(s):
Canada/Nova Scotia Business Service Centre
1575 Brunswick Street
Halifax, Nova Scotia
B3J 2G1
Toll-free: 1-800-668-1010 (Atlantic region only)
Toll-free TTY: 1-800-797-4188 (Atlantic region only)
Telephone: (902) 426-8604
Fax: (902) 426-6530
TTY: (902) 426-4188
E-mail: halifax@cbsc.ic.gc.ca
Web site: http://www.cbsc.org/ns
Voice Web: http://vweb.cbsc.org/english/forms/ns/talktous.jsp

Nunavut Contact(s):
Iqaluit
Canada-Nunavut Business Service Centre
P.O. Box 1000, Station 1198
Parnaivik Building
Iqaluit, Nunavut
X0A 0H0
Toll-free: 1-877-499-5199
Toll-free Fax: 1-877-499-5299
Telephone: (867) 979-6813
Fax: (867) 979-6823
E-mail: cnbsc@gov.nu.ca
Web site: http://www.cbsc.org/nunavut

Kugluktuk
Canada-Nunavut Business Service Centre
Enokhok Centre, Box 316
Kugluktuk, Nunavut
X0E 0H0
Toll-free: 1-877-499-5199
Toll-free Fax: 1-877-499-5299
Telephone: (867) 982-7256
Fax: (867) 982-3701
E-mail: cnbsc@gov.nu.ca
Web site: http://www.cbsc.org/nunavut

Rankin Inlet
Canada-Nunavut Business Service Centre
Siniktarvik Building
Bag 002
Rankin Inlet, Nunavut
X0C 0G0
Toll-free: 1-877-499-5199
Toll-free Fax: 1-877-499-5299
Telephone: (867) 645-5067
Fax: (867) 645-2346
E-mail: cnbsc@gov.nu.ca
Web site: http://www.cbsc.org/nunavut

Ontario Contact(s):
For information on programs, services and regulations contact:
Canada-Ontario Business Service Centre
Toronto, Ontario
M5C 2W7
Toll-free: 1-800-567-2345 (in Ontario only)
Telephone: (416) 775-3456
Fax: (416) 954-8597
TTY: (416) 973-0306
E-mail: ontario@cbsc.ic.gc.ca
Web site: http://www.cbsc.org/ontario
Voice Web: http://vweb.cbsc.org/english/forms/on/talktous.jsp

P.E.I. Contact(s):
Canada/PEI Business Service Centre
P.O. Box 40
75 Fitzroy Street
Charlottetown, Prince Edward Island
C1A 7K2
Toll-free: 1-800-668-1010 (Atlantic region only)
Telephone: (902) 368-0771
Fax: (902) 566-7377
E-mail: pei@cbsc.ic.gc.ca
Web site: http://www.cbsc.org/pe
Voice Web: http://vweb.cbsc.org/english/forms/pe/talktous.jsp
Office Hours: 8:30 a.m. to 4:30 p.m.

185

Québec Contact(s):
Info entreprises
380 St-Antoine West, local 6000
Montréal, Quebec
H2Y 3X7
Toll-free: 1-800-322-INFO (4636)
Telephone: (514) 496-INFO (4636)
Fax: (514) 496-5934
E-mail: infoentrepreneurs@cbsc.ic.gc.ca
Web site: http://www.ccmm.qc.ca/Infoentreprises
Voice Web: http://vweb.cbsc.org/english/forms/qc/talktous.jsp
Office Hours: Regulars Hours: 9:00 a.m. to 5:00 p.m., Monday to Friday
Documentation Centre (Library) Hours for On-Site Research:
9:00 a.m. to 3:00 p.m., Monday to Friday

Québec
Ressources Entreprises
2014, Jean-Talon North Street, suite 290
Sainte-Foy, Quebec
G1N 4N6
Toll-free: 1-800-322-INFO (4636)
Telephone: (418) 649-INFO (4636)
Fax: (418) 682-1144
E-mail: ressourcesentreprises@cbsc.ic.gc.ca
Web site: http://ressourcesentreprises.org
Office Hours: 9 a.m. to 5 p.m., Monday to Friday

Saskatchewan Contact(s):
business infosource
Canada-Saskatchewan Business Service Centre
345 - 3rd Avenue South
Saskatoon, Saskatchewan
S7K 2H6
Toll-free: 1-800-667-4374
Toll-free TTY: 1-800-457-8466
Voice Web: http://vweb.cbsc.org/english/forms/sk/talktous.jsp
Telephone: (306) 956-2323
Fax: (306) 956-2328
E-mail: saskatchewan@cbsc.ic.gc.ca
Web site: http://www.cbsc.org/sask

Yukon Contact(s):
Canada-Yukon Business Service Centre
Suite 101
307 Jarvis Street
Whitehorse, Yukon
Y1A 2H3
Toll-free: 1-800-661-0543
Telephone: (867) 633-6257
Fax: (867) 667-2001
E-mail: yukon@cbsc.ic.gc.ca
Web site: http://www.cbsc.org/yukon

186

Lawyer referrals services across Canada:

Alberta	1-800-661-1095
British Columbia	1-800-663-1919
Manitoba	1-800-262-8800
New Brunswick	1-506-458-8540
Newfoundland	1-709-722-2643
Northwest Territories	1-867-873-3828
Nova Scotia	1-800-665-9779
Nunavut	1-867-979-2330
Ontario	1-800-268-8326
Prince Edward Island	1-902-566-1666
Quebec Montreal	1-514-866-2490
Quebec	1-418-529-0301
Hull	1-819-777-5225
Longueuil	1-450-468-2609
Laval	1-450-686-2958
Laurentides Lanaudière	1-450-752-6774
Saskatchewan	1-800-667-9886
Yukon	1-867-668-4231

Business Related sites :

- Bank of Montreal - http://www.bmo.com/smallbiz
- Business Development Bank of Canada - http://www.bdc.ca
- Business Opportunities Classifieds Online - http://www.boconline.com
- Canada Business Service Centre - http://www.cbsc.org
- Canada Revenue Agency - http://www.cra-arc.gc.ca
- Entrepreneur Magazine - http://www.entrepreneurmag.com
- Franchise Annual - http://www.infonews.com/online.html
- Human Resources and Skills Development Canada - http://www.hrdc-drhc.gc.ca
- Idea Café: The Small Business Directory - http://ideacafe.com
- Inc. Online: Resource for Growing your Small Business - http://www.inc.com
- Internet World Magazine - http://www.iw.com
- MERX - http://www.merx.com
- SBA: Small Business Administration Home Page - http://www.sbaonline.sba.gov
- Small and Home Based Business Links - http://www.bizoffice.com
- Strategis - http://strategis.gc.ca
- Find a Lawer at: http://www.canadianlawlist.com/

E-Business Related Sites

Community Access Program
This program provides support for public computer access to the Information Highway via the Internet at the local community level. The overall objective is to provide all Canadians with affordable, convenient access to the global knowledge-based economy and the opportunity to use its technologies.
Web site: http://cap.ic.gc.ca

Consumers and Electronic Commerce, Consumer Connection
http://strategis.gc.ca/epic/internet/inoca-bc.nsf/vwGeneratedInterE/h_ca01192e.html

Office of Consumer Affairs discussion papers, links to other Strategis electronic commerce documents such as case studies.

E-commerce in Service Industries
http://strategis.gc.ca/SSG/ss00006e.html
Practical information on e-commerce in service industries, including associated benefits, company and industry profiles, statistics, and examples of utilizing e-commerce.

Building Trust in the Digital Economy: Authentication
http://e-com.ic.gc.ca/epic/internet/inecic-
ceac.nsf/vwGeneratedInterE/h_gv00090e.html
Discusses the use of cryptographic technologies to establish user's identity.

The Canadian Internet Registration Authority (CIRA)
http://www.cira.ca
The CIRA is a not for profit Canadian corporation that has the mandate to set policy for and operate the .ca domain.

ecommerce - guide.com http://e-comm.internet.com
Offers a broad range of articles and links.

Electronic Commerce and the European Union
http://europa.eu.int/information_society/topics/ebusiness/ecommerce/index
_en.htm
A large site with an introductory section on electronic commerce, an issues section and information on the G7 E-Commerce initiative.

Electronic Commerce and the Organization for Economic Cooperation and Development (OECD)
http://www.oecd.org/subject/e_commerce
A site providing documentation and background information on electronic commerce initiative in the OECD countries.

Protecting Yourself When Buying Online, US Federal Trade Commission
http://www.ftc.gov/bcp/menu-internet.htm
A basic overview of the potential hazards and how to avoid them.

ECnow.com http://www.ecnow.com

ECnow.com is a high-end electronic commerce consulting firm helping companies satisfy customers through electronic commerce & electronic communication.

Canadian Bankers Association http://www.cba.ca
Accepting payment by credit card usually requires a business bank (merchant) account with financial institutions that deal with each specific card. See your financial institution or the Canadian Bankers Association Web site for information on electronic commerce

Canadian Electronic Commerce Technology Suppliers
http://strategis.ic.gc.ca/epic/internet/inict-
tic.nsf/vwGeneratedInterE/h_it06122e.html
Section of Industry Canada's Canadian Company Capabilities Web site that lists suppliers of electronic commerce technology.

SES http://www.sesresearch.com
SES is a full-service market research firm, drawing on a wide range of disciplines including marketing, research, management consulting and business administration.

ZD-Net http://www.zdnet.com/ecommerce
This site includes a comprehensive Internet and e-commerce related search engine as well as Business Shopping links.

Forrester Research http://www.forrester.com
Even without a subscription to their research material, this site has a reference library, highlights from their reports and other e-commerce related information.

IBM http://www.ibm.com/e-business
This site has a small business section, with resource information to help small businesses with understanding what it takes to successfully set up shop on the Internet, as well as lots of other links to e-commerce related information.

econsumer.gov http://www.econsumer.gov/english/index.html
This site offers information about consumer protection laws and activities in participating countries.

Statistics Canada
Statistics Canada produces statistics that help Canadians better understand

their country, its population, resources, economy, society and culture. The following data and reports on the use of Internet and E-business are available:

- Internet Use http://www.statcan.ca/english/Pgdb/cultur.htm#int
- Household Internet use in rural Canada, 1998 to 2000
  http://www.statcan.ca/Daily/English/040106/d040106a.htm
- E-commerce: Household shopping on the Internet, 2002
  http://www.statcan.ca/Daily/English/031211/d031211b.htm
- Electronic Commerce and Technology - 2003
  http://www.statcan.ca/Daily/English/040416/d040416a.htm

Step-by-Step Guide to Exporting –
 Networking the Wold: E-Business for Exporters
http://exportsource.ca/gol/exportsource/interface.nsf/engdocBasic/1.2.11.html

E-commerce Overview Series: Plastics Industry and Plastics Processing Sector in Canada
http://strategis.ic.gc.ca/epic/internet/inecom-come.nsf/en/qy00061e.html?OpenDocument&source=Headlines
Learn about how firms in Canada's plastics industry and plastics processing sector are using the Internet and e-commerce to improve their business processes.

E-commerce Overview Series: Agri-food Industry in Canada
http://strategis.ic.gc.ca/epic/internet/inecom-come.nsf/en/qy00065e.html?OpenDocument&source=Headlines
Learn about how firms in Canada's agri-food industry are using the Internet and e-commerce to improve their business processes.

For other resources available, please contact your local CBSC.
For detailed information on setting-up your Web site, contact your Web developer or your Internet Service Provider

Employer's Introduction to Workplace Safety and Insurance

What is the WSIB?

If you are hiring workers, contact the Ontario Workplace Safety and Insurance Board (WSIB). It's important because most businesses - by law - must have this insurance coverage for work-related injuries and illnesses.

The WSIB provides workplace insurance coverage and oversees Ontario's workplace safety education and training system.

The WSIB collects premiums from most employers in Ontario, pools them in a collective liability fund, and distributes benefits to workers who are injured or who develop an occupational disease resulting from their employment.

Workplace insurance protects you and your business against worker lawsuits related to workplace injury and illness. It also provides benefits to injured workers. Benefits include:

- compensation for lost earnings due to work-related injury or illness
- payment of health care costs
- help with returning injured workers to work
- survivor benefits for work-related deaths
- access to health and safety training for you and your workers

Learn more about the WSIB - visit the WSIB Web site at:
http://www.wsib.on.ca/wsib/wsibsite.nsf/public/Home_e.

For more information, refer to the *Workplace Safety and Insurance Act* online at
http://192.75.156.68/DBLaws/Statutes/English/97w16_e.htm.

193

Benefits to Employers

In addition to protecting your workers, workplace safety insurance provides employers with important benefits that help keep your business productive and profitable. Benefits include:

- **Protection from lawsuits** - WSIB benefits replace the worker's right to sue the employer for similar benefits.

- **No-fault insurance** - The WSIB generally does not consider who is at fault when determining benefits.

- **Workplace insurance benefits for your workers** - WSIB insurance replaces lost earnings and covers health care costs resulting from work-related injuries and illnesses.

- **Prevention and training programs** - Workplace illness or injury can deprive you of essential staff and can seriously affect your company's productivity. The WSIB provides numerous **prevention, training, and education programs** (http://www.wsib.on.ca/wsib/wsibsite.nsf/public/Prevention TIP) that help you prevent injuries and illness before they cost you money.

- **Help in returning workers to the job** - Getting valuable staff back on the job sooner means your business can return to full productivity sooner. It also means your insurance claim will be smaller and your premium may be reduced. The WSIB claims management team will help you ensure that your worker gets effective health care and gets back to work as soon as safely possible.

Sole owners, partners, independent operators, and executive officers are not automatically covered under the *Workplace Safety and Insurance Act*, but can apply for optional insurance. When you buy optional insurance, you receive the same coverage as workers.

Learn more about **optional insurance** at http://www.wsib.on.ca/wsib/wsibsite.nsf/public/EmployersOptionali nsurance.

Small Business Services

Small Business Services is an area of the WSIB dedicated to helping the small business employer. If you employ **less than 20 workers**, Small Business Services can provide you with insurance coverage and health and safety services in a way that's as simple and easy for you as possible.

For more information, please visit **WSIB Small Business Services** online at http://www.wsib.on.ca/wsib/wsibsite.nsf/public/EmployersSBS or

contact the **Small Business Office** nearest you (http://www.wsib.on.ca/wsib/wsibsite.nsf/public/EmployersSBSOffices).

Registering with the WSIB

Most businesses in Ontario that employ workers (including family members and sub-contractors) must register with the WSIB within **10 days** of hiring their first full- or part-time worker. It's the law.

Registering with the WSIB provides workplace insurance coverage for all of your workers and gives you access to experts in health and safety for your business sector.

Employers who should register but do not are subject to fines, penalties and, in some cases, prosecution.

Learn more about **registering with the WSIB** at http://www.wsib.on.ca/wsib/wsibsite.nsf/public/EmployerRegisterWSIB.

For more information, please refer to the document **Registering with the WSIB.**

Paying Premiums

Anyone on your payroll, either working full- or part-time under a contract of service or as an apprentice is your worker and is covered under the WSIB premium. This includes family members.

Your premium payments depend on the health and safety risk of your type of business, the size of your payroll, and your company's health and safety record.

For more information, please refer to the WSIB document **Workplace Insurance Premiums and Financial Incentives**.

Learn more about WSIB Premiums at
http://www.wsib.on.ca/wsib/wsibsite.nsf/public/EmployersPremiuminfo.

REPORTING

Reporting incidents

If one of your workers has a workplace injury or illness for which they must obtain health care, or that results in loss of earnings, you must notify the WSIB within three days of learning of the incident.

Learn more about **reporting** at
http://www.wsib.on.ca/wsib/wsibsite.nsf/public/EmployersIIshouldreport.

Reporting material changes in your situation

If you have a change in circumstances that affects your employer obligations relating to WSIB, you must report that change to us within 10 days. For example, a material change in your situation could be a change in business name, address or payroll.

Forms

Employers can easily download most **WSIB forms** at
http://www.wsib.on.ca/wsib/wsibsite.nsf/public/FormsEmployers.

Remember that you must print, sign and then mail or fax your forms to the WSIB.

When reporting earnings information on Form 7s and similar forms, include both your **federal** and **provincial** net claims for exemptions and net claim **codes**.

Preventing Injuries in the Workplace

Safe workplaces not only mean better health and quality of life for workers, they also mean more profitable businesses and lower premiums for employers.

Visit the **WSIB Prevention section** at http://www.wsib.on.ca/wsib/wsibsite.nsf/public/Prevention to find information and resources that will help you maintain a safe workplace, and help you understand your health and safety rights and responsibilities. You'll also find out what we're doing to promote health and safety in Ontario's workplaces.

For more information please see refer to the WSIB document **Preventing Injuries and Illness in the Workplace.**

Your Health and Safety Obligations
To fulfill your legal obligations, all employers must:

- Post the "In Case of Injury- poster in a location visible to all staff **- download the poster online** at http://www.wsib.ca/wsib/wsibsite.nsf/public/InCaseOfInjury Poster or call the **WSIB Office nearest you** (http://www.wsib.on.ca/wsib/wsibsite.nsf/public/ContactWS IBOffices) to order one.

- Obtain and post a current copy of the *Occupational Health and Safety Act* - to get your copy, call Publications Ontario at 416-326-5300 or toll-free at 1-800-668-9938.

- Obtain a **first aid kit** for your first aid station - download the **WSIB First Aid brochure** at http://www.wsib.on.ca/wsib/wsibsite.nsf/public/FAP to ensure your first aid kit is stocked with the supplies appropriate to your firm's number of workers

- Have at least one certified first aider per shift - see a **list of first aid providers** at http://www.wsib.on.ca/wsib/wsibsite.nsf/public/FATrainers

Learn More About the WSIB

Employers can learn more about workplace safety insurance by visiting the **WSIB Employers page** at http://www.wsib.on.ca/wsib/wsibsite.nsf/public/Employers. You'll find answers to the following questions:

- What is the definition of work-related injury and illness?
- What are the benefits of having workplace insurance?
- How much will I pay in premiums?
- How can I reduce my premiums?
- How can I prevent injuries and illness in my workplace?
- What happens when one of my workers gets injured or ill?
- What items are included in Short-term Average Earnings?
- What constitutes fraud or non-compliance?
- What happens if I'm audited?

Find out more by calling the **WSIB office nearest you** (http://www.wsib.on.ca/wsib/wsibsite.nsf/public/ContactWSIBOffices).

Service in Other Languages

The WSIB provides service and information to employers and workers in English and French, as well as in many other languages. For service or materials in other languages, please ask your WSIB Customer Service Representative. You can also call our toll-free Language Services hotline at 1-800-465-5606 or 416-344-4999. Telephone service for the deaf (TTY) is available at 1-800-387-0050.

Appealing WSIB Decisions

Any employer or worker who disagrees with a decision made by the Workplace Safety and Insurance Board has the right to appeal that decision. The WSIB provides a variety of approaches to dispute resolution. These range from informal and timely approaches for quick resolution of simple issues, to more in-depth and formal approaches for more complex disputes.

Learn more about the **WSIB Appeals process** at http://www.wsib.on.ca/wsib/wsibsite.nsf/public/EmployersAppeals, or call **1-800-387-0773** for more information.

Helping Employers Meet WSIB Requirements

The Office of the Employer Adviser (OEA), an independent agency of the Ontario Ministry of Labour, is funded by employer WSIB premiums. The OEA provides employers (primarily those with less than 100 workers) with independent advice, education, and information on workplace safety insurance.

For further information on the services of the Office of the Employer Adviser (OEA), please refer to the document **Office of the Employer Adviser - Services**, contact the OEA at **(416) 327-0020** or **1-800-387-0774** or visit the OEA Web site at http://www.gov.on.ca/lab/oea.

WSIB Partners

The WSIB works with many valuable partners to promote workplace health and safety and return to work for injured workers in Ontario.

Learn more about the **WSIB's partners** at http://www.wsib.on.ca/wsib/wsibsite.nsf/public/Partners

Ontario Contact(s):

The WSIB's head office is located in Toronto and is supplemented by district offices in Hamilton, London, Ottawa, Sudbury, Thunder Bay and Windsor. Area offices in Kingston, Kitchener, North Bay, Sault Ste. Marie, St. Catharines and Timmins, round out the group of locations serving Ontario businesses and workers.

To find the office nearest you, please visit http://www.wsib.on.ca/wsib/wsibsite.nsf/public/ContactWSIBOffices or call 1-800-387-5540

Employment Regulations

1. What are the rules on workplace safety in Ontario?

Almost every worker, supervisor, employer and workplace in Ontario is covered by the *Occupational Health and Safety Act* and regulations. As an employer in Ontario, you have a number of obligations, including a duty to instruct, inform and supervise your workers to protect their health and safety. The Ministry of Labour produces a "Guide to the Occupational Health and Safety Act" that can help you understand the rights and duties of all parties in the workplace. This Guide is published on the Internet at http://www.gov.on.ca/lab/ohs/ohse.htm or can be purchased from Publications Ontario at **(416) 326-5300** or **1-800-668-9938**.

> **Note:** Some industries (such as highway and air transportation, radio and television broadcasting, banks, etc.) fall under the federal government's *Canada Labour Code*, rather than the Ontario regulations. For more information on the Code and its occupational health and safety requirements, see the document **Occupational Safety and Health in Canada**.

2. What are the rules on working conditions in Ontario?

The Employment Standards Branch of the Ontario Ministry of Labour is responsible for the administration and enforcement of the *Employment Standards Act,* which provides for minimum terms and conditions of employment in most industries. You may wish to confirm the details of legislation currently in force directly with the Ministry of Labour's Employment Practices Branch at **(416) 326-7160** or **1-800-531-5551**.

Note: Some industries (such as highway and air transportation, radio and television broadcasting, banks, etc.) fall under the federal government's *Canada Labour Code*, rather than the Ontario regulations. For more information on the Code and its rules on employment standards, please see the document **Labour Standards in the Federal Jurisdiction Workplace**.

The following are some of the aspects of the ***Employment Standards Act*** that employers should consider.

i. Vacation and Vacation Pay

Full-time, part-time, temporary and student workers are all eligible for vacation pay. However, certain types of workers are not covered by the Act's rules for vacations, and do not get vacation with pay or vacation pay.

- **Vacation with Pay**: minimum 2 weeks time off with pay each year for employees who have worked for an employer for 12 full months.

- **Vacation Pay**: minimum 4% of total earnings instead of time off with pay for employees who worked for an employer less than 12 months.

For further information on vacation and vacation pay (including a list of occupations not covered by the Act), see the document **Vacation**.

ii. Public Holidays

Ontario has 8 paid public holidays: New Year's Day, Good Friday, Victoria Day, Canada Day, Labour Day, Thanksgiving Day, Christmas Day, December 26th (Boxing Day). For further information on public holidays, see the document **Public Holidays**.

iii. Minimum Wage

Effective January 1, 1995, the minimum wages are the following:

- **General Workers** Minimum Wage - **$6.85** per hour *(Note: Effective February 1, 2004, the minimum wage has been increase to $7.15 per hour)*

- **Liquor Server** Minimum Wage - **$5.95** per hour (**Note:** Applies to employees serving liquor directly to customers in licensed premises as a regular part of their work).

- **Student** Minimum Wage - **$6.40** per hour (**Note:** Applies to students under age 18. If more than 28 hours a week are worked during the school year, the General Minimum Wage applies to **all** hours worked in that week. Effective February 1, 2004, the student minimum wage will increase to **$6.70** per hour).

- **Homeworkers** Minimum Wage - **$7.54** per hour (**Note:** This wage applies to all homeworkers whether they are full-time or part-time, or students under 18 years of age).

For further information on minimum wage, see the document **Ontario Minimum Wage**.

iv. Termination of Employment

Under the ***Employment Standards Act***, an employer can terminate employment at any time. However, the employer must give proper notice of termination, or termination pay instead ("in lieu") of notice. If an unexpected event, such as a fire or flood (not including bankruptcy or insolvency), makes it impossible for an employer to keep staff employed, the employer does not have to give notice or termination pay.

Wrongful dismissal is not covered by the ***Employment Standards Act***. If an employee feels that he or she has been wrongfully dismissed, the employee may wish to consult a lawyer and pursue the matter through the court system. For further information on termination of employment, see the document **Termination of Employment & Severance Pay**.

v. Severance Pay

An employer may have to pay severance pay to workers who lose their job. This money is paid in recognition of their years of service. Qualifying workers are entitled to receive one week of regular pay for each year of employment, up to 26 weeks. Severance pay must be paid to workers within 7 days following termination of employment. For further information on severance pay, see the document **Termination of Employment & Severance Pay**.

vi. Hours of Work and Breaks

Under the ***Employment Standards Act***, the normal limits on hours of work for most workers in Ontario are 8 hours each day and 48 hours per week. Workers cannot work more than 5 hours in a row without getting a meal break lasting 30 minutes or more. Employers are not required to pay for the time workers are on a meal break. If workers (or their union) agree, meal breaks can be shorter than 30 minutes, but this agreement must be approved by the Ministry of Labour.

Coffee breaks, or other rest periods, are determined by the employer. When workers must stay at their station or workplace, these breaks are included as part of the working time and cannot be deducted from workers' pay. For further information on hours of work and breaks, see the document **Hours of Work & Overtime.**

vii. Overtime Pay

For most workers, overtime pay begins after working 44 hours during any 7 days in a row. Through established practice, employers set the day on which a work week starts. Overtime pay is calculated at a minimum rate of 1.5 the regular wage. For further information on overtime pay, see the document **Hours of Work and Overtime**.

viii. Pregnancy and Parental Leave

Under the ***Employment Standards Act***, pregnant women have the right to take an unpaid pregnancy leave of at least 17 weeks from work and new parents have the right to take an unpaid parental leave from work to care for their child. The right to pregnancy and parental leave applies to both part-time and full-time workers. For further information on pregnancy and parental leave, see the document **Pregnancy Leave & Parental Leave**.

For information on specific aspects of employment standards in Ontario, you should contact the Ministry of Labour directly at **(416) 326-7160** or **1-800-531-5551** or visit the Ministry's Web site at http://www.gov.on.ca/LAB/es/ese.htm. This site also includes the "Your Guide to the Employment Standards Act", (the guide can also be purchased from Publications Ontario at **(416) 326-5300** or **1-800-668-9938**).

3. What are the rules on taxation, contributions and deductions?

i. Federal Employment-Related Requirements, Taxes and Deductions

Social Insurance Number (SIN)

Employers who will remit income tax deductions and Canada Pension Plan and Employment Insurance premiums based on an employee's income must ensure that a new employee produces a SIN card within 3 days after being hired. Employers also have a legal obligation to ensure that anyone hired with a SIN beginning with "9" has a valid authorization to work in Canada. This document is issued by Citizenship and Immigration Canada. For more information about hiring foreign workers, please visit **http://www.hrdc-drhc.gc.ca/hrib/lmd-dmt/fw-te/common/intro.shtml**

Application forms for SIN cards are available from any Human Resource Centre of Canada, listed in the blue pages of your telephone book or visit http://www.hrdc-drhc.gc.ca/sin-nas/.

Personal Information Protection - Privacy Commissioner of Canada

The Guide to Canada's *Personal Information Protection and Electronic Documents Act* (PIPEDA) helps businesses understand their obligations and comply to the Act. From January 1, 2004, the PIPED Act also covers the **collection, use** or **disclosure** of **personal information in the course of all commercial activities in Canada**, except in provinces which have enacted legislation that is deemed to be substantially similar to the federal law.

For more information, call **1-800-282-1376**, see the document **Protection of Personal Information : Your Responsibilities** or

visit the Privacy Commissioner's Web site at http://www.privcom.gc.ca/information/guide_e.asp

Employment Insurance (EI), Canada Pension Plan (CPP) and Income Tax

As an employer, you are responsible for making a number of deductions on behalf of your employees. Under federal law, it is required that all employers collect Employment Insurance Premiums, Canada Pension Plan Contributions and Personal Income Tax on behalf of the federal government. Remittances for Employment Insurance and the Canada Pension Plan are shared by the employer and employee. The deductions made on behalf of employees must be placed in a trust account.

The Canada Revenue Agency (CRA) offers personalized visits to new employers to help them understand withholding procedures. For more information on new employer visits, see the document **New Employer Visits.** For more information on federal deductions, see the document **Trust Accounts Division**, visit the CRA Web site at http://www.ccra-adrc.gc.ca/tax/business/payroll/menu-e.html   or contact a CRA Business Window at **1-800-959-5525**. For a list of office locations, please visit the following Web site: http://www.ccra-adrc.gc.ca/contact/tso/ON-e.html.

Filing an Information Return (T4)

An information return is the T4 slip and the T4 Summary form used to report salary, wages, tips or gratuities, bonuses, vacation pay, employment commissions, and all other remuneration employers pay to employees during the year. Employers must file an information return and give information slips to employees by the last day of February following the calendar year to which the information return applies.

To order blank copies of T4 slips, call **1-800-959-2221** or visit CRA's Web site at http://www.ccra-adrc.gc.ca/formspubs/request-e.html. To obtain more information about filing the T4 form, please see the "Employers' Guide - Filing the T4 Slip and Summary Form" at **http://www.ccra-adrc.gc.ca/E/pub/tg/rc4120/README.html**. To view other forms and publications related to the T4 forms, visit the CRA Web site at http://www.ccraadrc.gc.ca/menu/EmenuLGA.html.

Record of Employment (ROE)

The *Employment Insurance Act* requires every employer to complete an ROE when an employee stops working. This is considered an interruption of earnings. This happens when the employment ends, or an employee leaves due to pregnancy, injury, illness, adoption leave, layoff, leave without pay, or dismissal. An ROE must be issued within 5 calendar days of an employee's interruption of earnings or the day the employer becomes aware of the interruption, whichever is later.

Blank ROEs can be ordered by mail, telephone or in person from the local Human Resources Development Canada - Employment Insurance office, listed in the blue pages of your phone book, or visit http://hrdc.gc.ca/ae-ei/yrs/4.1.1_e.shtml. For further information on the ROE, see the document **Record of Employment** by visiting http://hrdc.gc.ca/ae-ei/pubs/roe-2002.shtml.

ii. Provincial Employment-Related Requirements, Taxes and Deductions

Workplace Safety and Insurance

Most industries in Ontario are covered by the *Workplace Safety and Insurance Act.* Employers must pay into the insurance fund of the Workplace Safety and Insurance Board (WSIB) through assessments on their payrolls.

By contacting a WSIB office, you can obtain a registration kit, which includes information on assessments, coverage, accident reporting requirements and appeals procedures. Employers are required to contact the board within 10 days of hiring an employee. For further information on the WSIB, see the document **Employer's Introduction to Workplace Safety and Insurance**, contact the WSIB at **(416) 344-1000** or **1-800-387-5540** or visit the WSIB Web site http://www.wsib.on.ca.

Note: The Office of the Employer Adviser (OEA) provides employers with advice, education, and information on workplace safety insurance. For further information on the services of the OEA, see document **Office of the Employer Adviser - Services**, contact the OEA at **(416) 327-0020** or **1-800-387-0774** or visit the OEA Web site at http://www.gov.on.ca/lab/oea.

Employer Health Tax (EHT)

The EHT is a payroll tax applied to all employers in Ontario. Unless exempted, all employers with a permanent establishment in Ontario must register for the EHT. For the first $400,000 of the payroll, eligible private-sector employers are exempt from paying the EHT. For further information on the EHT, see the document **Employer Health Tax - EHT**. To obtain the telephone number for the Employer Health Tax office nearest you, call the Ontario Ministry of Finance Information Centre at **1-800-263-7965** or visit **http://www.trd.fin.gov.on.ca**

4. What about hiring someone as a "self-employed contractor"?

Contractors are people who own and operate their own business, and have to remit their own taxes and deductions to the government. For this reason, some businesses feel that dealing with a self-employed contractor is easier than dealing with an employee. However, sometimes the relationship between the business and the contractor is quite similar to the relationship it would have with an employee: the business dictates the hours of work, supplies equipment and tools, directs the tasks to be completed, etc.

Before you hire someone as a self-employed contractor, it is essential to find out if the government considers the relationship to be that of an employer to employee, or of a business to self-employed contractor. If the government feels that you treat the contractor as an employee, you will be responsible for submitting all of the taxes and contributions that apply in an employer-employee relationship.

You may contact the Canada Revenue Agency (CRA) for a ruling on your situation. The CRA has a form called "Request for a Ruling as to the Status of a Worker under the Canada Pension Plan or Employment Insurance Act" (form CPT1). The form can be requested from CRA at **1-800-959-5525** or downloaded at **http://www.ccra-adrc.gc.ca/E/pbg/tf/cpt1/README.html**.

CRA also has a guide titled "Employee or Self-Employed?" that may help you determine the worker's status. The guide can be requested from CRA or accessed at the following Web site: **http://www.ccra-adrc.gc.ca/E/pub/tg/rc4110/README.html**

PART TWO

TAXES DUTIES AND REGULATIONS

Guide for Canadian Small Businesses
From CCRA RC4070(E) Rev. 01

Success is 1% inspiration and 99% perspiration.

(*-Meenakshi.*)

How This Section Can Help You

This section will introduce you to the **Canada Customs and Revenue Agency (CCRA)** programs you need to know about, and give an overview of your obligations and entitlements under the laws that CCRA administer.

Many activities of a small business are subject to different forms of taxation. This section of the book will help you with each of these, and will explain how to plan for taxes, keep records, and make and report payments. It will also explain the different kinds of business structures, income tax reporting and payment, payroll deductions, importing and exporting, and how to prepare for and handle an audit.

Taxes can sometimes be difficult and complex. In such cases, CCRA will refer you to more detailed publications-all free of charge.

If you aren't familiar with some of the terms used in this section, refer to the Glossary of Terms.

Internet access

Many of CCRA publications are available on the Internet. the Web address is: **www.ccra.gc.ca**
You can also get copies of the guides and forms mentioned in this publication by calling us at **1-800-959-2221** (within Canada & USA) If, after reading this section, you need more information about businesses or professional activities, call CCRA Business Enquiries line at **1-800-959-5525**.

About the Canada Customs and Revenue Agency (CCRA)

The CCRA is the federal government agency responsible for administering Canadian tax, border, and trade policy, and they play a fundamental role in supporting Canada's social and economic progress. They oversee various tax credit programs, and collect federal and provincial individual income taxes (except in Quebec).

213

They also administer federal and provincial corporate income taxes for all provinces except Alberta, Ontario, and Quebec, and collect the goods and services tax/harmonized sales tax (GST/HST) (except in Quebec), Canada Pension Plan contributions, Employment Insurance premiums, customs and excise duties, tariffs, and excise taxes on gasoline and tobacco products.

The CCRA also administers the North American Free Trade Agreement (NAFTA), Canada's trade laws, and Canada's international tax agreements with other countries. CCRA therefore have a key role in helping Canadian business and industry compete in world markets by ensuring they have a fair environment in which to trade. Finally, they are responsible for protecting Canadian society against the illegal movement of goods and people across Canada's borders.

CCRA committed to helping small businesses in Canada. They recognize that, as entrepreneurs, you are very busy making your business profitable. You may not always have the time, expertise, or inclination to do it all yourself. In some circumstances, you probably consult with professionals, such as lawyers, accountants, or customs brokers to help you with your business. While these individuals are professionals and will help you, you are the one who is ultimately responsible for the actions of your business. You need to keep informed so that you can work in partnership with the professionals you hire and with the CCRA.

Setting Up Your Business

A business is an activity that you conduct for profit or with a reasonable expectation of profit. There are three types of businesses: sole proprietorships, partnerships, and corporations. The way your business is taxed has a lot to do with the way your business is set up.

Sole proprietorship

A sole proprietorship is an unincorporated business that is owned by one person. It's the simplest kind of business structure.
The owner of a sole proprietorship has sole responsibility for making decisions, receives all the profits, claims all losses, and does not have separate legal status from the business.

If you're a sole proprietor, you pay personal income tax on all revenue generated by your business. You also assume all the risk of the business. This risk extends even to your personal property and assets.

As a sole proprietor, you have to register for the goods and services tax/harmonized sales tax (GST/HST) if your worldwide annual taxable revenues are more than $30,000.

It's easy to set up a sole proprietorship. Simply operate as an individual or as a registered, unincorporated business. If you operate as an individual, just bill your customers or clients in your own

215

name. If you operate under a registered business name, bill your clients and customers in the business's name. If your business has a name other than your own, you'll need a separate bank account to process cheques payable to your business.

How does a sole proprietor pay taxes?

A sole proprietor pays taxes by reporting income (or loss) on a personal income tax and benefit return (T1). The income (or loss) forms part of the sole proprietor's overall income for the year.

If you're a sole proprietor, you must file a personal income tax and benefit return if you:

- have to pay tax for the year;
- disposed of a capital property or had a taxable capital gain in the year;
- are required to make Canada Pension Plan/Quebec Pension Plan (CPP/QPP) payments on self-employed earnings or pensionable earnings for the year; or
- received a demand from us to file a return.

The list above does not include every situation where you may be required to file. If you're unsure, call CCRA at 1-800-959-5525.

As a sole proprietor, your income tax and benefit return must include financial statements or one or more of the following forms, as applicable:

- Form T2124, *Statement of Business Activities*;
- Form T2032, *Statement of Professional Activities*;
- Form T2042, *Statement of Farming Activities;*
- Form T1163, *Statement A - NISA Account Information and Statement of Farming Activities for Individuals,* and Form T1164, *Statement B - NISA Account Information and Statement of Farming Activities for Additional Farming Operations*; or
- Form T2121, *Statement of Fishing Activities.*

CCRA will also accept a computer-generated version of the applicable form.

*Note:*As a sole proprietor, you may have to pay your income tax by installments. You may also need to make installment payments for Canada Pension Plan contributions on your own income. Remember to budget for these payments. For more information, see CCRA publication called *Paying Your Income Tax by Installments.*

For GST/HST, sole proprietors have reporting periods for which they have to file a return. For more information, see the "Reporting periods".

Partnership

A partnership is an association or relationship between two or more individuals, corporations, trusts, or partnerships who join together to carry on a trade or business.

Each partner contributes money, labour, property, or skills to the partnership. In return, each partner is entitled to a share of the profits or losses in the business. The business profits or losses are usually divided among the partners based on the partnership agreement.

Like a sole proprietorship, a partnership is easy to form. In fact, a simple verbal agreement is enough to form a partnership. But if money and property are at stake, you should have a written agreement.

The partnership is bound by the actions of any member of the partnership, as long as these are within the usual scope of the operations.

How does a partnership pay taxes?

A partnership by itself does not pay income tax on its operating results and does not file an annual income tax return. Instead, each partner includes a share of the partnership income or loss on a personal, corporate, or trust income tax return.

Each partner also has to file either financial statements or one of the forms referred to in the section on sole proprietorship (or a computer-generated version of one of these forms). You do this whether or not you actually received your share in money or in credit to your partnership's capital account.

A partnership has to file a partnership information return if, throughout the fiscal period, it has six or more members or if one of its members is a member of another partnership. CCRA publications called *Guide for the Partnership Information Return* and Information Circular 89-5, *Partnership Information Return,* and its Special Release, have more details.

For GST/HST purposes, a partnership is considered to be a separate person and must file a GST/HST return and remit tax where applicable.

Corporation

A corporation is a separate legal entity. It can enter into contracts and own property in its own name, separately and distinctly from its owners.
Since a corporation has a separate legal existence, it has to pay tax on its income, and therefore must file its own income tax return. It must also register for the GST/HST if its taxable worldwide annual revenues (including those of associates) are more than $30,000.

You set up a corporation by filling out an article of incorporation, and filing it with the appropriate provincial, territorial, or federal authorities.

How does a corporation pay taxes?

A corporation must file a corporation income tax return (T2) within six months of the end of every taxation year, even if it doesn't owe taxes. It also has to attach complete financial statements and the necessary schedules to the T2 return. A corporation pays its taxes in monthly installments. CCRA publication called *T2 Corporation - Income Tax Guide* has more details on installment payments and the filing requirements for corporations.

For GST/HST, corporations have reporting periods for which they have to file a return. For more information on reporting periods, see the "Reporting periods".

The taxation year for a corporation is its fiscal period. For more information on fiscal periods, see the section "Fiscal period".
For more details, visit CCRA Web site at:
www.ccra.gc.ca/t2return/

Are you responsible for your corporation's debts?

As a shareholder of your corporation, you have limited liability. In the strict sense, this means you and the other shareholders are not responsible for the corporation's debts. However, limited liability may not always protect you from creditors. For example, if a smaller, more closely held corporation wants to borrow money from a bank or other creditor, the creditor may ask for the shareholder's guarantee that the debt will be repaid. If you agree to this condition, you'll be personally liable for that debt if the corporation does not pay it back.

This applies to taxes owing as well. If your corporation owes taxes, and you have personally guaranteed any loan on behalf of your corporation, CCRA will claim the amount of the taxes owing up to the limit of the loan guarantee.

Keeping Records

Five reasons why keeping records can benefit you

1. **Good records can help you identify the sources of your income.**

   You may receive cash or property from many different places. If you don't have records showing your income sources, you may not be able to prove that some sources are non-business or non-taxable.

2. **Well-kept records can mean tax savings.**

   Good records serve as a reminder of deductible expenses and input tax credits. If you don't record your transactions, you may forget some of your expenses or input tax credits when you prepare your income tax or GST/HST returns. For more information read under heading input tax credits.

3. **Well-kept records can prevent most of the problems you might encounter if CCRA audit your income tax or GST/HST returns.**

   If your records are so incomplete that auditors cannot determine your income from them, the auditors will have to use other methods to establish your income. This will cost you time. If your records do not support your claims, they could be disallowed.

4. **Your records will keep you better informed about the financial position of your business.**

   You need good records to establish your profit or loss, and the value of your business. Information from good records can also tell you what is happening in your business and why. The successful use of records can show you trends in your business, let you compare performance in different years, and help you prepare budgets and forecasts.

5. **Proper books and records may help you get loans from banks and other creditors.**

   Creditors need accurate information about your current financial position before they give you a loan. You can't give them this information if you don't keep organized records. Also, good records show potential creditors that you know what's going on with your business.

Legal requirements for keeping records

All records such as paper documents, as well as those stored in an electronic medium (e.g., on computer disk), must be kept in Canada or made available in Canada at CCRA request. You can keep these documents outside Canada if you get written permission from CCRA.

What records should you keep?

Make sure you keep orderly records of all income you receive. Also, keep all receipts, invoices, vouchers, and cancelled cheques indicating outlays of money. Such outlays include:

- salaries and wages;
- operating expenses such as rent and advertising, and capital expenditures; and
- miscellaneous items, such as charitable donations.

If you import goods into Canada, your records must substantiate the price you paid for imported goods, and list their origin and description. They must also include any documentation about the reporting, release, and accounting of the goods, as well as the payment of duties and taxes. For more information, see the chapter 5 called "Importing/Exporting"

You should keep these records at your place of business or residence in Canada (unless you get written permission from CCRA to keep them elsewhere). You have to make them available to CCRA if you're asked to do so.

Your records must be permanent

Whichever accounting or record-keeping method you use, your records must be permanent. They must contain a systematic account of your income, deductions, credits, and other information you need to report on your income tax and GST/HST returns.

What information should your records contain?

It's not hard to keep records that meet the requirements of the law. However, sketchy or incomplete records that use approximate instead of exact amounts, are not acceptable.
Your books and records must:

- allow you to determine how much tax you owe, or the tax, duties, or other amounts to be collected, withheld, or deducted, or any refund or rebate you may claim; and
- be supported by vouchers or other necessary source documents. If you do not keep your receipts or other vouchers to support your expenses or claims, and there is no other evidence available, CCRA may reduce the expenses or claims you have made.

Retaining And Destroying Records

The six-year requirement

You must retain books and records (other than certain documents for which there are special rules) for six years after the goods are imported or exported, for six years from the end of the last taxation year to which they relate for income tax, or for six years from the end of the year to which they relate for GST/HST purposes.

If you filed your income tax return late, keep your records and supporting documents for six years from the date you filed the late return.

The minimum period for keeping books and records is usually measured from the last year you used the records, not the year the transaction occurred or the record was created. For example, let's say you bought some restaurant equipment in 1999 and sold it in 2001. In this case, even though the records relating to the purchase of the equipment were created in 1999, you need them to calculate the gain or loss on the sale in 2001. Therefore, you must keep the records until 2007.

You have to keep every book and supporting record necessary for dealing with an objection or appeal until it is resolved and the time for filing any further appeal has expired, or until the six-year period mentioned above has expired, whichever is later.

Request for early destruction

If you want to destroy your books or records before the six years are up, you must apply in writing to the director of the tax services office in your area to obtain written permission from the Minister of National Revenue. To do this, either use Form T137, *Request for Destruction of Books and Records,* or prepare your own written request. In addition to CCRA requirements, there are other federal, provincial, and municipal laws that require you to keep books and records. CCRA have no authority to approve destruction of books and records that these other laws require you to keep.
6
For more information on keeping books and records for income tax purposes, refer to Information Circular 78-10, *Books and Records Retention/Destruction.* For GST/HST, refer to Chapter 15, "Books and Records," of the GST/HST Memoranda series.

Bringing Assets into A Business

Fair market value

You may find yourself in a situation where you would like to take assets that belong to you personally and transfer them to your business.

If you are operating a sole proprietorship, this is a reasonably simple process. The *Income Tax Act* requires that you transfer these assets to the business at their fair market value (FMV). This means that CCRA consider you to have sold these assets at a price equal to their FMV at that time. If the FMV at the time of the transfer to the business is greater than your original purchase price, you must report the difference as a capital gain on your income tax and benefit return.

You can claim a GST/HST input tax credit based on the **basic tax content** of the assets you transfer to your business. For more information on basic tax content, call CCRA at 1-800-959-5525.

Your business will show a purchase of these assets, with a cost equal to the FMV at the time of the transfer. This is the value that you will add to the capital cost allowance schedule for income tax purposes.

For income tax purposes, when you transfer the property to a Canadian partnership or a Canadian corporation, you may transfer the property to the partnership or the corporation for an **elected amount**. This amount may be different from the FMV, as long as you meet certain conditions. The elected amount then becomes your proceeds for the property transferred, as well as the cost of the property to the corporation or partnership.

The rules regarding these transfers of property are technical in nature. For more detailed information, please refer to Interpretation Bulletin IT-291, *Transfer of Property to a Corporation under Subsection 85(1)*, Information Circular 76-19, *Transfer of Property to a Corporation under Section 85*, and Interpretation Bulletin IT-413, *Election by Members of a Partnership under Subsection 97(2)*.

Buying an existing business

When you are considering becoming a business owner, you will find that you have the option of either **buying an existing business** or **starting up a new business**. The option you choose will have a significant effect on how you account for the purchase of the business assets for income tax purposes.
6
When you buy an existing business, you generally pay a set amount for the entire business. In some cases, the sale agreement sets out a price for each asset, a value for the inventory of the company and, if applicable, an amount that you can attribute to goodwill.

If the individual asset prices are set out in the sale agreement, and the prices are reasonable, then you should use these prices to claim capital cost allowance. If the individual asset prices are not set out in the contract, you have to determine how much of the purchase price you should attribute to each asset, how much to inventory, and how much, if any, to goodwill. These amounts should coincide with the amounts the vendor determined when reporting the sale.

The amount you allocate to each asset should be the fair market value (FMV) of the asset. You should allocate to goodwill the balance of the purchase price that remains after you allocate the FMV to each asset and to inventory.

Example You purchase a business for a total purchase price of $120,000. The FMV of the net identifiable assets of the business is as follows:	
Accounts receivable	$ 20,000
Inventory	10,000
Land	30,000
Building	50,000
Total net identifiable assets	$110,000
You can determine the value of the goodwill by subtracting the total value of the net identifiable assets from the purchase price:	
Purchase price	$ 120,000
Minus net identifiable assets	110,000
Amount attributed to goodwill	$ 10,000

Once you have determined the values for the assets and the goodwill, add the fixed assets (e.g., buildings and equipment) into the appropriate classes for the purpose of claiming the capital cost allowance. The goodwill is considered to be an **eligible capital expenditure**, which is treated in a manner similar to assets eligible for capital cost allowance.

Treat the value of the inventory as a purchase of goods for resale, and include it in the cost of goods sold in your income statement at the end of the year.

For GST/HST purposes, if you buy a business or part of a business and acquire all or substantially all of the property that can reasonably be regarded as necessary to carry on the business, you and the vendor may be able to jointly elect to have no GST/HST payable on the sale by completing Form GST44, *Election Concerning the Acquisition of a Business or Part of a Business*. You must be GST/HST registrants, and you both have to agree that the sale will not be subject to GST/HST. In addition, you must buy all or substantially all of the property, and not only individual assets.

Usually, for the election to apply to the sale, you have to be able to continue to operate the business with the property acquired under the sale agreement. You have to file Form GST44, on or before the day you have to file the GST/HST return for the first reporting period in which you would have otherwise had to pay GST/HST on the purchase.

Another way of buying an existing business is to buy the shares of an incorporated business. This does not affect the cost base of the assets of the business. As explained previously, a corporation is a separate legal entity and can own property in its own name. A change in the ownership of the shares will not affect the tax values of the assets the corporation owns.

The Business Number (BN)

Your first step to doing business with the CCRA

The BN is a numbering system that simplifies and streamlines the way businesses deal with us. It is based on the idea of "one business, one number." This helps businesses reduce costs and be more competitive. It also increases government efficiency. You get your BN the first time you register to do business with us. Eventually, businesses will be able to use their BN for other government programs.

The BN consists of two parts-the registration number and the account identifier. The four major CCRA business accounts and the account identifiers are as follows:

- corporate income tax (RC);

- import/export (RM);
- payroll deductions (RP); and
- GST/HST (RT).

Businesses that register for the BN will get one-stop business services from CCRA, including integrated new business registration, a consolidated approach for updating account information, and integrated business account enquiries.

Your BN, and all information relating to it, are confidential.

> **Note**: There are other types of CCRA accounts that the BN does not yet include. For example, some manufacturers and wholesalers need an excise tax licence for excise tax purposes, and some businesses need a filer identification number for filing information returns. Contact CCRA at 1-800-959-5525 if you want to find out about these other accounts and register for them.

Are you doing business in Quebec?

For businesses in Quebec, the BN does not include GST/HST accounts. The ministère du Revenu du Québec administers the GST/HST on behalf of the CCRA. If you plan to register for the GST/HST in Quebec, please contact the ministère du Revenu du Québec for more information at this address:

> Ministère du Revenu du Québec
> 3800 de Marly Street
> Ste-Foy QC G1X 4A5
> Telephone: 1-800-567-4692
> Outside Canada: (514) 873-4692

Do you need a BN?

If you need at least one of the four CCRA business accounts listed before, you will need a BN.

However, before you register for the BN, you need to know a few things about the business you plan to operate. For instance, you should know the name of the business, its location, its legal structure (sole proprietorship, partnership, or corporation), and its fiscal period end. You should also have some idea of what the sales of your business will be. Without this information, you won't be able to complete the BN registration form.

> *Note:* If you are a sole proprietor or a partner in a partnership, you will continue to use your social insurance number (SIN) to file your individual income tax and benefit return, even though you may have a BN for your GST/HST, payroll deductions, and import/export accounts.

For more information on the BN, please see CCRA publication called *The Business Number and Your Canada Customs and Revenue Agency Accounts,* or call CCRA at 1-800-959-5525.

Why it pays to plan ahead

In considering when to register for your BN, keep several things in mind.

Remember your legal obligations. For example, you become a registrant who must register for GST/HST when your taxable worldwide revenues (including those of your associates) exceed $30,000 over four consecutive calendar quarters, or in one calendar quarter. This threshold is $50,000 if you are a public service body. If you think your sales will exceed $30,000 (or $50,000 if you are a public service body), it's probably wise to register for the GST/HST sooner rather than later. Remember, registering for the GST/HST is the same as registering for the BN.

Registering early gives you certain advantages, such as the right to claim the GST/HST you pay on your business's start-up expenses from the time you register. For more information, see the section "Input tax credits" in the chapter on GST/HST. Also see the section "Can you deduct business start-up costs?".

If you intend to import goods into Canada, you should open an import/export account before you import the goods. This will avoid delays at the port of entry.

228

You should open a payroll deductions account as soon as you know when you will have employees. This account will allow you to make regular payroll deductions for your employees and make remittances on time. For information on how to make payroll deductions, see the chapter called "Payroll Deductions".

If you decide to incorporate, you will need a BN to pay your corporate income taxes and to make installment payments to your corporate account

The Goods and Services Tax (GST) and Harmonized Sales Tax (HST)

What is the GST/HST?

The GST is a tax that applies at a rate of 7% to the supply of most goods and services in Canada. Three provinces (Nova Scotia, New Brunswick, and Newfoundland) harmonized their provincial sales tax with the GST to create the harmonized sales tax (HST). The HST applies to the same base of goods and services as the GST, but at a rate of 15%. Of this, 7% is the federal part and 8% is the provincial part.

Although the consumer ultimately pays the GST/HST, generally businesses are responsible for collecting and remitting it to the government. Businesses that must register or that register voluntarily for the GST/HST are called **registrants**.

Registrants collect the GST/HST on most of their sales, and pay the GST/HST on most purchases they make to operate the business.

Registrants can claim a credit, called an **input tax credit (ITC)**, to recover the GST/HST they paid or owe on the purchases they will use in their commercial activities. They do this by deducting the amount of the credit from the GST/HST they collected. If they pay more than they collect, they can claim a refund.

230

On which goods and services do you charge GST/HST?

As a GST/HST registrant, you charge 7% GST or 15% HST on the taxable goods and services (other than zero-rated) you sell, lease, transfer, or provide in some other way. You can claim an input tax credit to recover the GST/HST you paid or owe on purchases and expenses you use, consume, or supply in your commercial activities. Examples of goods and services taxable at **7%** or **15%** include:

- commercial real property and newly constructed residential property;
- rentals of commercial real property;
- clothing and footwear;
- car repairs; and
- hotel accommodation.

Certain goods and services are subject to GST/HST, but at a rate of 0%. These goods and services are referred to as zero-rated supplies. You do not charge tax on these supplies, but you are still able to claim an ITC to recover the GST/HST you paid or owe on purchases made to provide them.

Examples of **zero-rated** goods and services include:

- basic groceries such as milk, bread, and vegetables;
- most farm livestock;
- medical devices such as hearing aids and artificial teeth;
- prescription drugs and drug dispensing fees; and
- exports (most goods and services taxable at 7% or 15% in Canada are zero-rated when exported).

Which goods and services are tax-exempt?

Some goods and services are exempt from the GST/HST. You do not collect GST/HST on these goods or services. You cannot claim an ITC to recover the GST/HST you pay or owe on purchases and expenses relating to such supplies.

You cannot register for the GST/HST if you're selling or providing **only** tax-exempt goods and services.

Tax-exempt goods and services include:

- sales of previously owned residential housing;
- residential rents of one month or more and residential condominium fees;
- most health, medical, and dental services that are performed by licensed physicians or dentists for medical reasons;
- day-care services provided for less than 24 hours per day primarily to children 14 years of age and younger;
- bridge, road, and ferry tolls;
- legal aid services;
- many educational services such as those courses supplied by a vocational school that lead to a certificate or diploma and allow the practice of a trade or a vocation, or tutoring services made to an individual in a course that follows a curriculum designated by a school authority;
- most services provided by financial institutions (e.g., arrangements for a loan or mortgage);
- arranging for and issuing insurance policies by insurance companies, agents, and brokers;
- most goods and services provided by charities; and
- certain goods and services provided by non-profit organizations, governments, and other public-sector organizations such as municipal transit services and standard residential services such as water.

Who registers for the GST/HST?

You have to register for and charge GST/HST if:

- you provide taxable goods and services in Canada; **and**
- you are not a small supplier.

You do not have to register if your only commercial activity is the sale of real property otherwise than in the course of a business or if you are a non-resident who does not carry on business in Canada. If you are a non-resident, see CCRA guide called *Doing Business in Canada - GST/HST Information for Non-Residents.*

Small supplier

You are a small supplier if you meet one of the following conditions:

- if you are a sole proprietor, your total taxable revenues (before expenses) from all your businesses are $30,000 or less in the last four consecutive calendar quarters and in a single calendar quarter;
- if you are a partnership or a corporation, the total taxable revenues of the partnership or corporation are $30,000 or less in the last four consecutive calendar quarters and in a single calendar quarter; or
- if you are a public service body (charity, non-profit organization, municipality, university, public college, school authority, or hospital authority), the total taxable revenues from all the activities of your organization are $50,000 or less in the last four consecutive calendar quarters and in a single calendar quarter. A gross revenue threshold also applies to charities and public institutions. For more information, see the CCRA guide *GST/HST Information for Charities.*

In all cases, total taxable revenues means your worldwide revenues from your sales of goods and services subject to GST/HST at a rate of 7% and 15% respectively, and your zero-rated sales. However, it does not include goodwill, financial services, and sales of capital property. You also have to include the total taxable revenues of all your associates in this calculation. Contact us if you need help to determine if you are associated to another person.

If your total taxable revenues exceed $30,000 ($50,000 for public service bodies) in a single calendar quarter or in four consecutive calendar quarters, you will no longer be considered a small supplier and you have to register for the GST/HST. Contact CCRA if this occurs.

Exception

Taxi and limousine operators, for their taxi operations, and non-resident performers selling admissions to seminars and other events must register for the GST/HST, even if they are small suppliers.

Voluntary registration

Although you do not have to register for the GST/HST if your taxable worldwide revenues are less than $30,000 (or $50,000 if you are a public service body), you can register voluntarily.

How to register for the GST/HST

If you have to register, or if you are a small supplier and wish to do so, call CCRA or visit your nearest tax services office. You may provide the necessary information to CCRA over the telephone or by facsimile transmission. Alternatively, you can complete Form RC1, *Request for a Business Number (BN)* and return it to CCRA. For more information, call at 1-800-959-5525.

Remember that if your business is in Quebec, you should contact the ministère du Revenu du Québec at 1-800-567-4692.

Reporting periods

CCRA will assign you a reporting period for filing your GST/HST returns when you register for the GST/HST. For each reporting period, you must file a GST/HST return.

The GST/HST reporting period is based on your estimated total annual taxable revenues in Canada as well as the annual taxable revenues of all your associates, if applicable.

The following chart shows the assigned GST/HST reporting periods based on your annual taxable revenues.

234

Annual Taxable Revenues	Reporting/Filing Period
$500,000 or less	annually
more than $500,000 to $6,000,000	quarterly
more than $6,000,000	monthly

If your annual taxable revenues are $500,000 or less, you may elect to file your GST/HST return quarterly or monthly.

If your annual taxable revenues are more than $500,000, but less than $6,000,000, you may elect to file your GST/HST return monthly.

For more information, refer to CCRA publication called *General Information for GST/HST Registrants.*

How to collect GST/HST on the taxable goods and services you provide.

As a GST/HST registrant, you generally charge 7% GST or 15% HST on the taxable supplies you make (other than zero-rated supplies).

> **Note**
> If you make taxable supplies (other than zero-rated) to customers in Nova Scotia, New Brunswick, or Newfoundland, including supplies shipped or mailed to recipients in these provinces, you are required to collect and remit the 15% HST.

Provincial sales tax

When you have to charge both GST and the provincial sales tax (PST), calculate GST on the price before you calculate the PST. For more information on how to calculate PST in relation to GST, contact your provincial tax office. You'll find the phone numbers of the provincial tax offices in the government section of your telephone book.

Informing your customers

As a GST/HST registrant, you must show your customers the total tax payable or let them know that the amount payable includes the tax. You can show this to your customers on the invoice, receipt, or contract, or by displaying acceptable signs. If you show the tax on your invoice, receipt, or contract, you must show the total tax or the total of the tax rate, that is, 7% or 15%.

What to put on your invoices

At the request of your customers who are GST/HST registrants, you must provide them with specific information that will allow them to support their input tax credit claim. The following chart shows what information you should put on your invoices, sales receipts, or other documentation.

Information required	Total sale under $30	Total sale of $30 to $149.99	Total sale of $150 or more
Your business or trading name	x	x	x
Invoice date or, if you do not issue an invoice, the date on which the GST/HST is paid or payable	x	x	x
Total amount paid or payable	x	x	x
An indication of items subject to GST at 7% or HST at 15%, or that the items are exempt. Also, an indication of either the total amount of GST/HST charged, or a statement that the GST/HST is included and the total rate of tax.		x	x
Your Business Number		x	x
The purchaser's name or trading name			x
Terms of payment			x
A brief description of the goods or services			x

Input tax credits

As a GST/HST registrant, you can get back the GST/HST you paid or that you owe on purchases and expenses related to your commercial activities. You do this by claiming an input tax credit.

You can recover the GST/HST you pay or owe on goods and services such as:

- merchandise to resell;
- advertising services;
- real property and capital property, such as office furniture, vehicles, and other equipment; and
- general operating expenses such as office rent, utilities, office supplies, and the rent of equipment such as computers, vehicles, photocopy machines, and other office appliances.

Where goods or services are used partly for personal use or for making exempt supplies, you are entitled to a partial input tax credit to the extent that they are for use in commercial activities.

In addition, you can claim input tax credits for purchases of land and purchases eligible for capital cost allowance under the *Income Tax Act*, such as buildings, computers, vehicles, and other large machinery and equipment.

Expenses for which you cannot claim an input tax credit include the following:

- employee wages;
- interest and dividend payments;
- most federal, provincial, and municipal taxes;
- most fees, fines, and levies;
- tax-exempt goods and services;
- items for your personal use or enjoyment;
    o capital property that is not primarily for use in your commercial activities; and
    o membership fees or dues to any club that provides recreational, dining, or sporting facilities (e.g., fitness clubs, golf clubs, hunting and fishing clubs), unless

you acquire the memberships to resell in the course of your business.

How to claim an input tax credit

To find out the total input tax credits you're entitled to claim for a reporting period, simply add up the GST/HST that you paid or owe on your business purchases made during the reporting period.

Most registrants claim their input tax credits when they file their GST/HST return for the reporting period in which the related purchases were made. However, you can generally claim your input tax credit in any return filed by the due date of the return for the last reporting period that ends within four years after the end of the reporting period in which the tax became payable on the purchase that qualifies for the credit.

Simplified accounting methods

There are two simplified accounting methods available for small businesses to calculate the GST/HST they owe. They are the Quick Method and the simplified input tax credit method.

The Quick Method

The Quick Method is an easy way to calculate the amount of GST/HST you owe. Generally, if your worldwide taxable annual sales (including zero-rated sales and sales of associates) are $200,000 or less (including GST/HST), you can use the Quick Method.

Certain persons, such as accountants, bookkeepers, and financial consultants, cannot use the Quick Method.

How do you use the Quick Method?

You collect GST at 7% or HST at 15% on taxable supplies to your customers in the usual manner. To find out how much GST/HST to remit to CCRA, multiply your total GST/HST-included sales for the reporting period by the Quick Method remittance rate that applies to those sales. The remittance rate will depend on whether you provide services or goods for resale, where your business is located, and whether you charged GST at 7% or HST at 15% on your taxable sales.

When using the Quick Method, you do not have to separately track the GST/HST you paid or owe on most of your business purchases. The remittance rates take into account the tax payable on general operating expenses. Therefore, you do not claim an input tax credit on your operating expenses (such as utilities, rent, and telephone), meal and entertainment expenses, and inventory purchases.

If you are using the Quick Method at the beginning of a fiscal year or on the day you become a registrant, you are entitled to a credit equal to 1% of your first $30,000 of supplies that are taxable at 7% or 15%. For more information, see the CCRA booklet called *Quick Method of Accounting for GST/HST.*

The simplified input tax credit method

The simplified input tax credit (ITC) method is an alternative way of determining the input tax credit part of your GST/HST return. You can use this method if you are registered for GST/HST and you and your associates have worldwide annual taxable sales totaling $500,000 or less in your immediately preceding fiscal year. You do not include supplies of financial services or sales of capital real property in the calculation of total sales.

To use the simplified ITC method, your taxable purchases (excluding zero-rated purchases) in Canada must also not exceed $2 million in the immediately preceding fiscal year.

If you qualify, you can begin using the simplified ITC method at the beginning of any reporting period in a fiscal year. You do not have to file a separate form with us to use the simplified ITC method. With the simplified ITC method, you do not have to separate the amount of GST/HST payable on each invoice. Instead, you only need to track the total amount of your taxable purchases. You will, however, need to separate your purchases that are taxable at 7% from those that are taxable at 15%. To calculate your ITC, you simply multiply your total taxable purchases by **7/107** for GST purchases and **15/115** for HST purchases. For audit purposes, you

240

will also have to keep the usual documents to support your input tax credit claims.

For more information on the simplified ITC method refer to CCRA publication *General Information for GST/HST Registrants.*

How to calculate the GST/HST you owe and file your return

For each reporting period, you calculate:

- the GST/HST collected or collectible on your taxable supplies during the reporting period; **and**
- the GST/HST paid or payable on your purchases for which you can claim an input tax credit.

The difference between these two amounts, plus or minus any adjustments, is your GST/HST payment or your refund. If you charge more GST/HST than you paid or owe, you pay CCRA the difference. Make cheques payable to the Receiver General. If you paid or owe more GST/HST than you charged, you can claim a refund.

Chapter 3

Excise Taxes and Excise Duties

What are excise taxes and excise duties?

They are two types of federal levies on products manufactured or produced in Canada.

These levies are applied to a limited range of goods at different rates and in different ways, depending on the product. Excise tax and excise duty apply to the goods before the GST/HST is added on.

Excise taxes

Excise taxes are charged on goods such as:

- tobacco;
- wine;
- jewellery;
- some heavy automobiles;
- automobile air conditioners; and
- gasoline, diesel fuel, aviation gasoline and aviation fuel.

The *Excise Tax Act* sets out the rates of tax for each of these goods. When goods are manufactured in Canada, excise tax is payable at the time the goods are delivered to the purchaser. When goods are imported, excise tax is payable by the importer, at the time the goods are imported.

Under certain circumstances, you may be able to claim a refund of the excise taxes you paid.

Manufacturers need an excise tax licence ("E" licence) unless they qualify as a small manufacturer. You qualify as a small manufacturer if your total annual sales are not more than $50,000.

A wholesaler licence ("W" licence) allows you to buy goods for resale without paying excise taxes. You may qualify for a "W" licence under certain limited circumstances, thereby enabling you to buy goods exempt of excise tax and to collect and remit the excise tax at the time you sell the goods.

For information on licensing, returns, and refunds, contact us and explain your situation.

Excise duties

Excise duties are charged on spirits, beer, and tobacco products manufactured in Canada. The *Excise Act* sets out the rates of duty for these goods.

Duty is charged on goods at the point of manufacture rather than sale. It is based on the quantity of goods you produce.
[6]
All manufacturers of these goods must be licenced and are subject to the bonding provisions set out in the *Excise Act* and Regulations.
For more information, contact CCRA. You will be referred to the excise duty manager in your area.

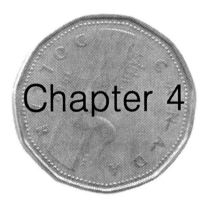

Chapter 4

Payroll Deductions

If you are an employer, you must make regular deductions from your employees' paycheques.
You are an employer if:

- you pay salaries, wages (including advances), bonuses, vacation pay, or tips to the people working for you; or
- you provide certain taxable benefits or allowances such as board and lodging to the people working for you.

Payroll deductions can be complicated. If you're having trouble with them, give CCRA a call. One of their representatives will come to your business and help you get started. Just call the nearest tax services office.

What to deduct from your employees' paycheques

You're responsible for deducting income tax, Canada Pension Plan (CPP) or Quebec Pension Plan (QPP) contributions, and Employment Insurance (EI) premiums from your employees' paycheques. You are also responsible for remitting this money to CCRA at regular intervals, usually on or before the 15th day of the month following the month in which you deducted it.

For example, if you make your deductions from an employee's paycheque on the 10th of May, you then have to remit the money to CCRA on or before the 15th of June. If the 15th of June falls on a Saturday, Sunday, or holiday, the remittance is due on the next business day after the 15th.

It's a good idea to remit payroll deductions on time. If your payment is late, you will have to pay a penalty.

Canada Pension Plan (CPP)/Quebec Pension Plan (QPP)

The Canada Pension Plan (CPP) came into effect as a way to provide financial assistance to Canadians when they retire from the workforce. Every person who works in Canada is eligible to get benefits when he or she retires.

If you run a business in Quebec, you deduct Quebec Pension Plan (QPP) contributions instead of CPP. You remit the payments to the ministère du Revenu du Québec instead of to the Receiver General for Canada.

Both employees and employers contribute to the CPP or the QPP. But you, as an employer, are responsible both for deducting CPP/QPP contributions from your employees' paycheques and for matching those contributions yourself.

Employees fall into many different categories, which determine how and when you should deduct CPP/QPP. To learn more about this, see CCRA guide called *Payroll Deductions (Basic Information)* and the *Payroll Deductions Tables* for your province or territory.

How to deduct CPP/QPP contributions

To deduct CPP/QPP contributions, you consult the payroll deductions publications mentioned above. These publications indicate how much CPP/QPP to deduct from your employees' paycheques, depending on their salaries and pay periods.

The rates for CPP/QPP deductions may vary from year to year. Each edition of the payroll deductions publications gives information on current rates. Make sure you have an up-to-date edition.

Remember : you must match each employee's contribution. This means that if you deduct $100 from an employee's paycheque, you must also contribute $100. You must then send us $200 for that employee.

To find out when you should deduct CPP/QPP contributions from your employees' paycheques and remit them, see CCRA guide *Payroll Deductions (Basic Information)* and the *Payroll Deductions Tables* for your province or territory.

Employment Insurance

Employment insurance (EI) is a federally administered insurance program that gives financial assistance to people who are unemployed. It also helps people get training for jobs.

How to deduct EI premiums

As an employer, you are responsible for deducting EI premiums from your employees' paycheques. To deduct EI premiums, consult the payroll deductions publications. These publications indicate how much EI to deduct from your employees' paycheques, depending on their salaries.

The rates for EI premiums may vary from year to year. Each edition of the payroll deductions publications gives information on current rates. Make sure you have an up-to-date edition.

Remember-you must also make your own contributions to EI on behalf of your employee. Generally, the employer's contribution will be slightly more than the employee's.

To find out when you should deduct EI premiums from your employees' paycheques and remit them , see CCRA guide called *Payroll Deductions (Basic Information)* and the *Payroll Deductions Tables* for your province or territory.

Types of employment for which you do not deduct EI premiums

There are certain types of employment which are not considered insurable and for which you do not deduct EI premiums.

For example, you do not deduct EI premiums when you and your employee do not deal with each other at arm's length. This includes individuals connected by blood relationship, marriage, or adoption. However, an employee who does not deal with you at arm's length can be in insurable employment if you would have negotiated a similar contract with a person that you deal with at arm's length. This decision is based on the terms and conditions of employment, and the remuneration paid for the work done.

For more information, see CCRA publication called *Payroll Deductions (Basic Information)*.

Income tax

As an employer, you're responsible for deducting income tax from the salaries, wages, or other remuneration you pay your employees. Since employees fall into various categories, you need various forms, such as federal and provincial TD1 forms, to help you decide what to deduct from their paycheques. For more information on these forms, please see CCRA guide called *Payroll Deductions (Basic Information)*.

How to make income tax deductions

To deduct income tax from your employees' paycheques, consult the payroll deductions publications for your province or territory. These publications indicate you how much income tax to deduct from your employees' paycheques, depending on their salaries and pay periods.

Workers' Compensation

As an employer, you may be required to make payments, and be subject to certain regulations under Workers' Compensation legislation. For more information, see the guide called *Payroll Deductions (Basic Information)*.

247

How to report payroll deductions

The T4

You report your employees' salary, wages, and taxable benefits, as well as any deductions, on the T4 form. You can get this form from your nearest tax services office.

You have to fill out and give your employees their copies of the T4 no later than the end of February following the calendar year to which the form relates.

Quarterly remittances

Most employers are required to remit withholding amounts on a monthly basis; large employers remit more frequently. As a small business employer, you may be able to make quarterly remittances of taxes and payroll deductions. CCRA will automatically notify you if you qualify for this program. No application is required. You can continue to remit monthly if you prefer.

Do you have a computer?

If you have a computer, you can use it instead of the paper tables to calculate your employees' payroll deductions. CCRA provide a computerized version of the *Payroll Deductions Tables* (T4032) and *Payroll Deductions Supplementary Tables* (T4008) called *Tables on Diskette* (TOD) (T4143). This diskette contains the information you need to calculate deductions from your employees' pay for all pay periods.

Tables on Diskette (T4143) are available on the Internet. For more information, see the *Payroll Deductions Tables* (T4032) or call at 1-800-959-5525.

If you'd like to create your own payroll deduction calculations, a publication containing the formulas you need (except for Quebec provincial tax and QPP), is available. You can get the publication called *Payroll Deductions Formulas for Computer Programs* (T4127) from CCRA, or download the publication from their Web site. A printed version is also available.

248

You can use any version of the tables to calculate your employees' payroll deductions for CPP, EI, and federal/provincial (except Quebec) income tax. The *Payroll Deductions Tables* (T4032) *and Payroll Deductions Supplementary Tables* (T4008) are available for each province and territory, and also for employees working outside Canada.

In summary, your responsibilities as an employer are to:

- deduct CPP/QPP contributions, EI premiums, and income tax from amounts you pay to your employees;
- remit these deductions **along with your share** of CPP/QPP contributions and EI premiums that you have to pay throughout the year on your employees' behalf; and

- report the employees' income and deductions on the appropriate information return and give information slips to your employees by the last day of February following the calendar year to which the information return applies.

Chapter 5

Importing/Exporting

Before you import commercial goods...

Before you import commercial goods into Canada, you need to know the answers to the following questions:

- Are the goods admissible to Canada?
- What will it cost to import the goods to Canada?
- How will you account for the goods and pay the duties and taxes?
- Must the goods be marked?
- What are the tariff classification, value for duty, and origin of the goods?
- Should you get a National Customs Ruling or an Advance Ruling before importing?

Importing and exporting can sometimes be complicated. Some businesses use customs brokers to help them.

Are the goods admissible to Canada?

Before you import anything to Canada, make sure it is admissible. For information, contact your nearest customs office, listed in the government section of your telephone book.

250

What will it cost to import the goods to Canada?

There are three different costs that go along with importing.
First, there is the purchase cost-what you pay for the goods in their country of origin, converted to Canadian dollars.

Second, there are **duties,** which are taxes that may be associated with importing. The taxes could include customs duty, excise tax, excise duty, and the goods and services tax (GST) or the harmonized sales tax (HST). To find out what duties and taxes apply to what you're importing, contact your customs office, listed in the government section of your telephone book.

Third, there are the costs of other services, such as transportation, brokerage, and insurance.

Also, you may incur additional costs, such as examination charges, to have the goods you import loaded or unloaded so that CCRA may examine them.

How will you account for the goods and pay the duties and taxes?

In most cases, you'll need to fill out Form B3, *Canada Customs Coding Form.* You will need to provide information such as your importer name, your Business Number, a description of the goods, shipment dates, tariff treatment, country of origin, tariff classification, value for duty, and the duty and taxes owing.

You can't account for or pay duties and taxes on your goods unless you know their tariff classification, the country of origin, and their value for duty. Value for duty is usually the amount of money, converted to Canadian dollars, that you pay for the goods you import. In cases where there is no purchase price, you can contact your customs office for help in determining the value for duty.

Must the goods be marked ?

There are a number of categories of goods that must be marked with their country of origin before they will be permitted entry into Canada. CCRA require country of origin markings such as "Made

251

in...". You can find more information on the marking program in the D11-3 series of departmental Memoranda.

What are the tariff classification, value for duty, and origin of the imported goods ?

The tariff classification, value for duty, and origin determine the duty you pay on the imported goods. That's why it's necessary to know the classification, value for duty, and origin before you calculate any costs. An incorrect tariff classification, value for duty, and origin will result in an incorrect duty.

Should you get a National Customs Ruling before importing?

You can make sure you are working with the correct information if you obtain a National Customs Ruling (NCR) from CCRA that verifies the tariff classification, country of origin, and value for duty on imported goods. Getting an NCR is not required, but might save you time and paperwork in the future. For more information on National Customs Rulings, see Memorandum D11-11-1, *National Customs Rulings*.

You can also make sure you are working with correct free trade information if you obtain an advance ruling from the customs administration of a free trade country. For more information on advance rulings, see Memorandum D11-4-16, *Advance Rulings*.

INTRODUCTION TO IMPORTING

Form B3, *Canada Customs Coding Form*

In most cases, you have to document the importation of commercial goods on Form B3, *Canada Customs Coding Form*.

If you are a new importer, you may need help completing Form B3. For more information or clarification, contact your customs office before you import the goods. Also see the brochure called *Importing Commercial Goods into Canada*, or Memorandum D17-1-10, *Coding of Customs Accounting Documents*.

Commercial Cash Entry Processing System (CCEPS)

The Commercial Cash Entry Processing System (CCEPS) is used by small commercial importers to generate Form B3, *Canada Customs Coding Forms*. Using a personal computer located at the front counter, clients enter customs importation data (e.g., vendor name, value for currency conversion, and date of direct shipment) into CCEPS. CCEPS automatically calculates the duties and taxes owing. Form B3 is then entered into the Customs Commercial System (CCS) for validation and cash collection. CCEPS has been implemented at 33 locations across Canada.

For more information on CCEPS, contact your local customs office.

Import permits, health certificates, and other forms that government departments require

Some goods are subject to the requirements of other federal government departments. In these cases, you may need permits, certificates, and examinations to import the goods. CCRA administer the import portions of some legislation on behalf of these departments. You should know that CCRA refer many importations to the appropriate department for processing before they release them.

253

For more details on the import/export documents you need for other government departments, see the Memoranda D10-18 and D19 series.

Setting up your import/export account

To set up your import/export account, you need a copy of Form RC1, *Request for a Business Number (BN)*, which is available from any CCRA office. You'll receive an account as soon as they process your application. If you already have a BN for GST/HST, payroll deductions, or corporate income tax, call us at 1-800-959-5525. CCRA will update the BN system with your import/export account.

Use your BN on release documents and final accounting packages for most shipments that enter Canada.

You will need an exporter number for shipments valued at more than $2,000, if they are destined to a country other than the United States.

You can report shipments in two ways: by using an approved cargo control document (CCD), or by transmitting the cargo data via electronic data interchange (EDI). The CCD controls the shipments until CCRA release them. Cargo reporting and completion of the CCD are generally the responsibilities of the carrier or freight forwarder.

You do not need to use a CCD when you personally transport the shipment and you obtain its release by accounting for the goods and paying any duties at the customs office where they enter Canada.

For complete details on cargo reporting, see the Memoranda D3 series.

Examining your goods

To verify that shipments are acceptable, CCRA occasionally select shipments for examination. Some shipments are selected on a random basis and some are selected on the basis of compliance risk. The frequency of examinations will depend on your compliance record and the type of goods you are importing. Examinations may be done at the point of arrival or where the goods are released, depending on the circumstances.

Release, accounting, and payment: your options

There are several ways to obtain release of your goods. You can get:

- release with full accounting and payment (cash option);
- release on minimum documentation;
- release of goods imported by mail; or
- release of goods imported by courier.

Accounting for goods

The following sections describe several elements of the accounting process, many of which appear on Form B3, *Canada Customs Coding Form.*

Value for duty, tariff classification, origin of goods, and applicability of other duties are subject to strict legal interpretation. If you need help, contact the nearest regional customs client services office listed in the government section of your telephone book, or check the section called "How To Get Information From the CCRA".

Tariff classification

Each good has a unique tariff classification number. The tariff classification number determines the duty rate you pay when you import the goods into Canada. As you can see, it's important for you to have the correct classification. You don't want to pay any more duty than is necessary.

You can obtain a National Customs Ruling (NCR) on the tariff classification of the goods by requesting one in writing from your regional customs client services office. These rulings are binding on both parties. For more information, contact the nearest customs client services office, listed in the government section of your telephone book

Value for duty

You as an importer are responsible for determining and reporting an accurate value for duty. The value for duty is the amount on which percentage duties are calculated. There are six methods provided in the value for duty sections of the *Customs Act* (Sections 44 to 53). However, the primary method, and the method that is most often applicable, bases the value for duty on the price you pay for the goods (your purchase price). Certain additions or deductions to this price may be required to arrive at the value for duty you report. You must report the value for duty in Canadian funds, so you may need to convert the amount from foreign currency. Only one valuation method will be used for an importation and each has requirements and rules for its use. The methods must be applied in the proper order. Further information is provided in the D13 series Memoranda. Also, for more detailed information on how to determine the value for duty for your shipments, contact your nearest customs office.

Origin

The country of origin of your goods also affects the duty payable. Depending on the country of origin and whether it has signed a trade agreement with Canada, some goods may receive a lower rate of customs duty.

If certain conditions are met, CCRA do give preferential rates of duty to goods originating in developing countries.

For more information on the rules of origin and tariff treatments, see the Memoranda D11-4 and D11-5 series.

Certificates of origin

As an importer, you can benefit from lower rates of customs duty under several trade agreements, such as the North America Free Trade Agreement (NAFTA), Canada-Israel Free Trade Agreement (CIFTA), and the Canada-Chile Free Trade Agreement (CCFTA). You should get a certificate of origin from the American or Mexican manufacturer or vendor of any goods you import from the U.S. or Mexico.

For more details on the origin of goods and the certificate of origin, see the Memoranda D11 series.

Trade incentives - how to reduce or eliminate the duty

You can reduce or eliminate customs duty on qualifying goods through duties relief incentives. The following programs are examples of these incentives.

Duty deferral program

The duty deferral program includes three components enabling companies to defer or be relieved of the payment of customs duties: the duties relief program, the drawback program, and the bonded warehouse program.

Duties relief program

The duties relief program enables eligible companies to import goods without having to pay customs duties, as long as they eventually export the goods. These companies can further manufacture the goods before exporting them or export them in their unaltered state without having to pay customs duties. The North American Free Trade Agreement (NAFTA) regulates the amount of relief where the goods are exported to NAFTA-participating companies. For more information, please refer to Memoranda in the D7 series.

Drawback program

With the drawback program, customs duties are refunded on imported goods when these goods have been exported. You may export these goods in the same condition as they were at the time of import, or you may further their manufacture before exporting them, without affecting the amount of the refund. NAFTA regulates the amount of relief where goods are exported to NAFTA participating companies. For more information, please refer to memoranda in the D7 series.

Note : Most goods are subject to the GST/HST at the time of importation. While the GST/HST is considered a duty payable under the *Customs Act,* it cannot be exempted under the duties relief program or the drawback program.

Bonded warehouse program

A customs bonded warehouse is a facility operated by the private sector and regulated by the Customs Branch of the CCRA. In this warehouse, you may store imported goods without having to pay duties and taxes. Duties and taxes will only become payable if the goods enter the Canadian domestic market. If imported goods are to be exported, you can avoid having to pay duties or taxes by placing them in a bonded warehouse on their arrival in Canada.

Also, if you are an exporter and wish to claim a drawback for customs duties you paid when you imported goods, you may stock the goods in a customs bonded warehouse while waiting to export them. As soon as they enter the warehouse, the goods are considered exported and you may therefore claim a drawback. For more information, please refer to Memoranda in the D4 and D7 series.

- Memorandum D4-1-2, *Customs Bonded Warehouse Regulations*
- Memorandum D7-4-1, *Duty Deferral Program*
- Memorandum D7-4-2, *Duty Drawback Program*
- Memorandum D7-4-3, *NAFTA Requirements for Drawback and Duty Deferral*

Remissions

Under remissions programs, some goods can enter Canada duty-free.

For more information on remissions, see the Memoranda D8 series, or contact your nearest customs office.

Refunds

CCRA can grant refunds of full or partial duties you paid on exported or destroyed goods, defective goods, shortages, or equipment you removed from the goods and returned to the manufacturer for credit. You can also use the refund process to claim the benefit of relief programs you didn't know about at the time of importation, or in other situations where you may have overpaid duties in error. For more information on refunds, see the Memoranda in the D6 series.

REVIEW, ASSESSMENT, AND APPEALS

Review of your accounting package

CCRA review your final accounting package no later than 30 days after you give it to them. If your final accounting package is found to be incorrect, a refund or reassessment can be issued, or they may ask you to provide more information or documentation to substantiate your claims.

Your reassessment rights

As the importer, you have the right to a review of the value for duty, tariff classification, or origin of imported goods (subject to some exceptions) either because you wish to make changes, or because you don't agree with the changes they made. You may request a review at any customs office in the region where the goods were released within one year of CCRA initial review.

For more information on the redetermination and reappraisal process, see Memorandum D11-6-1, *Determination/Re-determination and Appraisal/Re-appraisal of Goods.*

Your appeal rights

If you don't agree with the CCRA's decision, you have the right to appeal it to the Canadian International Trade Tribunal (CITT). To do so, you file a written appeal notice with the Commissioner of the CCRA and the Secretary to the CITT no later than 90 days after they issue their decision.

For more information about your appeal rights, contact your customs office.

Seizures and forfeitures appeal process

If you do not report goods, or report goods falsely to customs, the *Customs Act* allows CCRA to seize the goods. In most cases where the goods can't be found, they can assess an amount in lieu of seizure.

If you disagree with a seizure or an assessment in lieu of seizure, you can request a ministerial review. You do this by writing to the CCRA office where the seizure took place, or to the following address:

> Adjudications Division
> Appeals Branch
> Canada Customs and Revenue Agency
> Ottawa ON K1A 0L5

You must request a CCRA review within 30 days of the date of the seizure or the date they mailed you the notice of assessment.
CCRA review your request and give you the opportunity to provide them with additional information. They will let you know whether they will uphold or overturn the seizure or notice of assessment, and whether they will maintain, eliminate, or reduce the amount of the assessment.

If you don't agree with CCRA decision, you can appeal to the Federal Court of Canada - Trial Division, within 90 days of the date they mail you their decision.

Exporting

You have to file an export declaration when exporting goods that are:

- valued at CAN $2,000 or more; and
- the final destination of the goods is a country other than the United States, Puerto Rico, or U.S. Virgin Islands. This

includes goods travelling through the United States (U.S.) to a foreign destination or directly to a non-U.S. destination.

You **do not** need to file an export declaration for :

- goods you are exporting for domestic consumption in the U.S.; or
- any foreign, in-bond goods that are in transit through Canada for export to a foreign destination.

If you are exporting goods that are controlled, prohibited, or regulated, you have to submit the appropriate permit, certificate, or licence before you export them, regardless of the goods' destination or value. To obtain more information on controlled exports, contact the Export Controls Division of Foreign Affairs and International Trade at (613) 996-2387 or by fax at (613) 996-9933.

Exporters may use one of the following three methods to provide export declarations:

- The Canadian Automated Export Declaration program (CAED);
- Form B13A, *Export Declaration*; or
- Summary reporting.

Exporters are required to keep records in Canada in paper or electronic format for six years after the goods have been exported. For more information on export requirements and records maintenance, refer to the brochure called *Exporting Goods from Canada*.

Income Tax

This chapter introduces you to the process of reporting earnings and paying income tax on your business's profits. It will explain how to account for what your business earns, and what kinds of income you have to report. It also tells you what expenses you're allowed to deduct.

Accounting for your earnings

Generally, you have to report business income (other than farming or fishing income) using the accrual method of accounting. Farmers or fishers may use the cash method or the accrual method, but not a combination of both.

The accrual method

Under the accrual method, you have to report income in the fiscal period you earn it, regardless of when you receive payment.
Similarly, you deduct allowable expenses in the fiscal period in which you incur them, whether or not you pay for them in that period.

The cash method

Under the cash method, you report income as it is received and you deduct allowable expenses as they are paid. If you are a farmer, fisher, or self-employed commissioned sales agent, you can use the cash method.

For more information about the cash method, see the tax guides called *Farming Income, Fishing Income,* or *Business and Professional Income.*

How to keep sales and expense journals

You should keep a day-to-day record of your receipts and expenses. A book with columns and separate pages for income and expenses is good for this. Keep this record along with your duplicate deposit slips, bank statements, cancelled cheques, and receipts. This will support your expenditure claims.

How to record your business expenses

You can generally deduct business expenses if you incur them for the sole purpose of producing income. If you claim expenses, you have to be able to back up your claim. You do this by keeping all your business-related vouchers and receipts, and recording all your expenses in a journal.

The simplest method of recording these expenses is a basic sheet with columns that list the common categories of expenses. At the end of each month, total each column, and then start a new sheet for the next month.

Fiscal period

You have to report your business income on an annual basis. For sole proprietorships, professional corporations that are members of a partnership, and partnerships in which at least one member is an individual, professional corporation, or another affected partnership, your business income is generally reported on a calendar-year basis.

If you are a sole proprietorship or in a partnership in which all the members are individuals, you can elect to have a non-calendar year fiscal period. To do this, use Form T1139, *Reconciliation of Business Income for Tax Purposes* (revised annually) to file your election. You need to file this form by a certain date. For more

263

information, see the guide called *Reconciliation of Business Income for Tax Purposes.*

A corporation can choose a fiscal period that ends on any date. The corporation has to file its income tax return within six months of the end of its fiscal period.

The rules governing fiscal periods are complicated. It's a good idea to get familiar with them before you get into business. For more information, see CCRA income tax guide called *Business and Professional Income.*

> **Note**: If you are a GST/HST registrant, your decision about your fiscal period end for income tax purposes may affect your GST/HST reporting periods, as well as your filing and remitting due dates. For more information, call us at 1-800-959-5525 or see CCRA publication called *General Information for GST/HST Registrants.*

Income

This part gives you an overview of the business income that you should account for in your records for income tax purposes.

Types of income

During the year, you may receive income from your business and from sources other than your actual sales. If they relate to your business, you have to include them in your business income.

What is business income?

Business income includes money you earn from a profession, a trade, a manufacture or undertaking of any kind, an adventure or concern in the nature of trade, or any other activity you carry on for profit or with a reasonable expectation of profit. For example, income from a service business is business income. However, business income does not include employment income, i.e., wages or salaries received from an employer.

How to account for your business income

Business owners have to provide information about their business income and expenses.

Although CCRA accept other types of financial statements but encourage you to use the following forms if they apply to you:

- Form T2124, *Statement of Business Activities*;
- Form T2032, *Statement of Professional Activities*;
- Form T2042, *Statement of Farming Activities*; and
- Form T2121, *Statement of Fishing Activities*.

While they are not meant to be standard financial statements, these forms include optional balancing fields so that you can use them as financial statements. You'll find instructions on completing them in the appropriate income tax guides available at your tax services office or on CCRA Web site.

CCRA have designed these forms to accommodate the most common types of income and expense categories used in business, so it should be easy for you to set up your records of account. You may use the categories included on these forms when you establish your records of account.

You must support all income entries in your records with original documents-sales invoices, cash register tapes, receipts, fee statements, and contracts. Keep the supporting documents in chronological or numerical order and make them available if CCRA ask to see them.

You should also keep a separate record of your income from all other sources, such as professional fees, income from property, investments, taxable capital gains, estates, trusts, employment, and pensions.

Bad debts

If you received any amount during the year that you wrote off as a bad debt in a previous year, you have to include the amount in your income for the current year.

There may be GST/HST implications on the recovery of bad debts. For more information, see the GST/HST guide called *General Information for GST/HST Registrants* from CCRA.

Reserves

You have to bring any reserve you claimed in a given year back into income in the following year. The *Income Tax Act* allows you to take a new reserve based on your circumstances at that time.

Vacation trips and awards

If you received vacation trips or other awards of any kind (e.g., jewellery, or furniture) as a result of your business activities, you must include the value of these awards in your business income.

Vacation trips and awards may have GST/HST implications. For more information, see the GST/HST guide called *General Information for GST/HST Registrants*.

Government grants and subsidies

If you get a grant or subsidy from a government or government agency, you'll have to report it either as income or as a reduction of an expense. Generally, a grant or subsidy:

- increases your income or reduces your expenses;
- relates to an income deficiency; or
- relates to specific expenses.

For example, if you are a farmer and you received a payment to subsidize your income in a drought year, you would add the payment to your income. However, if you are a business which receives a government employment grant to let you hire more students, you would generally deduct it from the wage expense you are claiming.

Government assistance that enables you to acquire capital property does not increase your net income. However, in the case of depreciable property, you reduce the capital cost of the property by the amount of the assistance you received. In the case of other capital property, reduce the adjusted cost base accordingly.

For more information, see Interpretation Bulletin IT-273, *Government Assistance - General Comments.*

Surface rentals for petroleum or natural gas exploration

If you have land that you usually use in your farming or business operation, and you are leasing it out for petroleum or natural gas exploration, you may have to include the leasing proceeds in your income either as a capital receipt or as an income receipt.

For more detailed information, see Interpretation Bulletin IT-200, *Surface Rentals and Farming Operations.*

Rental income

Rental income can be either income from property or income from business. Income from rental operations is usually income from property.

To determine the type of rental income you have, and how to report it, refer to CCRA guide called *Rental Income.*

Barter transactions

A barter transaction takes place when any two persons agree to an exchange of goods or services, and carry out that exchange without using money.

If you are involved in a barter transaction, the goods or services you received could be considered proceeds from a business operation. If you are in a business or profession that provides goods or services, and you offer these goods or services in a barter transaction in exchange for other goods or services, you have to include the value of the goods or services you provided in your income.

Barter transactions may also have GST/HST implications. For more information, call us at 1-800-959-5525.

Selling a property

If you sell a capital property, you may have to include certain amounts in your income, such as:

- a recovery of capital cost allowance, known as **recapture**; and
- part of any capital gain you realize on the sale.

Generally, you have a capital gain or a capital loss when you dispose of capital property. For example, if you sell a piece of land for more than it cost, you have a capital gain as a result. Similarly, if you sell the land for less than it cost, you have a capital loss.

For more information on capital gains and capital losses, see the CCRA's income tax guide called *Capital Gains*. For special rules relating to farmers, see the income tax guide called *Farming Income*.

Also, there may be GST/HST implications when you sell a property. For more information, see the guide called *General Information for GST/HST Registrants*.

Inventory and cost of goods sold

To match expenses with income, you need to prepare an annual inventory. This is usually a list of goods held for sale. If you are a manufacturer, this includes raw materials as well as packaging material and supplies, work-in-progress, and finished goods that you have on hand.

However, if you have a professional practice and you are an accountant, dentist, lawyer, medical doctor, notary, veterinarian, or chiropractor, you may elect to exclude your work-in-progress when you determine inventory.

How to value your inventory

The value you place on the items in your year-end inventory is important in determining your income. For income tax purposes, the two acceptable methods of valuing your inventory are by determining:

- the fair market value of your entire inventory (use either the price you would pay to replace an item, or the amount you would get if you sold an item); or

- the value of individual items (or classes of items, if specific items are not readily distinguishable) in the inventory, at either their cost or their fair market value, whichever is lower.

Once you choose a method of inventory valuation, you must continue to use this method in subsequent years. For more information about valuing inventory, see Interpretation Bulletin IT-473, *Inventory Valuation*, and its Special Release.

Expenses

This section gives you an overview of the business expenses that you can claim for income tax purposes.

What are business expenses?

A business expense is a cost you incur for the sole purpose of earning business income. You must back up business expense claims with a sales invoice, an agreement of purchase and sale, a receipt, or some other voucher that supports the expenditure. If you pay cash for any business expenses, be sure to get receipts or other vouchers. Receipts should include the vendor's name and the date.

Remember to keep your cancelled cheques if you receive them from the bank. This is part of your proof that the bill was paid or the asset purchased. Keep the cancelled cheques in an orderly manner so CCRA can easily review them.

Running a business from your home

You can deduct expenses for the business use of a work space in your home, if the work space is either:

- your principal place of business; or
- you use the space only to earn your business income, and you use it on a regular and ongoing basis to meet your clients or customers.

You can deduct a portion of your maintenance costs, such as heating, home insurance, electricity, and cleaning materials. You can also deduct a portion of your property taxes, mortgage interest, and capital cost allowance (CCA). To calculate the portion you can deduct, use a reasonable basis, such as the area of the work space divided by the total area of your home.

For more information, see the income tax guide called *Business and Professional Income.*

TYPES OF OPERATING EXPENSES

Personal or living expenses

In most cases, you cannot deduct personal and living expenses, except for travelling expenses you incur in the course of carrying on a business while away from home.

The general rule is that you cannot deduct outlays or expenses that aren't related to earning business income.

Prepaid expenses

A prepaid expense is an expense you pay ahead of time. If you use the accrual method of accounting, claim any expense you prepay in the year or years in which you receive the related benefit.

For more information, see Interpretation Bulletin IT-417, *Prepaid Expenses and Deferred Charges.*

Accounting and legal fees

You can deduct the fees you incurred for external professional advice or services, including consulting fees.
You can deduct accounting and legal fees you incur to get advice and help in keeping your books and records. You can also deduct

270

fees you incur for preparing and filing your income tax and GST/HST returns.

Advertising expenses

You can deduct expenses for advertising. This includes printed materials, as well as ads in Canadian newspapers and on television or radio.

However, you cannot deduct expenses for advertising directed mainly to a market in Canada when you advertise:

- with a foreign broadcaster; or
- in an issue of a non-Canadian newspaper or periodical.

This second restriction does not apply to ads in a special issue of a newspaper published twice a year or less, and devoted to news or features mainly about Canada.

Business tax, fees, licences, and dues

You can deduct any annual licence fees and business taxes you incur to run your business.

You can also deduct annual dues or fees to keep your membership in a trade or commercial association. You cannot deduct club membership dues (including initiation fees) where the main purpose of the club is to provide dining, recreational, or sporting facilities for its members.

Insurance expenses

You can deduct all regular commercial insurance premiums you incur on any buildings, machinery, and equipment that you use for your business.

Interest and bank charges

You can deduct the interest you incur on money you borrow to run your business. However, there are some limits.

There is a limit on the interest you can deduct on money you borrow to buy a passenger vehicle. For more detailed information, see the section "Motor vehicle expenses" in the income tax guide called *Business and Professional Income.*

There is also a limit on the amount of interest you can deduct for vacant land. See the section "Interest" in the income tax guide called *Business and Professional Income.* If you need more information, call CCRA at 1-800-959-5525.

You can choose to capitalize the interest you pay on the money you borrow for the following purposes:

- to buy depreciable property;
- to buy a resource property; or
- for exploration and development.

In the case of exploration and development, when you choose to capitalize interest, you add the interest to either the cost of the property or the exploration and development costs.

Do not deduct the capitalized interest as a current expense.

For more detailed information about capitalizing interest, see Interpretation Bulletin IT-121, *Election to Capitalize Cost of Borrowed Money.*

Maintenance and repairs

You can deduct the cost of labour and materials for any minor repairs or maintenance done to property you use to earn income. You cannot deduct the value of your own labour.

You cannot deduct costs you incur for repairs that are capital in nature. However, you may be able to claim capital cost allowance on the repaired property. For more information about capital cost allowance, see the income tax guide called *Business and Professional Income.*

Meals and entertainment

You can deduct up to 50% of the cost of meals and entertainment that you incur to earn income in your business.

The 50% limit also applies to the cost of your meals when you travel or go to a convention, conference, or similar event. However, special rules can affect your claim for meals in these cases. For more details, see the sections "Meals and Entertainment," "Convention expenses," and "Travel" in the income tax guide called *Business and Professional Income*.

For more information, see Interpretation Bulletin IT-518, *Food, Beverages, and Entertainment Expenses*.

Motor vehicle expenses

You can deduct expenses you incur to run a motor vehicle that you use to earn business income. However, several things can affect your deduction.

What kind of vehicle do you own?

The kind of vehicle you own can affect the expenses you deduct. For income tax purposes, there are three types of vehicles.

1. *Motor vehicle* - Any automotive vehicle designed or adapted for use on highways and streets.

2. *Automobile* - A motor vehicle designed or adapted primarily to carry people on highways and streets. It seats a driver and no more than eight passengers.

3. *Passenger vehicle* - An automobile you bought after June 17, 1987. A passenger vehicle is also an automobile that you leased under a lease you entered into, extended, or renewed after June 17, 1987.

With certain exceptions, most cars, station wagons, vans, and some pick-up trucks are considered passenger vehicles. If you own or lease a passenger vehicle, there may be a limit on the amounts you can deduct for capital cost allowance, interest, and leasing costs.

For definitions and more detailed information about capital cost allowance limits, interest limits, and leasing costs, see the income tax guide called *Business and Professional Income*.

How to record motor vehicle expenses

You can deduct motor vehicle expenses only when they are reasonable and you have receipts to support them.

To get the full benefit of your claim for each vehicle, keep a record of the total kilometers you drove, and the kilometers you drove to earn business income. For each business trip, list the date, destination, purpose, and the number of kilometers you drove.

Be sure to write down the odometer reading of each vehicle at the start and end of the year. If you change motor vehicles during the year, write down the odometer reading at the time you buy, sell, or trade the vehicle.

Record the dates of these readings.

What kind of vehicle expenses can you deduct?

The types of expenses you can deduct include:

- fuel and oil;
- maintenance and repairs;
- insurance;
- licence and registration fees;
- capital cost allowance;
- interest you pay on a loan used to buy the motor vehicle; and
- leasing costs.

Joint ownership

If you and another person own or lease a passenger vehicle together, the limits on capital cost allowance, interest, and leasing still apply.

Business use of a motor vehicle

If you use a motor vehicle for both business and personal use, you can deduct only the portion of the expenses that relates to earning income.

To support the amount you deduct, keep a record of both the total kilometers you drove, and the kilometers you drove to earn income. The following chart shows you how to keep this type of record.

Jay owns a stereo retail business and has a van that he uses for the business. In keeping his records, Jay wrote down the following information for the current year:

Kilometres driven to earn business income		27,000
Total kilometres driven		30,000
Gas and oil	$	2,400
Capital cost allowance		4,500
Insurance		800
Licence and registration fees		100
Maintenance and repairs		200
Total expenses for the van	$	8,000

Jay calculates the expenses he can deduct for his van in the current year as follows:

$$\frac{27,000 \text{ (business kilometres)}}{30,000 \text{ (total kilometres)}} \times \$8,000 = \$7,200$$

> Note: When you use more than one motor vehicle to earn income, calculate the expenses for each vehicle separately.

Interest expenses on vehicle loans

You can deduct interest on money you borrow to buy a motor vehicle, automobile, or passenger vehicle that you use to earn income.

Include the interest as an expense when you calculate your allowable motor vehicle expenses. However, when you use a passenger vehicle to earn income, there's a limit on the amount of interest you can deduct.

The income tax guide called *Business and Professional Income* has more information on claiming this kind of expense.

Vehicle leasing expenses

You can deduct the leasing costs of a motor vehicle that you use to earn income. Include the leasing costs when you calculate your allowable motor vehicle expenses.

However, when you use a passenger vehicle to earn income, there is a limit on the amount of leasing costs you can deduct.
To calculate your eligible leasing costs, see the income tax guide called *Business and Professional Income*.

Office expenses

You can deduct the cost of office expenses, i.e., small items such as pens, pencils, paper clips, stationery, and stamps. Office expenses do not include items such as calculators, filing cabinets, chairs, and desks, which are capital items. For more information, see the income tax guide called *Business and Professional Income*.

Salaries, including employer's contributions

You can deduct salaries you pay to employees. You report these salaries by the end of February on a T4 or T4A slip. For more details on how to complete these forms, see the chapter "Payroll Deductions" in this guide, or the publication called *Payroll Deductions (Basic Information)*.

Can you deduct business start-up costs?

To be able to deduct a business expense, you had to have carried on a business in the fiscal period in which the expense was incurred. Because of this, you have to be very clear about the date your business started.

Determining exactly what you can claim as a start-up expense can be difficult. For more information, see Interpretation Bulletin IT-364, *Commencement of Business Operations*.

Chapter 7

Audits

What is an audit?

Auditing is a way for the CCRA to monitor and inspect GST/HST and income tax returns, customs import documents, and payroll records. Although there is a high standard of compliance with the law in Canada, audits help us maintain public confidence in the fairness and integrity of Canada's tax system.

How CCRA select files to audit

Your tax return is recorded in a computer system that enables CCRA to select returns to be audited. The system also lets them sort returns into various groups to help with their selection.

In some cases, CCRA compare selected financial information for current and previous years of clients engaged in similar businesses or occupations. From computer-generated lists of returns for potential audit, CCRA then choose specific returns.

Most returns are selected in this way. But there are three other common ways of selecting files

1. Audit projects

In some cases, CCRA test the compliance of a particular group of clients. If the test results indicate that there is significant non-compliance within the group, CCRA may audit its members on a local, regional, or national basis.

2. Leads

Leads include information from other audits or investigations, as well as information from outside sources.

3. Secondary files

Sometimes CCRA select files for audit because of their association with other previously selected files. For example, if you are in partnership with another client, and that person's file has been selected for audit, it is usually more convenient to examine all the records at the same time.

How CCRA conduct audits

If you are selected, an auditor will contact you to arrange a convenient date and time to start the audit. The auditor will then review the following records:

- the return or customs documents selected for audit;
- financial statements;
- audit reports from previous audits, if any; and
- any other information in the file.

On arriving at your place of business, the auditor will present an identification card. Before examining your books and records, the auditor may want to discuss the general nature of your business, or tour the premises to get a better understanding of the transactions recorded in your books.

The audit usually includes an examination of your ledgers, journals, bank accounts, sales invoices, purchase vouchers, and expense accounts. Throughout the process, the auditor may need to get information and assistance from your employees, particularly those who do your accounting.

Delays in the audit, and how to avoid them

Audits usually take only one or two weeks, but could be delayed for a number of reasons. For instance, you may want to consult with advisers, or you may be called out of town on other business before the audit is completed. Similarly, the auditor may ask for an interpretation from CCRA Headquarters on a particularly complex or contentious point of law.

Well-kept records will reduce the time required to complete the audit. Refer to the record-keeping guidelines on page 8 of this guide.

Finalizing an audit

When the audit is completed, the auditor may propose certain adjustments to your return. He or she will prepare a summary of the proposed adjustments.

Initially, the auditor will discuss this with you or your representative. If you request it, or if it is reasonable to expect that you will need some time to analyze the proposed adjustments, the auditor will confirm the proposal in writing and allow a reasonable time for your reply.

If you provide additional information within this period, the auditor will consider it and will issue a new proposal letter, if applicable.
If there are no proposed adjustments to your return, the auditor will inform you of this when the audit is completed.

Once the audit assessment is finalized, you will be issued a *Notice of Assessment* or *Notice of Reassessment*.

Note: The auditor's role is to determine the correct amount of duty or tax payable. This may mean that your taxes are adjusted downward and you get a refund as a result.

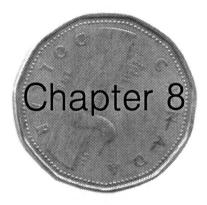

Objections And Appeals

What to do if you disagree with a tax assessment

If you do not understand or you disagree with an assessment, call or visit the Client Assistance Section of your tax services office or write to the tax centre that processed your return. CCRA resolve many problems with assessments in this way. If you employ the services of a tax professional, you may wish to consult with that person.

Extraordinary circumstances

CCRA can waive or cancel interest or penalties when they result from things that are beyond your control. Such things could include an illness which prevents you from filing an income tax or GST/HST return by the required deadline.

Fairness provisions in the *Income Tax Act* and *Excise Tax Act (*with respect to GST/HST*)* help us administer the legislation fairly. These provisions apply to individuals, testamentary trusts, small business owners, and corporations. All requests for relief under fairness legislation should be submitted in writing to your tax services office.

Problem Resolution Program

Most questions and concerns can be resolved quickly through CCRA's general enquiries service. However, from time to time, some people have concerns that need special attention.

CCRA Problem Resolution Program handles-on a priority basis-cases that cannot be resolved through regular channels. The program co-ordinators examine any concerns brought to their attention, trace the problem to its source, and determine whether the case is isolated or part of a larger trend that needs attention.

The objection process

Under income tax and GST/HST legislation, you can file an objection if you disagree with your *Notice of Assessment* or *Notice of Reassessment* and you think that the law has been applied incorrectly.

Income Tax - Send a letter, or complete and send Form T400A, *Objection,* to the Chief of Appeals at your tax services office or tax centre.

If you are an individual (other than a trust) or if you are filing for a testamentary trust, you must file your objection by the later of:

- one year after the due date of the return; or
- 90 days after the date CCRA mailed your *Notice of Assessment* or *Notice of Reassessment.*

In every other case, you have to file your objection within 90 days of the day CCRA mailed the *Notice of Assessment* or *Notice of Reassessment.* **GST/HST** - You must use form GST159, *Notice of Objection (GST/HST),* to file your objection. Send it to the Assistant Director of Appeals at your tax services office within 90 days of the day CCRA mail the *Notice of Assessment* or *Notice of Reassessment.*

When CCRA get your objection, the Appeals Division will conduct an independent review of the assessment. If the Assistant Director of Appeals agrees with you in whole or in part, CCRA will adjust your return and send you a *Notice of Reassessment.* However, if the

Assistant Director of Appeals disagrees, CCRA will send you a *Notice of Confirmation* confirming that the assessment was correct.

If you still do not agree, you can appeal CCRA decision to the Tax Court of Canada. You have 90 days from the date CCRA mail their decision on your objection (a *Notice of Reassessment* or a *Notice of Confirmation*). You can also file an appeal to the Tax Court of Canada if CCRA do not notify you of their decision within 90 days of the date you filed your income tax objection, or within 180 days of the date you filed a GST/HST objection.

Collection of disputed amounts

If you object to or appeal an income tax assessment, CCRA usually postpone collection action on amounts in dispute until 90 days after CCRA mail their decision to you. CCRA will not postpone collection action on some disputed amounts, such as taxes you had to withhold and remit. If you lose your appeal to the Tax Court, CCRA will resume collection action even if you appeal the Court's decision. However, CCRA will accept security for payment while your appeal is outstanding.

If you object to a GST/HST assessment, collection action may be postponed. However, you may post acceptable security while CCRA reviewing your objection.

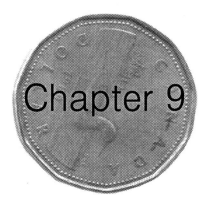

How To Get Information From the CCRA

You can get information and publications, and conduct other types of business, at most CCRA offices across Canada.

Some of these publications and services are also available at Government of Canada Info Centres. You can contact these offices for written information on income tax, customs duties and tariffs, and GST/HST programs.

Tax services offices

The tax services offices are your main points of contact with the CCRA. From your tax services office, you can get the forms and publications you need to complete your income tax returns, as well as GST/HST forms, publications, and information.

Employees at tax services offices answer telephone and over-the-counter enquiries about individual, employer, and corporate tax. They can give you information on refunds, assessment notices, paying tax in arrears, and late-filed returns.

Tax services offices also provide Business Number registration services.

285

Tax Centres

Staff members at the tax centres not only process and store income tax returns, but also provide a complete range of client services. They send assessment notices, arrange for refund cheques, and provide written explanations of tax assessments. They also process tax payments.

Each tax centre also has an enquiries counter to offer services similar to those offered by the tax services offices.

The International Tax Services Office

Canada's International Tax Services Office (ITSO), located in Ottawa, serves the special needs of clients whose income tax returns or information returns involve non-residents.

Staff members at the ITSO process non-resident individual and corporate tax returns, respond to written client enquiries, process requests for adjustments, and provide telephone and counter enquiry services.

The office also maintains the accounts of those individuals and institutions that issue payments to non-residents of Canada.

Customs information

You can get information on most customs-related matters by contacting the Automated Customs Information Service (ACIS). This service provides information on many topics, and also offers you the opportunity to speak with a customs official directly.

You can call ACIS toll free in Canada by dialing 1-800-461-9999 for service in English or 1-800-959-2036 for service in French.

Customs offices

You can get customs forms, publications, and information on importing and exporting goods from any of CCRA offices across Canada. CCRA employees handle enquiries and offer assistance on tariff classification, customs duty rates, accounting documentation, assessing the value of imported goods, methods of payment, import quotas and permits, customs assessments, refunds, duties relief, and appeals of customs seizures. You can enquire in writing, by phone, or in person.

Small business information seminars

The CCRA provides small business information seminars to inform new or prospective businesses about their rights and obligations regarding customs, GST/HST, income tax, and about the services CCRA offer to them.

These seminars are free of charge and cover many important topics, such as keeping adequate books and records, income and expenses, and business filing requirements.

To register for a seminar, simply contact the Business Enquiries Section of your tax services office.

New employer visit program

If you operate a small business, you may be too busy to attend an information seminar. If so, CCRA staff are available on request to visit you at your place of business.

This will give you a chance to ask questions about recording, withholding, or reporting employee earnings, tax, Canada Pension Plan contributions, or Employment Insurance premiums. CCRA do not charge for this service. If you are interested, call your tax services office to make arrangements.

Tax clinics

Every year during the filing season, the CCRA sets up tax clinics in various communities. These clinics are located in convenient places, such as shopping malls and public buildings, that are easily accessible to people who need information and advice about their tax returns. The clinics also have available a variety of forms, guides, and pamphlets that clients may need.

For the convenience of individual taxfilers in Quebec, whose provincial income taxes are administered by the Quebec government, the CCRA operates clinics jointly with the ministère du Revenu du Québec.

Government of Canada Info Centres may also host tax clinics in some smaller communities.

Government of Canada Info Centres

The CCRA is working with other federal government departments and agencies to provide improved service to Canadians in smaller communities, by offering a variety of government services from a single location. These new sites are called Government of Canada Info Centres and are usually located in Canada Employment Centres.

Canada Business Service Centres

The CCRA is also an active partner in the Canada Business Service Centre initiative, designed to help business clients through a single point of contact. These centres offer businesses access to information about the programs and services of various federal departments and agencies, including Industry Canada, and the CCRA, and economic development agencies such as the Atlantic Canada Opportunities Agency, Western Economic Diversification Canada, and the Federal Office of Regional Development (Quebec). Other partners include provincial and non-government agencies.
Twelve Canada Business Service Centres operate across the country. They are in Charlottetown, Edmonton, Fredericton, Halifax, Montréal, Saskatoon, St. John's, Toronto, Vancouver, Whitehorse, Winnipeg, and Yellowknife.

Business windows

Business windows are single-window service sites for CCRA business clients and are located in 45 tax services offices across the country. They are the initial point of contact for business clients who are looking for general information on programs and services or who would like to get a Business Number.

Publications

In addition to the services mentioned above, CCRA offer numerous tax guides, pamphlets, bulletins, and circulars. You can get information on any tax-related matter from these publications. Many of them are available on CCRA Web site at: **www.ccra.gc.ca**
You can also order copies of these publications by calling us at 1-800-959-2221.

The following publications may also be of interest:

- *CCRA Programs and Services* - An excellent way to find out about other CCRA services that meet your needs. This publication is available from the CCRA.
- *Your Guide to Government of Canada Services and Support for Small Business* - This publication lists every government resource for small businesses. If you're going to deal with government, you'll want to get this guide from Industry Canada.
- *Strategis* - Provides you with easy, direct access to Industry Canada's extensive expertise and information resources. You will find *Strategis* at: **www.strategis.ic.gc.ca**

Important Dates for Income Tax

Sole proprietorships and partnerships	
Monthly, by the 15th	Remit the payroll deductions from your employees' paycheques, along with your portion of Canada Pension Plan (CPP) contributions and Employment Insurance (EI) premiums, to us by the fifteenth of the following month.
Last day of February	File your T4 and T4A slips along with the related Summary form. Distribute the slips to your employees.
March 15	If you are self-employed, make your first instalment payment of tax and CPP contributions.
March 31	Partnerships (except those made up of corporations, or a combination of individuals, corporations, or trusts with different filing dates) must file a partnership information return.
April 30	File your T1 personal income tax and benefit return for the previous year. Pay any tax amounts owing. Self-employed individuals and their spouses or common-law partners have until June 15 to file their returns.
June 15	If you are self-employed, make your second installment payment. Self-employed individuals (and their spouses or common-law partners) must file their T1 personal income tax and benefit returns. However, you have to pay any balance owing by April 30, to avoid interest charges.

September 15	If you are self-employed, make your third instalment payment of tax and CPP contributions.
December 15	If you are self-employed, make your fourth instalment payment of tax and CPP contributions.
December 31	For farmers and fishers, calculate and pay the amount of your current-year instalment payment.

It is important that you file any required returns and remit payments on time. Penalties apply if you don't, and interest is charged on unpaid taxes and penalties.

Corporations	
Last day of February	File your T4 and T4A slips along with the related Summary form. Distribute the slips to your employees.
Monthly	Remit the payroll deductions from your employees' paycheques to us, along with your portion of Canada Pension Plan (CPP) contributions and Employment Insurance (EI) premiums, by the fifteenth of the following month.
Monthly	Corporations have to pay installments of their current-year taxes, by the last day of each month.
Two months from your taxation year-end	The balance of the corporation tax payable is due.
Three months from your taxation year-end	For corporations claiming the small business deduction, the balance of the corporation tax payable is due.
Six months from your taxation year-end	Corporations must file a *T2 Corporation Income Tax Return* no later than six months after the corporation's year-end.

HOW TO DOUBLE YOUR PRODUCTIVITY

There are many rules for success,
but none of them will work unless you do.

(Reed Markham, American educator)

HOW TO DOUBLE YOUR PRODUCTIVITY

A Secret of Success in Business & Life

All successful people are described as being very well organized and good time managers. Fortunately, time management skills are learnable with practice and repetition.

You can become one of the most productive people in your field by learning & following time management techniques.

What you are about to learn can change your life. These ideas, methods and techniques can increase your efficiency and effectiveness, boost your productivity, double your income, lower your stress levels and make you one of the most productive people in your field or business.

The fact is all successful people are very productive. They work longer hours and they work better hours, they get a lot more done than the average person. They get paid more and promoted faster. They are highly respected and esteemed by everyone around them.

They become leaders and role models for others, inevitably they rise to the top of their fields and to the top of their income ranges.

Every single one of these tested and proven strategies for managing your time and doubling your productivity is learnable through practice and repetition. Each of these methods if practiced regularly, will eventually become a habit of both thinking and working….lets begin

1. Make A Decision:

Every positive change in your life begins with a clear decision: either you are going to do something or going to stop doing something. Significant change starts when you decide to either get in or get out, either keep fishing or cut bait. Decisiveness is one of the most important qualities of successful and happy men and women and decisiveness is developed through practice and repetition as it becomes as natural to you as breathing in and breathing out.

The sad fact is people are poor because they have not yet decided to be rich. People are over-weight and unfit because they have not yet decided to be balanced and fit. People are inefficient time organizers because they haven't yet decided to be highly productive in everything they do.

Decide today that you are going to become an expert in time management and personal productivity. No matter how long it takes or how much you have to invest to achieve it. Resolve today that you are going to practice these principals over and over again until they become second nature. Discipline yourself to know that you need to be the very best in your field. Perhaps, the best definition of self-discipline is *"the ability to make yourself do, what you should do, when you should do it whether you feel like it or not"*. Its easy to do something when you feel like it. But when you do not feel like it and you force yourself to do it anyway, to move your life and career on the fast track

What decisions do you need to make in order to start moving toward the top of your field? Whatever they are, to get in or get out, make a decision today and then get started. This single act alone can change the whole direction of your life.

2. Develop Clear Goals And Objectives

Perhaps, the most important word in success for you for the rest of your life is "Clarity". About 80% of your success comes about as a result of your being absolutely clear about what it is that you are trying to accomplish. Unfortunately, probably 80% or more failure or frustration comes to the people who are unclear or fuzzy about what is they want in life and how to go about achieving it. The great oil billionaire HL Hunt (reportedly the world's first billionaire) once said that there are only two real requirements for success:

First he said "decide exactly what it is you want" , most people never do this. Second he said "determine the price that you are going to have to pay to get it and then resolve to pay that price" You can have just about anything that you really want as long you are willing to pay the price and nature always demand that you pay the price in full and pay it in advance. There is a powerful seven steps formula that you can use to set and achive your goals for the rest of your life. Every single successful person uses this formula or some variation of this formula to achieve success. As a result they accomplish vastly more then the average person and so can you:

a. Decide exactly what it is you want in each part of your life. Become a meaningful specific rather than a wondering generality . Decide how much you want to earn. Decide how much you want to weigh. Decide the kind family, relationship and lifestyle you want to enjoy. The vary act of deciding clearly, dramatically increases the likelyhood that you will achieve it.

b. Write it down clearly and in detail. Always think on paper. A goal that is not in writing is not really a goal at all, its merely a wish and it has no energy behind it. But when you take your goals out of your imagination and crystallize them on paper, you actually program them into your subconscious mind where they take on a power of their own.

c. Set a deadline for your goal. A deadline acts as a forcing system in your subconscious mind. A deadline motivates you to do the things necessary to make your goal come true. If it is a big goal then set sub-deadlines as well. Don't leave this to chance.

d. Make a list of everything you can think of that you are going have to do to achieve your goal. When you think of new tasks and activities, write them of on the list until your list is complete.

299

e.　　The 5th step in this goal setting formula for you is to organize your list into a plan. Decide what you will have to do first and what you will have to do second. Decide what is more important and what is less important and then write out your plan on paper. The same way you will develop a blueprint to build your dream house.

f.　　The 6th step is for you to take action on your plan. Do something, do anything but get busy, get going and don't delay.

g.　　Step seven and perhaps the most important of all is for you to do something every single day that moves you in the direction of your most important goal at the time. Develop the discipline of doing something 360 days of each year that is moving you forward. You will be absolutely astonished at how much you have accomplished when you utilize this formula every single day of your life.

Exercise:

Now here is an exercise that you can do that can change your life.

Take a blank sheet of paper and write out 10 goals that you want to accomplish in next 12 months and write each of these goals in present tense as though a year has passed and you have already achieved the goal. Start each of these goals with the word "I". For examples you can write down a goal such as

"I earned X no. of dollars this year" or
"I lost X no. of pounds in my weight" or
"I drive such and such a car"

Your subconscious mind only accepts instructions when they are phrased in present tense and when they are perceived with the word "I". Once you have your list of 10 goals, select the most important goal on that list and ask yourself "what one goal if I achieved right now will have the greatest positive impact on my life?" What ever it is put a circle around that goal and write it down at the top of a new sheet of paper, set a deadline, make a list, organize the list into a plan, take action on your plan and do something everyday until your goal is achieved.

This exercise has made more people successful than perhaps any other single exercise. From now on you should resolve to become intensely goal oriented.

Think and talk about your goals all the time. Write them and re-write them, review them everyday. Continually look for better ways to achieve them. This combination of goal setting formula and goal setting exercise will have more of a positive impact on your life than almost anything you can ever do. Give it a try.

3. Plan everyday in advance

Daily planning is absolutely essential for you to double your productivity. You should practice the *6P* formula for high achievement. This formula says *"Prior Proper Planning Prevents Poor Performance"*.

Proper planning is the mark of professionals. All successful men and women take a good deal of their time to plan their activities in advance. Remember the 10/90 rule which says that the first 10% of time that you spend planning your activity before you begin will save you as much as 90% of the time necessary to perform those activities once you start work

Always think on paper; something wonderful happens between your head and your hand when you write out your plans in detail on paper before you begin. Writing actually sharpens your thinking. It stimulates your activity and enables you to focus far better than if you are just trying to work out of your mind.

Begin by making a master list of everything you can think of that you have to do for the long term future. This master list then becomes the central control list for your life. Whenever you think of something new that you have to do, write it down on your master

301

list. At the beginning of each month make a monthly list covering everything that you can think of that you will have to do in the coming weeks, then break your monthly list down into a weekly list and specify exactly when you are going to start and complete the tasks that you have decided upon for the month.

Finally and perhaps the most important, make a daily list of your activities. Do this the night before so that your subconscious mind can work on your list while you sleep. Always work from a list, when something new comes up during the day, write it down on your list before you do it. As you work, you tick-off each item as you finish it. This tracking gives you an ongoing sense of accomplishment and personal progress. Crossing of items one by one motivates you and actually gives you more energy. A list serves as a scorecard and makes you feel like a winner. It tells you where you are making progress and what you have to do the next day. According to the time management experts, working from a list will increase your productivity by 25% the day you begin doing it. All highly effective people think on paper and work from written lists.

4. Set Your Priorities.

Also remember, the key to doubling your productivity is for you to spend more time doing things that are urgent and important and then working on activities which are important but less urgent. You increase your productivity by refusing to do things that are not important at all. Always ask yourself, what are the long term potential consequences of doing this task? What would happen if you did not do it at all? And whatever your answer is, let it guide you in your choice of priorities.

Use the law of forced efficiency; this law says that *"there is never enough time to do everything but there is always enough time to do most important things"*. Always ask yourself following question.

"What is the most valuable use of my time right now?"

Whatever your answer is, be sure that you are doing it most of the time. Discipline yourself to work only on your answers to the above question and this alone will double your productivity.

5. Apply the 80/20 Rule

The 80/20 rule, the Pareto principle is one of the most important and powerful of all time management principles. This rule comes from the Italian economist and political sociologist Wilfredo Pareto (1848-1923) who divided all activities into the vital few and the trivial many. This law says that 20% of the things that you do, the vital few, will account fully 80% of the value of all the things you do. The reverse of this principle is that 80% of the things you do will account for only 20% of the value of your activities. This 80/20 rule applies to all aspects of business and personal life. In business 80% of your sales will come from 20% of your customers. 80% of your profit will come from 20% of your products. 80% of your sales come from 20% of your sales people. 80% of you income, success and advancement will come from 20% of your activities. If you make a list of ten things that you have to do in a particular day, two of those items will turn out to be worth more than all the others put together.

Your ability to identify and focus on the top 20% of tasks will determine your success and productivity as much as any other factor. Here is an idea for you:

Practice creative procrastination with the 80/20 rule. Since you can't do everything, you have to procrastinate on something, therefore discipline yourself to procrastinate on the 80% of the activities that contribute very little value to you life and your results. The average person procrastinates on high value tasks but this is not for you. You must hold your own feet to the fire and procrastinate deliberately and continuously on those low value items that have very few consequences if they are done or not. Before you start work, always check to make sure that what you are doing is in the top 20% of all the things that you could be doing. Procrastinate on the rest.

6. Work at your Energy Peaks

One of the most important requirements for high productivity is high levels of physical, mental an emotional energy. All highly productive, highly successful, highly paid people have high levels of energy sustained over long periods of time. To generate and maintain high levels of energy you need to practice proper eating, proper exercise and proper rest. You need to eat light nutritious high protein foods and avoid fats, sugar, white flour products, pasta, potatoes, candy, soft drinks and desserts of all kinds. You need to get regular exercise, 3-5 times per week, 30-60 minutes each time. I have always been amazed to find that marathon and tri-athlon runners, people who sometime workout several hours a day are also among highly paid and most productive people in their fields.

There seems to be a direct relationship between physical fitness and energy on one hand and high levels of productivity on the other. Be sure to get lots of rest especially if you are working hard. You need at least 7 or 8 hours of sleep per night and sometimes even more. You need to take at least one full day off each week and two full weeks off each year if you want to perform at your best. You should identify the times of day that you are the brightest and most alert. For some people this is the morning, for others it's the afternoon or evening. Whatever it is for you, you should schedule your most creative and demanding task during that time of the day when you are at your very best.

7. Practice Single-Handling with key Tasks

Single handling is one of the most powerful of all time management techniques. This technique alone will boost your productivity by 50% or more the very first day you begin practicing it. When you make single handling a habit, you can actually double your productivity even if you do nothing else recommended above.

The way it works is really simple: you make a list of everything you have to do. You select the most important item on your list, that is the highest value use of your time then you start to work on it and you discipline yourself to stay at it until it is 100% complete.

Andrew Carnegie who became one of the richest men in the world after starting as a day laborer in a Pittsburgh steel plant attributed much of his wealth and success to this simple formula. He said it has transformed his life and the lives of everyone who ever worked for him. Remember the two keys to success are focus and concentration. Your ability to concentrate single mindedly without diversion or distraction on one thing, the most important thing and staying with it until it is complete will contribute more to your success than any other habit you will ever develop.

The fact is that if you start a task and then put it aside, coming back to it later and starting it again can eventually increase the amount of time required by 500% or 5 times. On the other hand if you pick-up a task and you discipline yourself to stay at it until it is done. You can decrease the amount of time it takes to do that task by as much as 80%. This is one of the greatest secret of time management and high productivity.

8. Organize Your Work Space.

Highly productive people work from a clean desk and a clean workplace. Inefficient, unproductive, confused people work from a messy desk. Their workplace often looks as though a grenade has gone-off, scattering papers and files everywhere. This is not for you.

Make it a habit of cleaning off your work space and do work from a cleaned desk all the time even if you have to take everything off the desk and put it behind on the floor or on a credenza. Keep your desk clean. 30% of the working time today is spent looking for something that has been misplaced in some way. When people say that they work better from a messy desk, it turns out not to be true at all. When these same people are forced to clean up their workspace and work on one item at a time, their productivity doubles within 24 hours. It amazes them to learn the truth.

Use what is called the *TRAF formula* on all your papers. The four letters stands for **Toss, Refer, Act and File.** Your waste basket is one of the most helpful time management tools in your office. **"Toss"** away and throw everything that you possible can before you get bogged down reading through it. This is especially true with direct mail advertising, unnecessary subscriptions for magazines, newspapers or any other material that you have no need of. The R stands for **"Refer"**. This is something that someone else should deal with. Make a note on it and send it off. Take every opportunity to delegate or refer everything that you possibly can so you have more time to do those things that only you can do. The A stands for **"Action"** Use a red file for this purpose to make it stand out. Your action file contains everything that you have to take action on in the foreseeable future. By putting things on your action file, you deal with them and get them out of the way. And the F stands for **"File"**. These are papers and documents that you think you will need to have available to you at a later time. *But remember, before you file things that 80% of all the items that are filed are never referred to again.* When you make a note to file something means you are creating work for someone else. Be sure that it is necessary before you file it.

There are time management specialists today who charge several hundred dollars to help executives clear-up their desks and offices. One of the first things these experts do to help their clients go through the piles of material that the executives have been saving up to read at a later time. And here is the rule *"if you have not read it in the last six months, its junk"* throw it away. When in doubt, throw it out. This also applies to old clothes, old furniture, old toys and anything else that is cluttering-up your life. Many people are pack rats in their attitude towards saving magazines, newsletters, newspapers and other information that comes in the door. The fact is that you will never be able to read all the information you receive on a daily basis. You must discipline yourself to throw it away as quickly as you possibly can. Keep your workspace clean and keep only one thing in front of you at a time. This will dramatically increase your productivity.

9. Use Travel Time Productively

The two major forms of travel time are driving and flying. You should turn both of these forms of transition time into highly productive time. When you drive always listen to educational audio programs. The average person in North America sits in his or her car 500-1000 hours each year. This is the equivalent of the 1-2 full-time university semesters. Experts at the University of Southern California recently concluded that you can get the same educational value as full-time university attendance by simply listening to educational audio programs as you drive from place to place. Turn your car into a university on wheels. View your car as a learning machine for the rest of your career. Many people have become highly educated and moved to the tops of their fields with audio learning. You should do the same. You should resolve from this day forward that your car will never be moving without something educational playing in the car.

When you are flying, you should use this time productively as well. Time management experts have found that every hour of working in an airplane is equal to three hours of work in a busy office. The reason for this is because you can work without any interruptions at all on an airplane if you plan and organize in advance. Plan your trip in advance; prepare your work schedule, write-up an agenda for the things that you are going to accomplish when you are in the air. Once the plane takes off you can lower your table, pull out your work and begin working immediately. Resist the temptation to read the magazine in the pocket in front of you or watch the movie they play on long flights. Do not drink alcohol of any kind; instead drink two glasses of water for every hour that you are in the air. This will keep you alert and refresh and will dramatically cut down on jet lack.

Every minute counts, turn your car into a mobile classroom and turn you airline seat into your flying office. Use them both to get ahead and stay ahead of your work.

10. Work in Real Time

This is an extremely important principle for increasing your productivity. Develop a sense of urgency. Develop a fast tempo, develop a bias for action. Pick-up the pace, do it now. Today there is an incredible need for speed. People who do things quickly are considered to be better, valuable and more competent than people who do things slowly.

Make decisions quickly, 80% of all decisions can be made the moment they come up. Don't delay or procrastinate on them. Slow decision making simply plugs up your pipeline and puts a drag on your activities. Complete all quick jobs as soon as they come up. Anything that will take you less than two minutes is usually something that you should do immediately. Always think about how much time it will take you to ramp up and do the job later if you don't do it now. Take an important phone call immediately and deal with it. Have an important discussion and take a decision to solve the problem right there. Respond to requests from your boss or your customers fast. Move quickly when need or opportunity arises. Develop a reputation for speed and dependability. Your goal should be to develop a reputation of being the person who is called by your boss when something needs to be taken care of quickly. This will open more doors to you than you can imagine. This will attract more and more opportunities to you to do more and more things quickly. Doing things quickly when they come up is the vital part of doubling your productivity.

11. Reinvent Yourself Annually

Reinvent yourself each year. We are living at the time of greatest change in all of human history. Things are changing so rapidly in all areas and all directions that you must be continually reevaluating and reinventing yourself and your life. At least once a year, you should stand back and look at every aspect of your life to determine whether or not this is something that you want to continue doing. Imagine for a moment that your company has burnt to the ground and that you have to walk across the street and start over again in a new building. What would you start-up immediately? What would you not start-up at all? Who would you bring from the parking lot to continue working in your company? Who would you leave behind in the parking lot if you had the choice?

Imagine that your job and your industry and business disappeared. Imagine that you are starting your career over again and you could go in any direction and do virtually anything. What would it be?

Evaluate where you live and how your family spends leisure time activities and vacations. Reevaluate your finances and your physical condition. If you could begin any part of your career and life over again like a painter standing before a white canvas, how would you design or reinvent your life today. When you stand back and look at your life from this point of view on a regular basis, you will begin to see all kinds of opportunities to change what you are doing; so that they are more inline with what you are really want. This is the real key to increasing your productivity.

12.   Practice Zero Based Thinking

Practice zero based thinking continuously. This is one of the best tools you will ever learn to clarify your thinking and to improve the quality of your life. Ask yourself on a regular basis "is there anything in my life that knowing what I know now, I wouldn't get into again today, if I have to do it over?" Is there anything that you are involved in today, any relationship, any investment that knowing what you now know today, you wouldn't get into, if you had to do it over? This is one of the most important questions you have to ask yourself.

When you think of time savers and time wasters, you usually think of interruptions and telephone calls. However the biggest time waster of all is for you to continue to peruse a course of action, a job, a career or a relationship that is the wrong one for you. Many people waste many years of their life working at something that they don't particularly like or enjoy and then in their thirties (30s) they have to start allover again in a completely new job, in a completely new career. Ask yourself "is there anything that you are doing today that based on your current knowledge and experience you wouldn't startup again, if you had the opportunity?

Because we are living in the time of rapid change, 70% of your decisions will turn out to be wrong in the fullness of time. This means that everyone is involved in at least one thing knowing what they now know, they wouldn't get into. The key indicator of a zero based thinking situation is "stress". Whenever you feel chronic stress, dissatisfaction or unhappiness with any person or situation that seems to go on and on, you should ask yourself, "knowing what I now know, would I get into this situation again today"? And if your answer is "No" then the next question is how can I get out of this situation and how fast?

Ask yourself these questions at least on quarterly basis, "is there any relationship in my life, business, social or personal activities that knowing what I now know, I wouldn't get into again? Is there any part of business, any product or service, expenditure or process that knowing what I now know, I wouldn't startup again today, if I had to do it over?

Remember, whatever the situation is, if it is an unhappy situation, it is probably not going to change on its own and going to verse over the time. The only question then is, "do you have the courage and character to deal honestly with your life as it really is today?" By applying the zero based thinking to every part of your life, you will be absolutely amazed that how much better your decisions become and how much more productive you become at the same time.

13. Set Clear Posteriorities

You have heard of setting priorities. Priorities are tasks that you do more of and sooner. A posteriority on the other hand is something that you do less of and later, if at all. The fact is that you are already overwhelmed with too much to do in too little time.

For you to do something new or different you must discontinue something that you are already doing. For you to do something new and different, you must begin systematically setting posteriorities on

310

activities in your life that are no longer as important as other activities. Practice what Peter Drucker calls creative abandonment with tasks and activities that are no longer as valuable as they were when you first started doing them.

The fact is that you have too much to do already therefore before you start doing something new, you have to stop doing something old. Picking up new task requires putting down an old task, getting in means getting out, starting up means starting off. Look at your life and your work. What sort of things that you should stop doing, so you can free up enough time to do more of the things that you should be doing more of the time? The fact is that you can only get your life under control to the degree to which you discontinue lower value activities. You can only double your productivity only when you free up time to do the things that can have significant pay-off for you in future.

Whenever you feel overloaded for any reason, whenever you feel that you have to too much to do in too little time, stop. Take a deep breath and just say to yourself that "all I can do is all I can do" and then sit-down, make a list of everything you have to do and begin setting posteriorities on your time. Sometimes the word "NO" can be the best time saver of all.

14. Keep Your Life in Balance

The reason you are working is so you can earn enough to enjoy your family, your health and the important parts of your personal life. You want to have a happy, healthy and harmonious relationship with your spouse and children. You want to be healthy and fit; you want to grow mentally and spiritually. You want to be as successful as possible in your work and career so that you have the resources to do all the things that you really care about that have nothing to do with your work

Unfortunately, most people get the cart before the horse. They become so preoccupied with their work that they loose sight of the reason for wanting to be successful at their work in the first place. This is definitely not for you. Remember that in life, relationships

311

are everything. 85% of your success in life will come from your happy relationship with other people. Only 15% of your happiness will come from your achievements in your work.

You must keep your life in balance. This will dramatically simplify your life and reduce your work hours. This will enable you to spend more time with your family and double your income over time, all simultaneously. The keys to balance are simple. Set your peace of mind, your happiness and your home life as your highest goals and organize the rest of your goals around them. Create blocks of time to spend with your family. Create time in the evenings, time on the weekends and time away on vacations. Remember the following formula for balance

"It is quantity of time at home that counts and quality of time at work and don't mix them up".

The simplest of all rules for balance is "put people first". Put the most important people in your life ahead of everything and everyone else. When you work, work all the time. Don't waste time with idle chatting and useless activities.

Remember that every minute you waste at work with idle socializing is a minute that you are taking away from your family and your important relationships. When you get your life in balance, you will actually accomplish more, be paid more, produce more and have vastly more time with your family. This is the whole reason for wanting to become more productive in the first place.

Adopted from "21 Secrets of Success" by Brian Tracy

Glossary of Terms

> Terms appearing in the glossary in upper case letters have their own listings elsewhere in the glossary.

Account - A formal record of transactions involving a particular item or person.

Accounts payable - Debts you have as a result of purchasing assets or receiving services on an open account or on credit. You have accounts payable when you have not yet paid for the assets or services you have received.

Accounts receivable - Amount of money you are owed. Generally, you are owed this amount because you sold assets or provided services.

Accrual method of accounting - With this method, income is reported in the fiscal period it is earned, regardless of when it is received. The expenses are also deducted in the fiscal period they are incurred, whether they are paid or not. This method is generally used by businesses or professionals.

Appeal - A process by which you ask a Court to review the decision the Appeals Division made on behalf of the Minister of National Revenue.

Articles of incorporation - Legal document filed with a provincial or territorial government, or the federal government, which sets out a CORPORATION's purpose and regulations.

Assessment - A formal determination of taxes to be paid or refunded. An assessment includes a reassessment. See NOTICE OF ASSESSMENT.

Assets - Any property owned by a person or business. Assets include money, land, buildings, investments, inventory, cars, trucks, boats, or other valuables that belong to a person or business. They also may include intangibles such as GOODWILL.

Bad debt - Money owed to you that you can't collect.

Balance - The amount remaining in an ACCOUNT after recording all deposits and withdrawals.

Balance sheet - Statement of the financial position of a business. It states the assets, liabilities, and owners' equity at a particular point in time.

Budget - A plan outlining an organization's financial and operational goals.

Business expenses - Certain costs that are reasonable for a particular type of business, and that are incurred for the purpose of earning income. Business expenses can be deducted for tax purposes. Personal, living, or other expenses not related to the business cannot be deducted for tax purposes.

Business Number (BN) - A number you get when you register to do any business with us. It is a single number which replaces the numbers that Canadian businesses previously needed to deal with the federal government.

Calendar year - The twelve-month period beginning January 1 and ending December 31. Depending on your business circumstances, you may or may not use the calendar year as your FISCAL PERIOD.

Canada Pension Plan (CPP) - An insurance program to help Canadians provide income for their retirement. It also gives them income if they become disabled. Contributions are directly related to annual earnings.

Capital cost allowance (CCA) - A yearly deduction or depreciation on the cost of certain assets. You can claim CCA for tax purposes on the assets of a business such as buildings or equipment, as well as on additions or improvements, if these assets are expected to last for some years.

Capital gains - The amount by which PROCEEDS OF DISPOSITION less outlays and expenses exceed the adjusted cost base of CAPITAL PROPERTY.

Capital loss - The amount by which the adjusted cost base and outlays and expenses of CAPITAL PROPERTY exceeds PROCEEDS OF DISPOSITION.

Capital property - Generally, any property of value, including DEPRECIABLE PROPERTY. Common types of capital property include principal residences, cottages, stocks, bonds, land, buildings, and equipment used in a business or rental operation.

Cash method of accounting - With this method, you report income in the year it is actually received. Similarly, expenses are deducted in the year they are actually paid. Farmers, fishers, and certain salespeople who work on commission may use the cash method.

Confidentiality - The privacy of income tax and GST/HST returns and other related tax information. The only people with access to this information are those who are authorized by law or those to whom the taxpayer has given permission in writing.

Corporation - A form of business authorized by federal, provincial, or territorial law to act as a separate legal entity. Its purpose and regulations are set out in its ARTICLE OF INCORPORATION. A corporation may be owned by one or more persons.

Cost of goods sold - The actual cost of the items sold in the normal course of business during a specific period.

Customs duties - Taxes you pay when you bring foreign goods into the country.

317

Debt - An amount which is owed. If you borrow money or purchase something on credit, you have created a debt.

Deemed - A legal term used when something is considered to be something else for certain purposes.

Depreciable property - Property that wears out as it is used over the years. For example, cars, farm equipment, and business machines are depreciable. See CAPITAL COST ALLOWANCE.

Depreciation - A decrease in the value of an asset through age, use, and deterioration. In accounting terminology, depreciation is a deduction or expense claimed for this decrease in value.

Disposition - Generally, the disposal of property by sale, gift, transfer, or change in use.

Election - A formal choice among specific options on how tax laws are applied to a taxpayer's financial affairs. Usually you make an election on your tax return.

Employment income - See SALARY.

Employment Insurance (EI) - A federal program that provides financial assistance to people who are temporarily out of work. It is an insurance program, with employers and employees making payments into the Employment Insurance Fund.

Employment Insurance premiums - Deductions that an employer must make from employees' paycheques and forward to the Receiver General for Canada. Employers must also contribute Employment Insurance payments.

Excise - Taxes on the manufacture, sale, or use of goods and items.

Fiscal period - This is the twelve-month period over which a business or profession reports its income-earning activities. The fiscal period may or may not coincide with the CALENDAR YEAR.

The business usually establishes its fiscal period when it files its first income tax return.

Goodwill - The excess of the purchase price of a business over the fair market value of the net assets of the business.

Gross profit - Sales minus COST OF GOODS SOLD.

Half-year rule - A provision in the *Income Tax Act* that allows you to claim only half of the capital cost allowance available on an asset in the year you purchased the asset.

Income - The sum of revenues earned in a specific period of time. It includes revenues from salaries, wages, benefits, tips, and commissions, profits from operating a business or profession, and investments earned.

Income statement - A financial statement that summarizes the results of business activities (income and expenses) for a given period of time. Sometimes called a PROFIT AND LOSS STATEMENT.

Income tax payroll deductions - Employers must deduct income tax from their employees' salaries or wages. They must base these deductions on the income tax deductions tables, which reflect each province's rates.

Information circulars - Publications that CCRA issue to give detailed explanations on a variety of tax subjects.

Information slips - Forms that employers, trusts, and businesses use to tell taxpayers and the CCRA how much income was earned, and how much tax was deducted.

Input tax credit - A credit GST/HST registrants may claim for GST/HST paid or payable on purchases relating to a commercial activity.

Instalment - A partial payment of a tax debt. The debt is divided into parts that are paid at different times within a certain period.

Interpretation bulletins - Publications that give CCRA interpretation of parts of the *Income Tax Act*.

Inventory - Generally, the total value of the goods on hand that a business intends to sell, use for manufacture, or use to render a service. In certain cases, inventory can also include services.

Investment - An expenditure to acquire property that yields or is expected to yield revenue or services.

Lease - A contract under which a property is rented from one person or business to another for a fixed period of time at a specified rate.

Liability - DEBT owed by a person or business.

Loss - The amount by which expenses exceed revenues.

Net income - Income subject to taxation after allowable deductions have been subtracted from gross or total income.

Notice of Assessment - A form that CCRA send to all taxpayers after CCRA process their returns. It tells taxpayers or GST/HST registrants if CCRA made any corrections to the returns or rebate applications and, if so, what they are. It also informs taxpayers or registrants if they owe more tax or what the amount of their refund will be.

Objection - A statement of facts and reasons detailing why a taxpayer or registrant disagrees with an assessment.

Operating expenses - The routine costs of running a business. They include expenses for gasoline, electricity, and office supplies. They do not include the cost of buildings or machinery that are expected to last for several years. See CAPITAL COST ALLOWANCE.

Payroll deductions - Income tax deductions, CANADA PENSION PLAN or QUEBEC PENSION PLAN contributions, and EMPLOYMENT INSURANCE premiums which are deducted from an employee's wages or SALARY and sent regularly to us. Employers also make their own contributions to the Canada Pension Plan or Quebec Pension Plan, and Employment Insurance.

Penalties - Amounts taxpayers or registrants must pay if they fail to file returns or remit or pay amounts owing on time, or if they try to evade paying or remitting tax by not filing returns. Penalties must also be paid by people who knowingly, or under circumstances amounting to gross negligence, participate in or make false statements or omissions in their returns, and by those who do not provide the information required on a prescribed form.

Personal tax credit return (Form TD1) - The first income tax form a person has to complete when starting a new job. It tells an employer how much income tax to deduct from the employee's pay.

Prepaid expense - An expense you pay for in advance; an expense you incur for goods and services you will receive in a later FISCAL PERIOD; amounts you pay in interest, income taxes, municipal taxes, rent, dues, or insurance for later fiscal periods. These amounts are included as assets on the balance sheet at the end of a fiscal period.

Proceeds of disposition - Usually, the selling price of property when it is disposed of. Proceeds of disposition also include compensation received for property that has been destroyed, expropriated, stolen, or damaged. It is also the fair market value of property when it is transferred to another person, or when there is a change in its use.

Professional dues - Membership fees paid to maintain a professional status recognized by law, such as lawyers' annual law society fees.

Profit and loss statement - Same as an INCOME STATEMENT.

Proprietorship - A non-incorporated business entirely owned by one person. Same as a SOLE PROPRIETORSHIP.

Quebec Pension Plan (QPP) - A pension plan equivalent to the CANADA PENSION PLAN (CPP) but maintained by the province of Quebec. The provincial government handles the contributions.

Rates of tax - Percentages of income that must be paid as tax. The Department of Finance sets the basic income tax rates, which vary progressively with the amount of income received.
For GST/HST purposes, the GST rate is 7%, while the HST rate is 15%.

Records - Documents such as account books, sales and purchase invoices, contracts, bank statements, and canceled cheques. You must keep records in an orderly manner at your business or residence in Canada for at least six years from the end of the last taxation year to which the records relate. You must make these books and other documents available to CCRA officers for audit purposes.

Refund - The overpayment of income tax returned to a taxpayer after CCRA assess the return.

Registrant - A person who is registered or required to be registered under GST/HST legislation.

Remittance - A payment of CPP or QPP, EI, income tax, or GST/HST that is paid to us through a financial institution, or that a business or individual sends directly to us. It also includes the employer's share of CPP contributions and EI premiums.

Research grants - Amounts of money given to individuals to explore areas in various fields of study. The grants cover the cost of research plus the researcher's income. These amounts are taxable but some of the researcher's expenses may be deductible for tax purposes. For more specific information, refer to Interpretation

Bulletin IT-75, *Scholarships, Fellowships, Bursaries, Prizes, and Research Grants.*

Reserves - Funds set aside to cover future expenses, losses, or claims.

Salary - The amount an employer pays an employee for work done. Each employer records this type of employment income on T4 slips. Same as EMPLOYMENT INCOME and wages.

Self-employment - The operation of your own business.

Social insurance number (SIN) - A number given to each contributor to the Canada Pension Plan, Quebec Pension Plan, and Employment Insurance Plan. It helps record the contributions and premiums paid into and the benefits paid out of the plans. Since these social insurance programs are connected to the tax system, the SIN is also used as an identifier for federal income tax purposes. Everyone who files an income tax and benefit return must provide a SIN.

Sole proprietorship - An unincorporated business entirely owned by one person. Same as a PROPRIETORSHIP.

Spouse - For purposes of the *Income Tax Act*, starting in 2001, the term **spouse** will mean only a married partner. The term **common-law partner** will include partners of the same sex or opposite sex, who meet certain conditions. For more information, see your General Income Tax and Benefit guide.

Statement of income and expenses - Form that summarizes revenue, income, and expenses for a specific period.

Statement of remuneration paid (T4 slip) - Information slip that shows the income that an employer pays to an employee. Taxable allowances and benefits, such as payments made on the employee's behalf to a provincial health care plan, are included as income. A T4 slip also shows how much the employer deducted for income tax,

CPP or QPP contributions, EMPLOYMENT INSURANCE premiums, and contributions to the employer's pension plan.

Supply - For GST/HST purposes, this generally means the provision of property or a service in any manner, including sale, transfer, barter, exchange, licence, rental, lease, gift, or disposition.

Tax centres - Offices in different regions of Canada where CCRA process tax returns.

Tax Court of Canada - A court that hears appeals about income tax and GST/HST assessments. In addition, the Court has jurisdiction to hear appeals under the Canada Pension Plan, *Employment Insurance Act* and several other acts. The Tax Court maintains four offices (Vancouver, Ottawa, Toronto, and Montréal) and regularly conducts hearings in major centres across Canada.

Tax payable - The amount of income tax that you must pay on taxable income for the taxation year. It is also the amount of tax payable on a taxable supply (for GST/HST purposes).

Tax services offices - Offices across the country that provide tax guides and forms, as well as consultation services.

Tax treaties - Government agreements signed between countries. They help citizens who earn foreign income avoid double taxation.

Taxable benefits - Amounts of money, or the value of goods or services, that an employer pays or provides in addition to salary. For example, the part of a health insurance plan that the employer pays is a taxable benefit.

Taxable income - The amount of income left after all allowable deductions have been subtracted from NET INCOME. This amount is used to calculate the tax payable.

Taxation year - The CALENDAR YEAR or FISCAL PERIOD for which income tax is to be paid.

Workers' compensation - Money paid to compensate a person injured on the job. It is an insurance plan paid for by employers and administered by the Workers' Compensation Board.

MOST COMMON HOME BASED BUSINESSES

1. Advertising Agency
2. Aromatherapist
3. Astrologer
4. Bookkeeping Service
5. Business Broker
6. Business Plan Writer
7. Caterer
8. Cleaning Service
9. Computer Programmer
10. Computer Repair/Tutoring
11. Copywriter
12. Consultant
13. Desktop Publisher
14. Drafter/CAD
15. Editing
16. Elder Companion
17. Errand Services
18. Export Agent
19. Executive Search
20. Facialist or Aesthetician
21. Family Child-Care Provider
22. Financial Planner
23. Fitness Trainer
24. Hauling Service
25. Home Inspector
26. Image Consultant
27. Indexing
28. Interior Designer/Decorator
29. Independent Sales Rep.
30. Mailing List Service
31. Make-up Artist
32. Mediator
33. Medical Billing
34. Meeting and Event Planner
35. Multimedia Production

36. Newsletter Publishing
37. Pet Sitting
38. Photography
39. Professional Organizer
40. Proofreading
41. Private Investigator
42. Real Estate Appraiser
43. Repair Services
44. Resume-Writing Service
45. Secretarial Services
46. Sign Maker
47. Tax Preparation Services
48. Technical Writer
49 Tour Operator
50. Translator /Interpreter
51. Travel Consultant
52. Web Designer
53. Web Merchant/Mail Order
54. Webmaster
55. Wedding Planner

USEFUL BUSINESS & SUCCESS QUOTES

1. Wherever you see a successful business, someone once made a courageous decision. *(Peter Drucker)*

2. In prison all expenses are paid by taxpayers, with no work required. At work you get to pay all the expenses to go to work & then they deduct taxes from your salary to pay for the prisoners."*(Unknown)*

3. For every dollar the boss has and didn't work for, one of us worked for a dollar and didn't get it. *(Big Bill Haywood)*

4. We do not go to work only to earn an income, but to find meaning in our lives. What we do is a large part of what we are.*(Alan Ryan)*

5. We are what we repeatedly do. Excellence, therefore, is not an act but a habit. *(Aristotle)*

6. If you see a snake, just kill it. Don't appoint a committee on snakes. *(Ross Perot)*

7. It's easy to make a buck. It's a lot tougher to make a difference. (Tom Brokaw)

8. Never disrespect people on your way up because you are going to pass them one day on your way down. (*Unknown)*

9. You can get everything in life you want if you will just help enough other people get what they want. *(Zig Ziglar)*

10. All paid jobs absorb and degrade the mind. (Aristotle)

11. A topnotch businessman offers the right products to the right people, in the right place, at the right time, with right prices, receiving his reasonable gain without violating the laws of the land and rights of the consumers. *(Jose B. Cabajar)*

12. Don't ask me 'When is our IPO?' My office overlooks the parking lot, and when I see the BMWs of investment bankers fighting for spaces, I'll know it's time.*(Jean-Louis Gassee)*

13. In these troubled economic times remember to beware of little expenses, a small leak will sink a great ship. Wasteful spending can sink a great organization .*(Reed Markham, American educator)*

14. The successful producer of an article sells it for more than it cost him to make, and that's his profit. But the customer buys it only because its worth more to him than he pays for it, and that's his profit. No one can long make a profit producing anything...unless the customer makes a profit from using it.*(Sam Pettengill, an American Congressman from the 1930's)*

15. It's not the employer who pays the wages - he only handles the money. It is the product that pays wages. *(Henry Ford)*

16. "An entrepreneur is someone that steals office supplies from home and brings them to work."*(-Auren Hoffman)*

17. Pay the people who know. *(Scott Anderson)*

18. Management cannot dictate creativity. Management cannot force loyalty. Management must create an atmosphere that fosters loyalty and encourages creativity. *(Tony Calabrese)*

19. **Sam's Rules for Building a Business:**

   a. COMMIT to your business.

   b. SHARE your profits with your associates and treat them as partners.

   c. MOTIVATE your partners.

   d. COMMUNICATE everything you possibly can to your partners.

   e. APPRECIATE everything your associates do for the business.

   f. CELEBRATE your success.

   g. LISTEN to everyone in your company

   h. EXCEED your customers' expectations.

   i. CONTROL your expenses better than your competition

   j. SWIM upstream.   *(Sam Walton (founder of Wal-Mart)*

20. Try a lot of stuff and keep what works *(From the book Built to Last)*

21. Tomorrow is two days late for yesterday's work *(Unknown)*

22. You either make money or make excuses.*(-Ryan Hunter)*

23. Money is a useless invention. All it has done is lead to war and poverty.*(Chae Richardson)*

24. Half the money I spend on advertising is wasted, and the trouble is I don't know which half. *(Viscount Leverhulme, 1851-1925)*

25. If all you have is hope, it's not enough. Hoping, wishing, praying without action is a waste of time. You will accomplish nothing by just

wishing it would happen. You must get off your butt and make it happen. (Tony Calabrese)

26. With business and technology progressing at such a pace, both the need and opportunity for an individual to continuously develop, improve and sometimes recycle their skills have never been greater

27. The Customer Bill of Rights

Customer have the right to:

Be "wowed"

Hear "yes"

Complain & receive satisfaction

Be served and served well

Prompt service (*Unknown*)

28. "Copy from one, it's plagiarism; copy from many, it's research."
(Wilson Mizner (1876-1933)

29. The only thing that can stop you is the doubt that you carry in your mind. (*Chae Richardson*)

30. To dream anything that you want to dream - that's the beauty of the human mind. To do anything that you want to do - that is the strength of the human will. To trust yourself to test your limits - that is the courage to succeed." (*unknown*)

31. There are many rules for success, but none of them will work unless you do. (*-Reed Markham, American educator*)

32. I find that the harder I work, the more luck I seem to have.
(*Thomas Jefferson*)

33. I have learned that success is to be measured not so much by the position that one has reached in life as by the obstacles which he has had to overcome while trying to succeed. (*Booker T. Washington*)

34. The higher your expectations get, the higher the mountain will stand on your way.(*Philippos Aristotelous*)

35. The only boundaries for your success are your emotions. If your fears and doubts control your mind they shall control your future. (*Rachel*)

36. 'To achieve success one must endure and learn from failure' (*Rich Grosso*)

37. Only through focus can you do world-class things, no matter how capable you are. (*Bill Gates (Fortune, July 8, 2002)*)

38. "Don't stay in bed, unless you can make money in bed."
(*George Burns (1896-1996)*)

39. The minute you start talking about what you're going to do if you lose, you have lost. *(George Shultz)*

40. Nothing great was ever achieved without enthusiasm.*(Ralph Waldo Emerson)*

41. Ability is what gives you the opportunity; belief is what gets you there. *(Apollo)*

42. Success requires long term dedication and patience on a short term pace. *(Philippos)*

43. "Every day I get up and look through the Forbes list of the richest people in America. If I'm not there, I go to work." *(Robert Orben)*

44. Success comes when it is no longer regarded merely as a desire, but as an irresistible need. *(Philippos)*

45. "Just do what you do best." *(Red Auerbach, Hall of Fame Basketball Coach)*

46. The secret to success is making your vocation your vacation.*(Mark Twain)*

47. The two hardest things in life for people to handle are failure and success. *(Oscar Wilde)*

48. "When you do the common things in life in an uncommon way, you will command the attention of the world." *(George Washington Carver (1864-1943)*

49. "Success in almost any field depends more on energy and drive than it does on intelligence. This explains why we have so many stupid leaders." *(Sloan Wilson)*

50. Challenge is an invitation to success. *(Jose B. Cabajar)*

51. Visualization is an unseen activity of a winner. *(Jose B. Cabajar)*

52. If there is something that you think you can do, chances are you can do it.*(Chae Richardson)*

53. Success is 1% inspiration and 99% perspiration.*(Meenakshi.)*

54 When Love and determination work together expect a masterpiece *(Tamz)*

55. What's money? A man is a success if he gets up in the morning and goes to bed at night and in the middle does what he wants to do. *(Bob Dylan)*

56. Nothing is impossible since when we first walked on the moon we though it was impossible. *(Dharma)*

57. "Work only half a day. It makes no difference which half - the first 12 hours or the last." *(Kemmons Wilson (founder of Holiday Inn)*

58. The only way to success is failure no failure, no success *(Lesley Heylen)*

59. Computers in the future may weigh no more than 1.5 tons."
(Popular Mechanics, forecasting the relentless march of science, 1949)

60. I think there is a world market for maybe five computers."
(Thomas Watson, chairman of IBM, 1943)

61 I have traveled the length and breadth of this country and talked with the best people, and I can assure you that data processing is a fad that won't last out the year."
(The editor in charge of business books for Prentice Hall, 1957)

62. There is no reason anyone would want a computer in their ome."
(Ken Olson, president, chairman and founder of Digital Equipment Corp., 1977)

63. This 'telephone' has too many shortcomings to be seriously considered as a means of communication. The device is inherently of no value to us." (Western Union internal memo, 1876.)

64. The wireless music box has no imaginable commercial value. Who would pay for a message sent to nobody in particular?"
(David Sarnoff's associates in response to his urgings for investment in the radio in the 1920s.)

65. The concept is interesting and well-formed, but in order to earn better than a 'C,' the idea must be feasible."
(A Yale University management professor in response to Fred Smith's paper proposing reliable overnight delivery service. (Smith went on to found Federal Express Corp.))

66. Who the hell wants to hear actors talk?"
(H.M. Warner, Warner Brothers, 1927.)

67. I'm just glad it'll be Clark Gable who's falling on his face and not Gary Cooper. (Gary Cooper on his decision not to take the leading role in "Gone With The Wind.")

68. A cookie store is a bad idea. Besides, the market research reports say America likes crispy cookies, not soft and chewy cookies like you make. (Response to Debbi Fields' idea of starting Mrs. Fields' Cookies.)

69. We don't like their sound, and guitar music is on the way out."
(Decca Recording Co. rejecting the Beatles, 1962.)

70. Heavier-than-air flying machines are impossible."
(Lord Kelvin, president, Royal Society, 1895.)

333

71. Professor Goddard does not know the relation between action and reaction and the need to have something better than a vacuum against which to react. He seems to lack the basic knowledge ladled out daily in high schools."
(1921 New York Times editorial about Robert Goddard's revolutionary rocket work.)

72. Drill for oil? You mean drill into the ground to try and find oil? You're crazy." (Drillers who Edwin L. Drake tried to enlist to his project to drill for oil in 1859.)

73. Stocks have reached what looks like a permanently high plateau."
(Irving Fisher, Professor of Economics, Yale University, 1929.)

74. Airplanes are interesting toys but of no military value."
(Marechal Ferdinand Foch, Professor of Strategy, Ecole Superieure de Guerre).

75. Everything that can be invented has been invented."
(Charles H. Duell, Commissioner, U.S. Office of Patents, 1899.)

76. Louis Pasteur's theory of germs is ridiculous fiction."
(Pierre Pachet, Professor of Physiology at Toulouse, 1872)

77. The abdomen, the chest, and the brain will forever be shut from the intrusion of the wise and humane surgeon."
(Sir John Eric Ericksen, British surgeon, appointed Surgeon-Extraordinary to Queen Victoria 1873.)

78. 640K ought to be enough for anybody." (Bill Gates, 1981)

FUN QUOTES – ALL UNKNOWN

1. Someday your prince charming will come. Mine just took a wrong turn, got lost, and is too stubborn to ask for directions.

2. People have the right to be stupid. Some people abuse that privilege.

3. Don't play stupid with me...I'm better at it.

4. Just remember, if the world didn't suck, we'd all fall off.

5. I was standing in the park wondering why Frisbees got bigger as they get closer. Then it hit me.

6. People say nothing is impossible, but I do nothing every day."

7. Before marriage, a man yearns for the woman he loves. After marriage, the 'Y' becomes silent .

8. I think-therefore I'm single.

9. There are three types of people in this world: those who make things happen, those who watch things happen and those who wonder what happened.

10. Beer is proof that God loves us and wants us to be happy.

11. When tempted to fight fire with fire, remember that the fire department generally uses water. (Judge your leader's competence)

12. When I die, I want to die like my grandmother, who died peacefully in her sleep. Not screaming like all the passengers in her car

13. The fact that no one understands you doesn't mean you're an artist.

14. I am not a vegetarian because I love animals; I am a vegetarian because I hate plants.

15. Only two things are infinite, the universe and human stupidity, and I'm not sure about the former.

16. I'm a nobody, nobody is perfect, therefore I am perfect!

17. If practice makes perfect, and no one is perfect, why practice?"

18. I was born intelligent but education ruined me!

19. A girl phoned me and said...Come on over there's nobody home. I went over... Nobody was home!

335

336

IN CLOSING

> *"To succeed in a small business, you need a dream to make you want to do it in the first place. Then you need the drive to get you started and keep you going. A lot of people have the dream, but not the drive and energy to see it through."*
>
> *- C.B., Dawson, Yukon*

This book has provided you with some information and advice about starting your own small business. But it is only a first step toward finding out all you need to know to ensure that your decisions are right ones.

GO SLOWLY — PLAN CAREFULLY

As you have heard from those who have started their own business, the work is hard and the risks are high. Take the time to explore the vast amount of information and resources available to you. Make sure you have a good idea of what you are getting into. Good and careful planning will be critical to your success.

> *"To succeed in your own business in today's tough market, you have to plan really well, work hard, continually take stock of where you are and where you want to go, provide a high–quality product and give excellent service. A bit of good luck along the way really helps too."*
>
> *- R.M., Halifax, Nova Scotia*

INCLUDE THOSE CLOSE TO YOU

When you are going through a change, those who are closest to you — your spouse, partner, family members — are going through it with you. Be sure to include them in your decision-making and planning process from the very beginning. Ask them what the implications of starting your own business are for them. Will it require using joint savings? Will they have to give up things that are important to them? If so, are they willing to do this? Change can put stress on relationships. Working through the transition together will make it easier on everyone.

MAKE LIFELONG LEARNING A HABIT

You know the world is changing rapidly when what you finally understood in the morning is already obsolete by that afternoon.

You are going to be learning a great deal as you shift careers to become an entrepreneur, but the learning can't stop once your business has started. Change will be a constant in Canadian life for the foreseeable future. The success of your business will depend on your capacity to learn about and adapt to social, demographic and technological changes. Continue to read, take courses and expand your knowledge and understanding of the world around you.

Wish you Good-luck

LIST OF USEFUL WEB SITES

NON PROFIT ORGANIZATION

Canadian International Development Agency	www.acdi-cida.gc.ca
Charity Village	www.charityvillage.com
Human Rights-Job Bank	www.Hri.ca/jobboard/joblinks.shtml
Online Resource for Non Profit	www.onestep.on.ca

WOMEN

Wired Women	www.wiredwoman.com

AGRICULTURE

Caffeine	www.caffeine.ca
The Farm Directory	www.farmdirectory.com/employment.asp

ARTS AND ENTERTAINMENT

Acting	www.madscreenwriter.com
ACTRA (film)	www.actra.com
Canadian Actor Online	www.canadianactor.com
Canadian Actors Equity Association	www.caea.com
Canadian film @ TV Production Association	www.cftpa.ca
Canadian Film Centre	www.cdnfilmcentre.com
Mandy	www.mandy.com
National Film Board	www.nfb.ca
Ontario Theatre	www.theatreontario.org
Playback Magazine	www.playbackmag.com

SPECIALIZED

Canadian Federation of Chefs & Cooks	www.cfcc.ca
Canadian Human Resource Counsellors	www.chrp.ca
Contact Point – Counsellors	www.contactpoint.ca
Oil and Gas Industry	www.pcf.ab.ca
Social Workers of Toronto	www.swatjobs.com

PEOPLE WITH DISABILITIES

Canadian Council for Rehabilitation & Work	www.ccrw.org
Canadian Hearing Society	www.chs.ca
Canadian Mental health Association	www.cmha.ca
Canadian Paraplegic Association	www.canparaplegic.org

339

Job Accommodation Network	http://janweb.icdi.wvu.edu
TCG for People with Disabilities	www.tcg.on.ca
U of T Adaptive Tech ERC	www.utoronto.ca/atrc

WEB SITES FOR YOUTH AND RECENT GRADUATES

Bridges	www.bridges.com
Canadian Youth Business Foundation	www.cybf.ca
Canadian Youth Business Foundation (B)	www.cybf.ca
Career Owl	www.careerowl.ca
Career Planning	www.alis.gov.ab.ca
Cdn.International Development Agency(B)	www.acdi-cida.gc.ca
Fedeal Student Work Experience Program (B)	www.jobs.gc.ca
MazeMaster	www.mazemaster.on.ca
National Graduate Register	http://ngr.schoolnet.ca
Strategies Business Info – By Sector (B)	Strategis.ic.gc.ca/sc_indps/en gdoc/homepage.html
Summer Jobs	www.summerjobs.com
Work Web (B)	www.cacee.com
Youth Canada (B)	www.youth.gc.ca
Youth Info-Job (B)	www.infojob.net
Youth Opportunities Ontario (B)	Youthjobs.gov.on.ca
Youth Opportunities Ontario (B)	www.edu.gov.on.ca

NEW COMERS

Citizenship and Immigration Canada	www.cic.gc.ca
Settlement.org	www.sttlement.org
Skills for change	www.skillsforchange.org
World Educational Services/Foreign Credentials Assessment	www.wes.org/ca

CAREER PLANNING AND JOB SEARCH STRATEGIES

Bridges	www.cxbridges.com
Career Cruising	www.careercruising.com
Counsellor Resource Centre (B)	http://crccanada.org
Essential Skills	www.essestialskills.gc.ca
Job Futures	http://jobfutures.ca
National Occupational Classification (NOC)(B)	www.hrdc.gc.ca/noc
Toronto Public Library	http://careerbookmarks.tpl.vrl.toronto.on.ca
What Colour is your parachute:	www.jobhuntersbible.com

LABOUR MARKET / INDUSTRY INFORMATION

Canada News Wire	www.newswire.ca
Canada Work InfoNet (B)	www.workinfonet.ca
HRDC Metro Toronto(B)	www.toronto-hrdc.sto.org
HRDC Sector Studies (B)	www.on.hrdc-drhc.gc.ca/english/lmi
Industry Canada	http://strategis.ic.gc.ca
Labour Market Information: Salary Ranges	www.Canadavisa.com/documents/salary.htm
Ontario Wage Information	www.on.hrdc-drhc.gc.ca
Workwaves Toronto	www.workwaves.com

NEWSPAPERS/MAGAZINE

Eye Magazine	www.eye.net/classifieds.
Globe and Mail	www.theglobeandmail.com
National Post	www.careerclick.com
Newswire	www.neweswire.ca
Toronto Star	www.thestar.com
Toronto Star / Globe and Mail	www.workpolis.com
Toronto Sun	www.canoe.ca

SMALL BUSINESS INFORMATION

Business Development Bank of Canada (B)	www.bdc.ca
Canada Business Service Centres (B)	www.cbsc.org
Canadian Company Capabilities (B)	Strategis.ic.gc.ca/engdoc/main.html
Canadian Women's business Network	www.cdnbizwomen.com
Educated Entrepreneur	www.educatedentrepreneur.com
Enterprise Toronto	www.enterprisetronto.com
Self Employment Assistance	http://www.sedi.org/html/prog/fs1_prog.html
Toronto Business	www.city.toronto.on.ca/business/index.htm

WEB SITES WHERE YOU CAN POST JOBS & RESUME

Electronic Labour Exchange	www.ele-spc.org
Job Canada	www.jobcanada.org
Job Shark (B)	www.jobshark.com
Monster Board (B)	www.monster.ca
National Graduate Register (B)	www.campusworklink.com

NetJobs	www.netjobs.com
Worklink	www.workink.com
Workopolis	www.workopolis.ca

TRAINING

Can Learn	www.canlearn.ca
Ellis Chart/Apprentice Training Programs	www.hrdc.gc.ca/hrib/hrpprh/redseal/ndex.shtml
Interactive Training Inventory (B)	www.trainingiti.com
Ministry of Eduction & Training	www.edu.gov.on.ca/eng/welcome.html
Onestep	www.onestep.on.ca
Ontario Universities' Application Centre	www.ouac.on.ca
Scholarships and Exchanges (B)	www.homer.aucc.ca
School finder(B)	www.schoolfinder.com

TUTORIAL SITES

Internet Stuff	www.webteacher.com
Learn the Net	www.learnthenet.com
Microsoft Office: word, excel, powerpoint	www.utexax.edu/cc/training/handouts
Mouse Tutorial	www.albright.org/Albright/computer-Lab/tutorials/mouse/

RELEVANT INFORMATION

City of Toronto	www.city.toronto.on.ca
Employment Resource Centres	www.tcet.com/ercs
Possibilities Project	www.possibilitiesproject.com

VOLUNTEER SITES

Charity Village	www.charityvillage.com
Rehabilitation	www.voc-reb.org
Volunteers	www.volunteer.ca

FREE EMAILS SITES

Excite	www.excite.com
Hotmail	www.hotmail.com
Mail City	www.mailcity.com
Yahoo	www.yahoo.com

SINGLE SEARCH ENGINES

www.google.com	www.altavista.com

www.excite.com	www.go.com
www.hotbot.com	www.yahoo.ca

META SEARCH ENGINES

www.search.com	www.profusion.com
www.megaweb.com	www.metacrawler.com
www.dogpile.com	

344

345

INDEX

About The Editor

The editor has a mechanical engineering background with more then 14 years of experience in his field with multi-national companies especially in project management and coordination. He is also a Cisco certified network and design professional (CCNP, CCDP, A+). He arrived in Canada as a skilled worker immigrant and faced numerous surprises and challenges as well as suffered a number of losses.

The editor has a flare to help and teach. This is 5th book under his belt including his bestselling book at Amazon "Immigrating to Canada and Finding Employment" (ISBN 0973314028).

He voluntarily helps clients from all over the world via e-mail, phone and personally wherever possible for him. He provides people necessary guidance and advises by answering to their questions about Canadian immigration, settlement, employment search and starting a small business in Canada especially to foreign trained professionals.

In "How to Start A Small Business in Canada", he is providing all necessary tools, guidance and information to Canadian men and women who are on paid jobs and wishes to start their own small business. He encourages and motivates foreign trained professionals to get self-employed, who are facing numerous barriers during their job search efforts and struggling for an opportunity where they can utilize their talent and skills to their full competence.

The Editor can be reached at *info@selfhelppublishers.ca* or *tariq_nadeem@sympatico.ca* for questions or feedback upon his publications. He has compiled this publication under a licensing agreement with Public Works and Government Services Canada 350 Albert Street, 4th Floor Ottawa ON K1A 0S5.

NOTES

354

Printed in the United States
137236LV00004B/6/A

9 780973 314069